D0065511

SCHIZOPHRENIA IN FOCUS

SCHIZOPHRENIA IN FOCUS

Guidelines for Treatment and Rehabilitation

David F.L. Dawson, M.D.
Heather Munroe Blum, M.S.W.
Giampiero Bartolucci, M.D.

McMaster University,
Hamilton, Ontario

HUMAN SCIENCES PRESS, INC.
72 Fifth Avenue
NEW YORK, NY 10011

Copyright © 1983 by Human Sciences Press, Inc.
72 Fifth Avenue, New York, New York 10011

Printed in the United States of America
23456789 987654321

Library of Congress Cataloging in Publication Data

Dawson, David F. L., 1941-
   Schizophrenia in focus.

   Bibliography: p.
   Includes index.
   1. Schizophrenia--Treatment. 2. Schizophrenia--Rehabilitation. I.
Blum, Heather Munroe, 1950-. II. Barotlucci, Giampiero, 1933-. III.
Title. [DNLM: 1. Schizophrenia--Rehabilitation. 2. Schizophrenia--
Therapy. WM 203 D271s]
RC514.D33   616'.89'8206   82-3016
ISBN 0-89885-096-7   AACR2

CONTENTS

> *For James Tyhurst, teacher*

PREFACE

In 1976 I began two projects. The first, with Heather Blum, was an attempt to develop a comprehensive treatment and rehabilitation program for the many schizophrenic patients being referred to our Community Psychiatry Service. The second project was a weekly meeting with Gian Bartolucci to discuss the application of language studies to schizophrenia. The first project resulted in the development of a course subsequently presented at the American Psychiatric Association Annual Meeting in 1979 and 1980. The second project culminated in a paper "Language and Schizophrenia" published in *Comprehensive Psychiatry,* January 1980.

In 1979 we decided to try to integrate the two endeavors; each project was already influencing the other. While language studies provide only one perspective on schizophrenia, it is a perspective particularly relevant for psychosocial management. The result of this collaboration is the book before you.

A special debt is owed all the staff (both past and present) of 43 Charlton, the Community Psychiatry Service of St. Joseph's Hospital, Hamilton, Ontario. They treated with good will the writing time of the principal author and previously had taught him a great deal of what he knows about the treatment and rehabilitation of schizophrenia.

Patricia Colton did our typing, searched for references, and offered editorial assistance. Linda Stewart proofread, edited, and provided much needed criticism. A number of our colleagues offered advice and suggestions, but of course, any errors and omissions in the text are our own responsibility.

David Dawson

INTRODUCTION

The thinker is one side; the mind's eye is separate. My
quandary lies between.—anonymous patient

Books on schizophrenia are legion. It is well to ask, Why another one?
Especially, why another book on schizophrenia when the very concept of
schizophrenia is being challenged?

There is general agreement that schizophrenia is not a single syndrome. In
professional usage the word refers to a collection of clinical entities and
specific diseases yet to be adequately catalogued. Its broader definitions
include a range of human reactions understood without recourse to a disease
concept. Some kinds of schizophrenia have a clear genetic component, while
others do not. In fact, we may all be predisposed to schizophrenic symptoms
in certain developmental and social circumstances.

Disease or reaction? The question is still unresolved. Classifications that
distinguish between disease (process schizophrenia) and reaction (schizophreniform, reactive psychosis) prove unreliable on an individual basis.
Worse yet, such classifications cause therapists to view some people with
schizophrenia as following an inevitable, progressive downhill course to
Kraepelin's dementia praecox and to treat others with unrealistic expectations. The first viewpoint creates an atmosphere of hopelessness conveyed to
and absorbed by the patient; the second leads to inadequate treatment.

The crucial question is not whether schizophrenia is a "disease" but
rather, "Does the disease concept offer any benefit to those people perceived
as having schizophrenia?" Forty years ago this question would have been
difficult to answer. Was lifelong incarceration in mental hospitals better than
other unknown fates? Were the medical treatments of the day more effective
and more humane than, say, religious asylum? Probably not.

One might argue that the medical model legitimized refuge and
humanitarian care for people who would otherwise have been subjected to
abuse and witch-hunts. This, too, is debatable. Certainly, throughout
history, some societies persecuted or banished those who would now be
considered mentally ill, but others offered protection and asylum. Before the
"invention" of asylums for the disenfranchised, foster-home care, funded by
the state, was prevalent in the original thirteen American colonies (Rothman,
1971). Other cultures have traditionally offered the mentally ill special status
and roles as soothsayers and healers.

5

Since the late eighteenth century, practitioners of the medical model, keepers of the disease concept, have distributed hope, asylum, succor, and relief from suffering to the mentally ill. During the moral-treatment era of the first half of the nineteenth century, psychotic individuals were "cured" with a regimen of hard work and instruction in etiquette and moral habits within a pastoral setting. Theories of cause were principally moral, but the prevailing social values of equality and fraternity provided the optimism necessary for good treatment programs. Unfortunately, society's institutions—much more powerful than individual physicians—ensured that common public attitudes about the mentally ill became operationalized in their treatment.

As the twentieth century approached, these same people were shelved in large warehouses, segregated from society and offered meager sustenance. Once admitted to these institutions, patients seldom left. Their plight was rationalized by the assumption that insanity was a hereditary disease of progressive brain deterioration, a condition that became more severe with each succeeding generation. Programs of sterilization were called for, and in many countries were instituted. Social Darwinism was the order of the day, so despite opposing beliefs and efforts of individual physicians, medical institutions enforced the status quo.

This history is presented as a caution to the authors as well as to readers. In this book a model will be proposed for understanding and organizing the treatment of schizophrenia. The foregoing serves to remind us that theories are often simply reifications of contemporary social values. What actually happens to people, especially low-status people, depends more on politics and economics than on the preoccupations of scholars.

Nonetheless, we do seem to be at the beginning of a good epoch for those suffering from schizophrenia. Contemporary values and economics have turned the old mental hospital inside out. The rights of all individuals, including mental patients, are collectively prized and promoted. Communities are becoming less segregated as in our pluralistic society there is more room for deviants of all kinds. Now, with medical treatments for schizophrenia that have proved effective, we possess the technology and the social climate to make major advances.

The disease concept for schizophrenia has been vindicated in the past dozen years. It offers much for the alleviation of suffering. The caution today should be aimed at the excesses of the medical model: paternalistic institutions, fostering of the sick role, undermining of people's responsibility for their own health, and blind belief in the efficacy of technology. Medical treatment, especially that of elusive diseases, must be accompanied by a vigilance for its harmful effects. Though two years in a hospital may provide an opportunity to eradicate hallucinations, it may also diminish a patient's chances of returning to independent community life.

Schizophrenia is, however, more than disease. People who develop schizophrenia are reacting to a host of environmental stresses as well as to the disease itself. Battie (1758), in *A Treatise on Madness,* put it this way:

> And indeed, with respect to Consquential Madness, whatever may accompany it as a symptom or follow it as a seeming effect, every such accidental disorder hath in reality no necessary connection to Madness itself; but is either resolvable into other injuries quite foreign to Maniacal affections; or, it is owing to any one remote cause of Madness, it is still not more than another effect of the same cause; which effect is just as capable of being thereby generated, whether Madness is or is not produced together with such symptom or before such consequence.

Many of the symptoms and behaviors of people with schizophrenia can be viewed as secondary; as stress responses, compensatory behaviors, and restitutive activities; as products of medical treatment and social responses to deviance; and as products of the interaction of the disease, the person, and the environment over long periods of time.

These secondary symptoms are relatively nonspecific. They may arise from processes only indirectly related to the illness "schizophrenia." Thus, clinicians find themselves working with a syndrome as yet not clearly defined, not knowing what part of what is seen is disease, what part is reaction, what part is projection or preconception, and what part has nothing to do with schizophrenia at all.

Some of the schizophrenias emanate from a core defect, although no core defect explains all the symptoms of schizophrenia without consideration of the interaction of this defect with neurophysiological, developmental, and social processes over time. This core defect of schizophrenia has thus far eluded discovery, although it has been hypothesized at every level of analysis, from molecular chemistry to social organization.

There may be other pathways to schizophrenia, or at least to the secondary manifestations of the disease. It is possible that some families drive their offspring mad, and indeed certain catastrophic social situations may produce similar results. In addition, each symptom of schizophrenia can appear as a component of other disease, as the product of quite different processes, and as part of the wide spectrum of normal (ethnologically, actuarially, and functionally) human behavior.

Herein lies a major dilemma for the practicing clinician. Clearly all that is seen is not simply disease when encountering a patient labeled "schizophrenic." No simple approach, be it neuroleptic medication, psychotherapy, or life-skill training, constitutes an adequate response. The problem is compounded by the fact that the schizophrenic patient's very presence in treatment may be determined by a social process beyond the reach and perhaps the grasp of the clinician. One may diagnose the problem as hallucinations while the landlady who sent the patient in may have defined the problem as uncleanliness. Having an illness and becoming a patient are two separate, although related, processes. Clinicians must pay attention to both.

To reiterate, then, the word "schizophrenia" refers to an illness or illnesses, the boundaries of which remain ill-defined, the components of which reside in all levels of organization, and the treatment of which must be multidimensional and individualized.

Further research may delineate the syndrome. A number of schizophrenias may be discovered and their pathogenesis mapped. A clearer distinction between these illnesses and other forms of madness may be made and simple treatment programs developed in the near future. Meanwhile, clinicians awaiting the unfolding of this research must continue to work with schizophrenic patients. They must rely on the publication of outcome studies, recent refinements in diagnosis and prognosis, heuristic theory, empiric evidence, the art of experience, the contributions of allied professionals, and, perhaps too often (though one shouldn't ignore their importance) deep personal convictions about the nature of human beings and their dilemmas. Such students and clinicians turn to the literature for help. Apart from being overwhelmed by quantity, they are usually disappointed. In a lengthy psychoanalytic interpretation of schizophrenia, one is unlikely to find a simple guide for what can be done for the ten schizophrenics in follow-up. One may find a complex outcome study showing that group treatment is better than individual therapy in aftercare, but therapy is of limited benefit during hospitalization, and that family therapy is less effective than either. One is unlikely, however, to find out what one should be doing in this group or what to say to the mother and father of the young boy one just admitted to a hospital.

Turning to the literature of the theoretician-therapists, one finds it an experience of having learned more about what it is to be human than about schizophrenia. Though this literature is rich and of immense help, clinician-readers must separate the wheat from the chaff, the sense from the nonsense, and uncover the hidden assumptions for themselves. This book is our synthesis and translation of research findings, clinical studies, proposed theories and models, and clinical experience into a practical framework and set of guidelines for the treatment and rehabilitation of people suffering from schizophrenia.

Emphasis will not be placed on the problem of diagnosis; this is left to the many general texts. One aspect of the problem, however, requires a further comment at this introductory point. American psychiatry has been justifiably criticized for the expansive manner in which it employs the diagnosis of schizophrenia. Certainly, common usage is too broad and too unclear. British psychiatry has been much more forthright in limiting the label "schizophrenia" to a clearly defined set of first-rank symptoms, permitting better research and population comparisons, and reducing the chance of someone being treated for a nonexistent disease.

There is, however, more to the American position than a simple problem of sloppiness. Defining absolute criteria for the diagnosis of schizophrenia, with our current state of knowledge, remains a somewhat arbitrary act. The symptoms upon which the diagnosis is made are always gathered in the context of a dyadic or larger relationship. They unfold in the communication between doctor and patient and between patient's family and doctor. They depend on form as much as content, and both of these are influenced by the human relationship and the social context. Perceptions and judgments of the verbal and behavioral productions of others tend to be socially constructed and culture bound (Berger and Luckmann, 1967). Furthermore, the closer one gets to a schizophrenic patient, the less crazy he or she seems. Karl Jaspers' distinction (1963) of psychotic symptoms as those phenomena that defy both logical and empathic understanding begins to break down when one tries very hard to understand them in the manner of Sullivan and Laing.

With these points in mind, then, it is possible to comprehend how the British psychiatrist (from a particular background of culture, social class, and objective-descriptive training) can diagnose schizophrenia consistently while the American counterpart cannot. The pluralistic culture of American society, with its pursuit of individual life-styles and its pervasive psychoanalytic orientation, breeds psychiatrists who tend to distrust diagnosis. Paradoxically, these same psychiatrists end up applying the devalued label "schizophrenia," too often.

British and American attitudes toward the treatment of schizophrenia also differ. Literature from Britain is dominated by a tone of acceptance of the realities of the disease and a therapeutic goal of learning to cope with handicaps. American literature often implies cure through psychotherapy, eradication of disease by research, and elimination of disablement through the funding of mental health programs. There seems to be benefit in taking a middle ground, aiming for the clarity of British perceptions, as exemplified by Wing (1978) and his colleagues, tempered with a touch of American optimism.

This book is divided into three major sections. Part I provides a model for understanding the origins and development of schizophrenic psychosis and the process of becoming a patient. Part II is devoted to providing a framework for conceptualizing and organizing comprehensive treatment, rehabilitation, and continuing care for people who suffer from schizophrenia. The framework consists of four models of illness and recovery guiding specific treatment tasks throughout six defined phases. Part III is divided into six chapters, each devoted to one phase of illness and recovery. When problems, issues, and interventions pertain to more than one phase, they are described in the chapter-phase in which they most commonly arise.

This book does not address the specifics of psychopharmacological management of schizophrenia. Our focus is the psychosocial component of treatment. This does not imply an antineuroleptic stance. On the contrary, the authors assume that appropriate neuroleptic medication will be offered. On the whole, the recommended use of neuroleptics is conservative: Drugs are to be prescribed in the lowest possible dosage to do the job; almost all patients should be treated at some point without drugs; the choice of medication is governed by the principle of least possible side-effects; chronic psychotic patients who do not benefit from drugs are not given them; and others are given self-control of dosage, schedule, and, on occasion, choice of neuroleptic. The following chapters will, however, address the interplay of drug and psychosocial treatments and special factors in neuroleptic management as they pertain to the problems of postpsychotic depression, rehabilitation, compliance, passivity, and the "sick role."

It is very difficult to address the complexity of schizophrenia and its treatment in a manner brief, specific, and clear enough to be of practical value to clinicians without being overly simplistic. Almost every statement made about schizophrenia and its treatment could rightly be accompanied by alternatives, exceptions, and multiple qualifications. To include them all, if it could be done, would make for poor reading. Our hope is that we have described a clear framework and that the reader will flesh it out with qualifications from his or her own experience and research.

Part I

TOWARD AN UNDERSTANDING OF SCHIZOPHRENIA

Chapter 1

ORIGINS

My problem is I can't tell the foreground from the background.
— anonymous patient

Introduction

The pursuit of an understanding of schizophrenia is treacherous. The very nature of the disease and our selective encounters with it allow for many facile social and psychological interpretations, each of which holds only temporary satisfaction. Yet perusing the research literature, one is unlikely to come away with a good and thorough explanation of the particular schizophrenic behavior one is trying to manage. One then probably falls back on reductionistic biochemical hypotheses or psychodynamic formulations. Cromwell (1975) pointed out that those aspects of schizophrenia to which clinicians usually attend (and must explain) may be far removed from the underlying deficit. As he expressed it:

> No schizophrenic has been arrested, held in jail or committed to a mental hospital for having a slow reaction time, a strong crossover effect between regular and irregular series, or any of the other phenomena [which are studied by] scholars of schizophrenia.

It is difficult to perceive a link between the rather fine and esoteric experiments of cognitive psychologists, the blatant characteristics of madness, and the frustrating and pathetic qualities of chronic schizophrenia.

One major aim of the model presented here is to create a bridge between the clinical observations, the facets of schizophrenia that demand treatment or managment, and the concepts generated outside the clinical field in information-processing theory, cognitive psychology, linguistics, and sociolinguistics. The concept of "thought disorder," examined from a new perspective, provides a starting point for this endeavor.

Thought Disorder

Thought disorder has long been considered the central problem in schizophrenia. Kraepelin (1919) collected many examples of thought disorder and described several types. Bleuler (1950) considered thought disorder a fundamental symptom and sought an explanatory principle in the concept of associations.

A great many authors have attempted to describe and/or explain thought disorder. Many descriptions that have found their way into clinical use are listed below:

    blocking
    symbolism
    associations (altered, bizarre, clang)
    displacement
    condensation (Bleuler, 1950)
    overinclusion
    interpenetration
    approximations (Cameron, 1964)
    fusion
    omission
    derailment
    driveling
    deprivation
    insertion
    broadcasting (Schneider, 1930)
    incoherence
    paralogia
    neologisms
    agrammatism (Kleist, 1914)
    Knight's move
    wooliness
    loose association
    circumstantiality
    cognitive slippage
    disorganization
    rambling

Despite these descriptions, thought disorder remains an elusive concept; in fact, the extensive number of descriptions is most likely a symptom of this elusiveness. Clinicians may agree on the presence of thought disorder, but seldom describe or explain it in the same manner. This difficulty may arise from several sources. The presence of thought disorder is an inference based on an observation of a disruption in the normal use of spoken language. Language, in turn, is one facet of communication, and communication is a complex social phenomenon.

Furthermore, thought disorder is not always present in schizophrenia and is quite variable within one patient. The interpretation of thought disorder always relies heavily on the bias of the examiner, and usually some meaning can be found in even the most bizarre productions of schizophrenic patients. In fact, some mild forms of thought disorder appear to be situation bound, apparent only during stressful or confusing interpersonal encounters. Lastly, thought disorder is not confined to schizophrenia; ordinary discourse between normal individuals, when taken out of context and put into print verbatim, may appear thought-disordered to a reader.

Several theorists have stressed the interpersonal-communication level of analysis of schizophrenic thought disorder. Cameron (1938, 1964) suggested that the genesis of schizophrenia lies in a developmental failure to acquire role-taking skills. The schizophrenic, encountering stressful interpersonal situations she or he cannot manage, abandons social communication and retreats into fantasy life. Sullivan (1962) presented a similar idea, that the withdrawal of the schizophrenic is brought about by an inability to attain satisfaction in interpersonal communication. The schizophrenic is seen to retreat to a childhood mode of communication, seeking security through magical manipulation. Haley (1963) suggested that schizophrenics actively withdraw; he explained thought disorder as an effort to deny relationships while attempting to communicate. The schizophrenic negates his or her communication (in various ways) by denying or disrupting those components of discourse that usually define and establish an interpersonal relationship.

While these theories (especially Cameron's) are attractive and clinically helpful, they fail to connect the general disruption of communication to the specific formal qualities of thought disorder. One must examine more closely both normal interpersonal communication and schizophrenic communication to make this connection.

Language and Communication

Until recently, the investigation and explanation of thought disorder were hampered by a rather limited concept of language. Language was studied out of context, the emphasis being placed on grammatical units of speech. It was assumed that thought disorder, as expressed in a communication disorder, would consist of a disruption of those rules of syntax (sentence structure) understood at the time. In fact, when schizophrenic speech is examined closely, it appears to follow the same set of syntactic and semantic rules as normal speech. Yet it is still obviously disordered. One must conclude, then, that the source of the disorder lies beyond syntactic and semantic considerations. A broader understanding of language in the context of social communication is required to clarify the phenomenon of thought disorder.

Contemporary language study considers the intent of language, its interpersonal and social dimensions. It moves from the study of single sentences to the study of "text" (larger semantic units), and from there to the study of interpersonal and social context, that is, the interpersonal and social variables that influence the use of language. In fact, these variables can be considered a part of the language event. As M. Gregory and S. Carroll in *Language and Situation* (1978) point out: "Language events do not occur in isolation from other aspects of human behaviour; rather, we know they operate within the manifold complex of human social behaviour and are mutually related to it. They take place in situations and situation is...[an] aspect of the language event: 'the environment in which text comes to life' (Halliday, 1973)...situation can be thought of as the relevant extratextual circumstances, linguistic and non-linguistic, of the language event/text in question."

A *text* is a semantic unit that finds realization in a certain number of sentences; continuity of meaning is present within text and finds expression in varying linguistic forms. For instance, in "Johnny was mad yesterday. He will be in a better mood today," "he" can be understood only by making reference to "Johnny" in the previous sentence. Similarly, "better" can be understood only by making reference to "mad" in the previous sentence. These items in the sentence are *cohesive* in the sense that they can be interpreted only by making reference to information already given in previous exchanges, and this link is necessary for the maintenance of semantic continuity. The two sentences constitute a textual unit; the first contains referents necessary for the comprehension of the second.

In other situations a necessary referent may be present in the physical environment in which the conversation occurs. An example of this would be "Put it on the table," where "the" indicates a specific table that, if the command is appropriate, should be in the physical environment of both the listener and the speaker along with the object referred to as "it."

The *context* of a language event or communication is equally important. This term refers to the extratextual circumstances within which the communication is occurring. Some elements of context are relatively static and formal while others may be considered specific and always unfolding.

The concept of role is important here. A key concept in Piaget's theory of development, and specifically of language development, is that of egocentrism and its resolution (Piaget, 1950). The young child utters words that succeed in conveying meaning to family members, but when engaged in a transaction with an unfamiliar adult or another child, shows an inability to adapt the coding of his or her message to the characteristics of the other. The young child, in other words, fails to focus upon and to use the interpersonal cues that suggest what information may or may not be available to others and which form his or her own language should take.

The child at the egocentric level of development will engage in parallel play with other children rather than engage them in a game. Games governed by rules, an important model of social interaction, do not appear until the child has overcome egocentrism in social communication and begins to approach adult competence. These skills develop over time and normally reach their complex adult form well into adolescence.

The interpersonal cues unavailable to the child are necessary both for the understanding of complex communication and for the establishment of adult relationships. Some of these interpersonal cues are rather static, such as the age, cultural, and social characteristics of the individual one addresses. Some characteristics are subsumed under the concept of "role," as in Flavell's studies of role taking and communication skills in children. Flavell (1975) emphasized the ability of the communicator to intuit the addressee's role, perceptual data, and cognitive set in initiating and maintaining communication. Role taking refers to the covert, cognitive process of adopting the perspective or attitude of another in a given situation. Adults engage automatically in this process, as do people of all cultures simplify linguistic form and modify content when addressing very young children.

Social psychologists and sociologists use the concept of role in similar ways. *Structural role theory* refers to those culturally defined roles (doctor, lawyer, wife) to which people more or less conform, while *dynamic role theory* involves the consideration of roles as tentatively unfolding rules of conduct created in the interactional process of any human encounter. These related concepts of role may be defined and refined in a variety of ways. For the purpose of this thesis, however, it can be simply stated that in order to understand a communication, one must perceive, comprehend, and integrate three categories of information other than the content and organization of a grammatical unit. The three categories are presented below:

1. Textual and extratextual referents, that is, referents from remote and recent communication or shared experience
2. Static situational variables, that is, the task at hand, the formal role relationship, the social structure and formal expectations (See Parsons, 1951, and Merton, 1968, on structural role theory.)
3. Changing situational variables, that is, role relationships as unfolding tentative rules of conduct that are created in the interaction (See Turner, 1962, and Goffman, 1959, on dynamic role theory.)

All but textual referents rely heavily on nonverbal components of language. Extratextual referents are signaled by gestures and eye movements. Formal role relationships are indicated by choice of words and tone. Unfolding rules of conduct are indicated by omissions, postures, and facial expressions. Nonverbal components of language are extensive. Clinicians often speak of metacommunication, covert messages and nonverbal communication, in referring to nonvocal signaling such as posture, facial expression and eye movements. Other signals more closely related to verbal and vocal language, such as emphasis, cadence, and tone, can also be considered nonverbal. Lyons (1972) classified these nonverbal components of language as *voice quality* (the permanent background invariable for an individual's speech), *prosodic components* (intonation, stress, and other coloring that convey meaning and communicate the attitude of the speaker), and *paralinguistic features* (signaling not so closely related to grammatical structure, such as gestures, facial expressions, and eye movements).

Nonverbal messages modify the meaning of verbal utterances. An utterance is interpreted as a question or a statement according to whether the intonational contour rises or drops toward the end of the utterance itself. For example, "John owes you." "John owes you?" In the question form of this single utterance, one's eyebrows tend to lift with the cadence of the sentence. Further modification of meaning is brought about by placement of *stress*. In the sentence "How much does John owe you?" the particular word or passage stressed would depend on intended meaning. If "how much" is stressed, the speaker is expressing a concern about the amount; if "you" is stressed, the speaker is expressing concern about the amount owed to the addressee, probably in relation to what John may owe someone else, and so forth.

As Argyle (1972) pointed out, these nonverbal components of language also play a major role in managing the immediate social relationship, while the verbal component is more closely associated with the cognitive function of language. From a social psychologist's perspective, it is the need to manage immediate social relationships without the commission of faux pas, intrusions, gaffes, presumptions, exposures, and ultimately obscenities that moderates much of our day-to-day behavior. Our interactions with others are guided by the imperative of creating and maintaining face (Goffman, 1967). When an encounter cannot be easily managed, we tend to withdraw from it.

The ability to receive and comprehend the categories of information listed above is to some extent interdependent. An ability to take on roles and try out rules of conduct developmentally is fundamental to a later quick understanding of static situational variables and formal role relationships. Similarly, the nonverbal cues that mold an understanding of relationship expectations are the same kind of cues that guide one's attention to specific textual and extratextual referents. It can also be seen that the ability to manage these categories of information would be most taxed in new social situations and unfolding (developing) relationships and least taxed in static, familiar relationships.

Schizophrenic Language and Communication

Those people likely to be labeled "schizophrenic" appear to have difficulty processing the kinds of information found in the three categories listed above. This failure, in its most severe form, can account for that clinical phenomenon which has been called "thought disorder."

Textual Failure

Rochester, Martin, and Thurston (1977) reported the results of their experiments on textual function in schizophrenic speakers. They found that *cohesive items* are used ambiguously by patients diagnosed as schizophrenic, particularly in those segments of their conversation that are considered thought-disordered by clinicians or disorganized by naive listeners. An example of such ambiguity would be this opening exchange between a clinician and a psychotic patient who have never spoken before:

How are you today?
They have already put me through the machine three times.

"They" and "the machine" imply shared information that actually was not given; an impression of disorganization and vagueness is created for the listener. While a clinician might call this problem tangentiality or loosened associations, it can be better understood as a loss of the schizophrenic speaker's ability to make adequate inferences about what information the listener may already have or to keep track of the information that has been exchanged in the course of the conversation.

A longer example of a thought-disordered response to a question is reproduced below. It can be seen that individual grammatical and semantic units (separated by slashes) remain intact but that referents are confusing and ambiguous. Those cohesive elements that require referents for their interpretation are in italics. They fail to link individual semantic units to one another or to other referents and thus the larger semantic unit or text is disrupted.

Interviewer:
Is this a word that you made up? [savage]
Patient:
No. If you hear it on the street/*then it* just goes to your brain/*because*/I am not one like *that* at all/*to say, that*/passing *pictures* around is really crazy/*because if* you have big pictures for grade nine/*and then*/you have small pictures/and/you cut the small pictures around the edges/that's what I did/well I had to use a ruler for that/and then *they* didn't have scissors *at the time*/and um/I said, I'll give *you* my picture *to Lucy*/because I didn't know what kind of girl *she* was at first/and she said okay/and she passed *it* on to *that boy*/She had the nerve to introduce me to him and I said

This phenomenon can be called "textual failure." It occurs primarily in florid-psychotic states and is generally responsive to neuroleptic medication. It may be a manifestation of a defect in very short-term memory or possibly of disturbances in the time-ordered, sequential information processing typical of the dominant hemisphere. Schizophrenia does not begin with textual failure, however, and it may be in fact a secondary phenomenon. It is also curiously variable and at times correctable by more active interviewing. Example:

"How are you today?"
"They have already put me through the machine three times."
"No, I mean how do you feel right now?"
"Oh, all right, I guess."

Contextual Failure

It has been suggested that "schizophrenic speakers fail to account for the listener's immediate needs...this arising from an inability to assess the listener's state of ignorance on a moment-to-moment basis" by Rochester, Harris, and Seeman (1978). While this conclusion derives from studies of schizophrenic language, it has a clear relationship to hypotheses emanating from cognitive studies and clinical observation.

A theory postulating that referential communication occurs by a process of selection and editing of possible associations from the individual's repertoire is presented by Cohen and others (1967, 1974, 1978). When schizophrenic patients were presented with an increasingly difficult discriminating task, they were unable to reject the initial dominant association and select a more appropriate one. A further assumption made by these authors is that an inability to disattend from immediate stimuli is at the basis of this language disturbance.

Cohen reasoned that schizophrenics are deficient in their ability to edit out situationally inappropriate responses. From the theoretical emphasis of this research, though it is cognitive and aimed at associative processes, one can surmise that the subject's judgment of what is relevant and irrelevant in selecting and editing associations is partially based on an ability to perceive and interpret the situational information discussed previously. In other words, the appropriateness and success of an association must be judged by the speaker according to the cognitive set of the listener and the social situation in which the exchange occurs. Cohen's findings are compatible with the assumption that the schizophrenic speaker is unable to grasp the characteristics of the listener in making judgments about linguistic form and content.

Clinical observations support this hypothesis. Schizophrenics are notoriously prone to misread or misinterpret others' roles and expectations in social exchanges, and have great difficulty assuming and fulfillng reciprocal roles (Cameron, 1938).

Similarly, it was noted that schizophrenics tend to overinclude similar but inappropriate objects in sorting tasks, in the work of Epstein (1953), Lisman and Cohen (1972), and Payne (1962). They also tend to respond to the dominant (more concrete) meaning of a word that has two or more meanings in common usage. This can be seen as a failure to interpret the contextual clues that would otherwise have led the subject to finer discrimination in the first category of experiments and to the selection of a less common meaning in the later set.

This phenomenon can be called "contextual failure." While the use of neuroleptics corrects textual failure and curbs the most extreme misinterpretations of context in the florid-psychotic phases of the illness, contextual failure tends to typify the premorbid development of the schizophrenic and to remain as a defect after recovery. In its more subtle form-inability to interpret the meaning of interpersonal exchanges in context—it is particularly impervious to pharmacological treatment.

The level of information processing from which this failure might emanate is a matter of conjecture. It is clear, however, that in social exchanges contextual information is principally nonverbal and that schizophrenics have little problem in hearing and comprehending the meaning of individual words. One might conclude therefore that schizophrenics have difficulty, at some level, processing the nonverbal components of interpersonal exchanges.

Nonverbal cues play an important part in signaling change in any relationship. A correct interpretation on the part of the receiver of such cues leads to a rejection of the initiative or the establishment of a different, mutually agreed-upon role relationship with its own new set of rules and expectations. What begins as a friendly relationship between two people may change, on the initiative of either party, to a sexual encounter. The initiative is usually subtle and nonverbal and may be accepted or rejected in kind. If rejected in this manner, the two participants can return to their previous relationship without loss of face.

Verbal and nonverbal messages are not usually interpreted in isolation, but their meaning is conveyed and interpreted by reciprocal relationship. The level of interpretation of verbal messages, particularly, is often based, in an interpersonal exchange, on the nonverbal cues that accompany it. The ambiguity of a sentence such as "Would you like to go to bed?" can be resolved only by proper grasp of the socio-situational context, the nature and continuity of the exchange that precedes the question, and the nonverbal component of the message. It is well known that schizophrenic patients show perplexity or "inappropriate" responses to mildly ambiguous messages or double entendre. They are aware of the possibilities of a relationship but unable to interpret the nonverbal or other situational variables that would otherwise direct them to an appropriate course of action.

Conclusion

In summary, then, it is suggested that schizophrenic thought disorder can be conceptualized as consisting of two components: *textual failure* and *contextual failure*. While textual failure is responsible for the more florid examples of formal thought disorder in psychotic states, contextual failure appears to be a more primary defect, present in the early stages of schizophrenia as well as in the post-psychotic recovery phases. The ability to receive, interpret, and exchange *nonverbal information* in interpersonal exchanges is an essential ingredient of context. A decay in the ability to manage this nonverbal information, then, would appear to be implicated as a fundamental defect in schizophrenia. This may be one aspect of a larger information processing problem for schizophrenics, but it encompasses the particular categories of information that establish social meaning, continuity, and, essentially, the cohesion of human groups. An inability to manage this information will have profound consequences for the development of relationships and ultimately for the maintenance of shared (socially validated) interpretations of experience.

While the information-processing problems of schizophrenics are being pursued by research scientists (see the reviews of Chapman and Chapman, 1973; Cromwell, 1975; and Maher, 1977), at neurophysiological and neuropsychological levels of analysis, the level of conceptualization presented here provides a link between their hypotheses and clinical realities. It also permits the consideration of developmental, psychological, and social influences on the course of the disease.

A failure to manage nonverbal contextual information will certainly have negative effects on any current relationship a schizophrenic might attempt. It can also be surmised that, in a longitudinal fashion, the management of contextual information is crucial to the development of adult social skills. The successful management of this information developmentally provides the building blocks for interpersonal and social competence.

Furthermore, by conceptualizing the deficit at this level it can be seen that the schizophrenic would be especially vulnerable to change, complexity, and ambiguity in interpersonal situations. Shakow (1963) labeled this common clinical observation "neophobia." Here one can see that simple, old, practiced relationships (e.g., parent-child) require minimal finesse in the day-to-day management of contextual information, while new or ambiguous relationships require a finely tuned and accurate feedback system.

While textual failure may be a way of describing the more severe types of formal thought disorder, contextual failure would appear to be a more fundamental and profound deficit. An inability or decay in the ability to interpret contextual information would seem to be the basis for the development of the many schizophrenic symptoms to which therapists must attend.

The authors propose then that the deficit that exists is related to specific aspects of information processsing and has fundamental significance in the development of schizophrenia. This deficit pertains primarily to that aspect of information processing concerned with the management of the nonverbal components of communication, related to one's ability to meaningfully and accurately interpret role relationships and expectations. This deficit also concerns that aspect of functioning involving integration of recent verbal information and extratextual referents. Thus, the potential schizophrenic with a deficit in these areas of information processing is seen as experiencing an inability to discern meaning in interpersonal interactions and to organize his or her social world. The prospective schizophrenic's failure to accurately perceive and interpret the messages being received from others will interfere with establishment or maintenance of consistent and functional role relationships and with the ability to respond to behavioral expectations.

Normally, a finely tuned nonverbal feedback system and a catalogue of previous experience will allow one to accurately anticipate responses in most interactions. This *transactional predictability* is an aspect of relationships that helps to maintain order and decrease anxiety. The schizophrenic's inability to interpret contextual clues leads to a failure to develop or maintain transactional predictability. This lack will, of course, be more apparent and more threatening in new relationships and less problematic in older relationships, such as those with parents.

It is suggested that this deficit is fundamental to the development of the full and complex syndrome of schizophrenia. All other manifestations of the syndrome can be considered secondary. Chapter 2 is devoted to a description of the way a decay in one's ability to interpret context might lead, over time, to the many and varied symptoms of schizophrenia.

\

Chapter 2

EVOLUTION OF SYMPTOMS

My periscope may have been a little too peripheral for city lights.
— anonymous patient

Overextension and Withdrawal

As an individual's ability to accurately interpret context—based on the ability to receive and interpret the moment-to-moment nonverbal components of language decays, he or she will experience a failure of knowing "what is expected of me." Ability to manage relationships will become impaired. This is, then, the phase of schizophrenic breakdown Docherty, Van Kammen, Siris, and Marder (1978) labeled "overextension." The subjective experience of this condition has been variously reported as, for example, "feelings of anxiety," "not fitting in," and "losing one's grip." This period of overextension could be precipitated by social, environmental, or developmental changes or, simply, a worsening of an underlying process. The consequences of this impairment will logically depend on two sets of factors: the first is the extent, severity, consistency, and speed of onset of the deficit; the second is the individual's age, developmental phase, personality structure, social relationships, and nature of involvement with family.

Most hypothetical situations described in this book refer to a young adult with parents and siblings but, of course, people suffering from schizophrenia can be found in a variety of social circumstances and the actual case examples reflect this.

The following is a description of the way in which such an impairment might interact with certain variables to produce a picture of schizophrenia.

In behavioral terms, a natural response to overextension would be withdrawal from the relationships and social experiences that create anxiety, and regression to simpler role relationships the individual has fulfilled adequately in the past. It would also seem likely, as so often is clinic-ally observed, that the subject's parents would respond to this regression by an ambivalent caring and protectiveness that reinforce the regression to a simpler parent-child relationship. If the answer to "What is expected of me?" is confusing and ambiguous (Laing and Esterson, 1970), then anxiety, withdrawal, and regression would be further enhanced. This state of affairs can remain stable for some time; the young schizophrenic remains in an immature, simple role relationship with mother, father, and family, withdrawing from or not attempting more complex role relationships with others. In this situation, an understanding of reciprocal roles is available and transactional predictability is maintained.

Case Example

The patient, a 30-year-old man, had suffered five acute psychotic episodes since the age of 19. Between hospitalizations he lived at home with his parents but developed no new relationships with peers of either sex. Now, at age 30, in conversation with his therapist and his brother, he reminisced about playing in the high school band, his one date and his one kiss before the onset of his illness. He spoke of these events as if occurring in the past week and in language more common to adolescents of the previous decade. His profanity had not progressed beyond "kripes, Kate," and his analysis of the anxiety-ridden transaction between himself and his date remained that of a shy adolescent.

It is interesting to note that the age of onset of schizophrenia is later for females than for males (Bland, 1977). This finding may be explained by earlier social and developmental pressures on males to move from a child-hood social position and assume an independent adult role; females, on the other hand, are often permitted a more extended period to remain at home without expectation, free from pressures to move from the daughter role. In some cultures, in fact, the girl may shift from her position in her family of origin to marriage without a major change in her behavioral functioning and role relationships. Other than those accompanying the physical act of sexual intercourse, expectations for her behavior may not change until the birth of a child; the shift from daughter to wife may impose far less strain than the shift from wife to mother. Thus, the male and female, equally impaired in their ability to interpret context, may not be subjected to the same developmental and social demands. Though the female may be able to maintain simple or childlike role relationships for longer periods, this pattern may change with increased impact of the women's movement. Commensurate changes in family and societal expectations could also affect other such sex-typed roles and tasks.

Transitional Crisis

If I could only color the vibes I would have something to fly by.
—anonymous patient

At some point new and potentially ambiguous expectations arise, making it impossible for the schizophrenic to sustain his or her limited and confined role relationships. Ill equipped, the person is pushed into considering or experiencing new relationships. Typically, this situation occurs during those years the subject is culturally expected to begin assuming adult responsibilities, although many cases exist in which families accommodate a prepsychotic's early-adolescent behavior well into his or her middle years. In this latter instance, the subject may not come to the attention of health authorities until a parent dies or the family is disrupted in another way.

More commonly, a transitional crisis is precipitated by developmental imperative and new social activity occurring in the novice stage of adulthood. To some extent the pressure to engage in such difficult social relationships as dating may be biological, while social class and ethnicity may fashion the immediate vocational and/or education expectations for the young adult. He or she may be thrust into new social situations by such accidental phenomena as a family move, parental separation, father's retirement, or siblings' leaving home. Whichever the source, new expectations do develop and the young schizophrenic is forced into considering or directly experiencing new role relationships. A similar pivotal or transitional point has been described by several authors under the various headings of "developmental impasse," "insoluble impasse," and "transition" (Bowers, 1974; Kubie, 1967; Semrad, 1966).

All people experience such transitional points at various periods throughout their lives. Normally these transitions are negotiated by careful, albeit anxious perception and interpretation of others' expectations on a moment-to-moment basis in interpersonal communication. More specifically, the novice must have a finely tuned ability to interpret context, to understand the situational and role characteristics of others, to scan for information, and to actively clarify expectations, and in doing so, to learn the transactional rules of the new, unfolding role relationship. These tools, most needed to effect successful transition, are denied the schizophrenic.

Anxiety, arousal, and perplexity appear as consequences of the subject's failure to master new situations. These, in turn, lead to behaviors designed to decrease anxiety, regain equilibrium, and reestablish transactional predictability.

A feedback mechanism operates here. With each failure to behave according to the role expectations of othes, these others will likely modify their expecations and/or limit their communications, compounding the schizophrenic's confusion (Gruenberg, 1967). He or she will experience what could be described as a profound loss of meaning and continuity or, as more poetically expressed by Mark Vonnegut in *Eden Express* (1976), "Putting it together was like to trying to make a movie from a bunch of slides that had nothing to do with each other."

Compensatory and Restitutive Activities

The attempts to resolve this dilemma can include a variety of reactions and compensatory activities that the authors see as mechanisms for regaining transactional predictability. These are listed below and then discussed on succeeding pages.

1. Further Withdrawal from Social Contact
   a. avoidance of new situations
   b. regression to or maintenance of earlier role relationships established with parents
2. Adoption of Restrictive Communication Patterns
   a. clinically described as "obsessional traits," "lack of spontaneity," and "poverty of ideas"
   b. understood as limited or simplified communication patterns that increase transactional predictability
3. Chaotic Searching Behavior
   a. travel
   b. preoccupation with religious documents, fads, and/or fringe groups
   c. use of consciousness-altering drugs and/or bizarre diets (As Mark Vonnegut described it, "I was trying out the new world and my new self.")
4. Conversion
   a. adoption of simplistic codes
   b. conversion to religious groups and social orders that provide simple and stereotyped role relationships (e.g., Hare Krishna sect or Scientology)
5. Assumption of a Stereotypical Role for Self
   a. Hysteric, Crazy, Bad Child, Infant, Parent, Savior, Rebel, Again from Mark Vonnegut, at the height of his perplexity, "Well, these people need a prophet and I guess, times being what they are, short notice and all, I'm the best they could do." (This concept might explain the common clinical argument over whether the patient is "really crazy" or "just acting crazy." Often, in fact, the answer is, most accurately, both).
6. Projection of Role Characteristics Onto Others
   a. may be caricatured notions of parent/teacher/religious figure/or doctor
   b. generally drawn from earlier experiences
   c. responses of others would, in most cases, not fulfill the projected role characteristics and thus the patient's perplexity would be enhanced
   d. in clinical settings, seen as a variety of thought disorders or as delusional ideas.

Withdrawal from social contact and adoption of restrictive communication patterns. Mechanisms one and two above resemble the state that Docherty refers to as "restricted consciousness." Whether or not an actual restriction of consciousness does occur is debatable. Certainly some schizophrenic patients spend an inordinate amount of time sleeping and others appear empty-headed, but a great number who appear out of touch for long periods of time report later that they were well aware of their surroundings, of other patients, and of their therapists and that their heads were full of things they wished to communicate but could not.

When these two mechanisms (withdrawal from social contact and restriction of communication patterns) are adopted over a long period of time, they create a diagnostic and treatment problem. Often patients engaging these mechanisms reveal very little when interviewed. There is a "praecox," or out-of-touch feeling about them, and their families report minor episodes of bizarre behavior. Though seeming totally unmotivated and leading impoverished lives, they display no positive symptoms of schizophrenia. The interviewer senses that there may be an underlying psychosis or, as described within the parameters of this model, that if stressed by social or developmental demands, the patient would become psychotic.

Chaotic searching behavior. The pursuit of continuity and meaning in travel, exotic locations, vegetarian diet, drugs, communal experiences, and fads is fairly widespread among North American youth. These can be creative and growth-promoting processes for healthy individuals, especially in times of widespread social change. But for young people suffering from schizophrenia, these are relatively unsuccessful restitutive mechanisms that eventually increase distress and alienation. Joining a commune, adopting an idiosyncratic diet, and heading west by thumb may temporarily establish a simplified context allowing for some transactional predictability, but they will, eventually, produce even more disjunction with the larger societal pattern, increasing the young schizophrenic's vulnerability.

Conversion. The schizophrenic may feel protected for a longer period if she or he is able to settle into one religious group or social order. In an organization in which the rules are simple, the relationships are similar to the parent-child experience, and where rational verbal communication is not valued, the young schizophrenic may go undetected for some time. There may be times, in fact, when conversion to a simple but stable and well-integrated religious code will offer the young schizophrenic more than psychiatric treatment. Unfortunately a number of young schizophrenic patients opt for joining such movements, becoming members of the Hare Krishna sect, the Sun Young Moon organization, or Scientologists, none of which is integrated within the larger social matrix. These fringe sects may offer initial protection as the schizophrenic enters the structure and confinement of the group. Over time, however, confusion and disorganization increase as the young person must make sense of the dissonant intersection between his or her group and the rest of society.

Assumption of a stereotypical role for self.

> I asked directions to the water fountain when they pegged me for the Virgin Mary (being so near Christmas and all)
>
> —anonymous patient

The roles we play, or simply the dominant patterns of behavior we display, are determined to a great extent by the expectations we perceive from others. This must be especially true for people like young schizophrenics, who have relatively unformed or inconsistent concepts of self. A young, suggestible girl, discerning that the staff of the psychiatric ward expect her to be trouble, might decide to give them her best. She can manage to fulfill their expectations, resolve her own conflict over being good or bad, and rebel against authority in one fell swoop.

The young schizophrenic patient, unable to decipher the expectations of others, may be forced to adopt a pattern of behavior that will fulfill some traditional and known role and thus provide, at least unilaterally, some transactional predictability. When this adopted role offers a disjunctive reciprocity for the roles of others, the others will see the patient as being inappropriate, crazy, deluded, or, sometimes, "acting crazy."

Projection of role characteristics onto others. This concept derives from an observation of the acute schizophrenic with thought disorder. It has been suggested that such a patient has difficulty interpreting the role characteristics of others. Many of these patients respond as if speaking to a parent or teacher, a friend or doctor—and sometimes to all of these roles and more—during the course of an interview. Thus, when asked about any recent illnesses, the adolescent responds as if answering an essay question put forth by her teacher. The response is then experienced by the examiner as thought-disordered. If she is having trouble interpreting the context of the situation, her natural adaptive response is to impose her own. This imposition may be fixed and shade into overt delusions, or be transitory and merely perplexing to the interviewer.

The compensatory and restitutive activities described above can occur as adaptive strategies in life situations other than schizophrenia. In his section in the *Comprehensive Textbook of Psychiatry* (1975), Lehmann illustrates this in the following case:

Case Example

A 20-year-old college dropout illustrates some aspects of this new problem for the clinician. The young man had been arrested in front of a gas station, where he was meditating and blocking traffic. [Inappropriate and bizarre behavior?] When he was arrested, he responded by laughing. [Inappropriate emotional reaction?] At the police station he expressed his need to "laugh or fuck" in order to "prevent thinking." [Bizarre and irrelevant, probably autistic, reasoning?] The police concluded that he was clearly insane and delivered him to a mental hospital.

The young man told the psychiatrist who examined him that he was a Zen Buddhist and that thinking and analyzing things inhibited true growth of personality, according to his philosophy. He was convinced that the two best ways of preventing himself from getting lost in thinking were "laughing and fucking" because both were incompatible with thinking. "Sort of reciprocal inhibition, if you believe in that stuff." Under certain circumstances—for instance, in the police station—he could use only the laughing method. He tried to make things "Buddhaful"; his smile indicated that this was a pun and not a neologism. Why had he chosen the gas station to meditate? "Well, that's where the winds of Karma blew me." After 30 minutes he terminated the interview by walking out of the room, remarking that he was becoming upset by the "very bad vibrations" he was getting from the psychiatrist.

The man was discharged after a few days' observation, with a diagnosis of behavior disorder in an eccentric personality with poor judgment. The psychiatrist suspected that he might develop schizophrenia eventually, but there were no grounds for making this diagnosis at the time.

In discussing this case, Lehmann emphasized the "differential culture currents and standards that now exist within the Western cultural sphere and [that we] must make allowances for them."

The young man seems to be utilizing, in varying degrees, the first five compensatory mechanisms. There is, however, a relatedness about him and, even more diagnostically significant, he sends and presumably receives nonverbal messages to clarify the context of the word "Buddhaful." It is interesting to note that the feature by which Lehmann decides "Buddhaful" is a pun rather than a neologism is the nonverbally signaled intention or attitude. Schizophrenic patients will often explain neologisms when asked to do so. The problem is that in using them they do not clarify or signal contextual elements, and thus they do not clarify their meaning. This out-of-context or unexplained use of neologisms, not the actual use of the word itself, is what is perceived as crazy.

Restatement of Symptoms of Schizophrenia as Interpersonal-Communicative Processes

At this point, then, it would be important to show how the full range of schizophrenic symptoms arise (in social and developmental contexts, over time) from the deficit described previously. One or more of these six compensatory mechanisms may protect the potential schizophrenic for an extended period of time. As they fail, he or she becomes further isolated from validating and structuring social experience. Isolation increases the likelihood of perceptual distortions, misinterpretations, and the full range of symptoms associated with schizophrenia. The clinical picture is usually a mixture of the compensatory mechanisms described above and the symptoms as follows:

Praecox experience or glass wall phenomenon. This is an elusive yet ubiquitous symptom of schizophrenia that proves to be remarkably reliable in diagnostic studies. It involves an examiner's feeling that the patient is not entirely present, detached, "not with me," or "it's as if there's a glass wall between us."

This experience can be understood as the schizophrenic's failure to process the bits of data (primarily nonverbal information emanating from the examiner) that would allow him or her to fully understand the context of the interview. The examiner in turn experiences the disjunction as it is expressed in the patient's verbal and especially nonverbal responses (or lack of responses). It is the nonverbal components of language (eye movements, voice tone) that signal affect, relatedness, purpose, and relationship boundaries. The moment-to-moment feedback circuit required is disrupted by the schizophrenic's inability to process the necessary bits of information.

Ideas of reference. It is common practice to hypothesize a reference point for observed events or overheard remarks. The more ambiguous the situation, the more mistaken the hypothesis might be. When this ambiguity of situation is coupled with personal anxiety and an unclear relationship between self and others, the assumed reference point might become the self. Normally, this tendency is dissipated by the activity of consensual validation, a comprehension of the situation, and the correct interpretation of contextual information.

For the schizophrenic, the loss of understanding of the relationship of self to others and to external situations is profound, and consensual validation is not easily available. The contextual information that would lead to referents other than the self is not available to the schizophrenic.

Delusions. Delusions may be understood as explanatory mechanisms for further resolving the major predicament arising from a decay in the ability to interpret context. From Freud onward, investigators have postulated that delusions are a means of explaining experiences that would otherwise be psychologically unacceptable. This remains a useful interpretation for the understanding of paranoid states. For the schizophrenic, however, such experiences are not simply unacceptable, but also unfathomable. Delusions provide the schizophrenic with a reliable and simplified *context* within which to interpret communication and bring meaning to otherwise meaningless events.

It is noteworthy that the *content* of delusional ideas is seldom trivial. Delusional beliefs are usually direct expressions of, or metaphors for, power and control, vulnerability and passivity, love, hate, and guilt. Indeed, these are extreme expressions of the very parameters by which we all manage relationships.

In the clinical setting, the schizophrenic's inability to understand the role and purpose of the psychiatric examiner might further support a conviction that something suspicious is happening, especially if the interviewer is vague and ambiguous. Again, Mark Vonnegut:

> Paranoia was the best way to deal with my situation, the most hopeful way to make any sense of the things that were happening to me. If there was no sense to what was happening, no intention, malignant or benign, then there was no hope. Would you rather be chased by a pack of wild dogs that were hungry or a pack of dogs that had a master who could, if he wanted to, call them off.

Hallucinations. As Horowitz (1975) pointed out, hallucinations can be seen as the product of avoidance of self-designation. He suggested that hallucinations are erroneous appraisals of information and intrusions into conscious awareness that must be seen as "not of the self." Still, this explanation does not quite come to grips with the auditory hallucinations experienced by schizophrenia sufferers. It is important to note that some schizophrenics report the source of the voices as internal while others report it as external. Our model suggests the following explanation.

Normally, listening to one's own thoughts—as opposed to unconscious thinking—requires the same appreciation of context and text as listening to the verbal productions of another person. It constitutes the conscious, essentially dyadic, communication between "I" and "self." The thought "I am evil" or simply "Evil!" requires, for comprehension, an extratextual referent: "[I think] I am evil." Here *textual* and *contextual failure* would lead to a loss of meaning to the "I." Thoughts become, in effect, disembodied—experienced without a clear link to the "I." Such thoughts are then experienced as free-floating voices, devoid of contextual meaning. It would be necessary to construct or infer a source of these thoughts, explain both their existence and their apparent unrelatedness. When these acknowledged communications to the self consist of fragmentary or unpalatable directives and/or accusations (e.g., "Break your mother's vase," "Whore!"), their source would need to be seen as other than "I."

As Wing (1978) pointed out, there seems to be a spectrum of phenomena, from "loud thoughts" (the experience of one's own thoughts being spoken aloud in the head...or simply "hearing one's own thinking") to "thought insertion" (the experience of thoughts being put into one's head from outside sources) to "thought broadcast" (the experience of feeling that one's thoughts are being heard by others) to "auditory hallucinations (source perceived within)" to "auditory hallucinations (source perceived as external)." Though a single patient does not exhibit this whole continuum, this is the likely pattern of progression followed. Specific symptoms documented by the examiner are determined by the extent of this progression at the time the patient was first examined and the extent to which the patient developed explanatory elaborations of his or her initial experience.

It is important to note that with chronicity, habit patterns may develop, and the "listening attitude" described by Arieti (1976) would be a natural consequence. Furthermore, the sense of self and the boundaries of the self, insofar as they are social constructs, are terribly damaged over time, leaving the patient more vulnerable to misperceptions. Our persistent human striving to organize our perceptions of the world about us and their relation to ourselves explains why these mechanisms may arise within the private world of the schizophrenic to provide consistency and meaning.

Therapists have long assumed that hallucinations were projected thoughts, unacceptable to the patient's self-image; the frustrating task of therapy has been to get the patient to accept these impulses, wishes, and accusations as his or her own. The disembodied, unrelated quality of the voices usually thwarts such theraputic maneuvers. It is not simply that patients *will* not accept these as their own thoughts, they *can* not; the tools by which they would relate them to the self are deficient.

NOW IS THE TIME FOR GODS TO STAND UP FOR BASTARDS.
The voices didn't even have the courtesy to tell me it was Shakespeare. As usual, it seemed like the voices were trying to help, trying to give me some clue about what was going on. As usual, it didn't help much. Who was and who wasn't a bastard? What sort of things are gods and bastards going to do? When is now? (Vonnegut, 1976)

Inappropriate and/or blunted affect. Affective response is primarily a social/interpersonal phenomenon. It depends on the ability to receive, interpret, and respond to subtle interpersonal, primarily nonverbal clues on a moment-to-moment basis. This is precisely the information with which the schizophrenic has the most difficulty. With a decay in the ability to manage this information, his or her own respones will appear inappropriate, off-key, or blunted. This pattern may be further reinforced by depression, anxiety, social isolation, and institutionalization.

Bizarre preoccupations. Many productions of schizophrenic patients are very strange and difficult to comprehend. It is equally difficult to explain this phenomenon as a whole, other than by invoking such nonspecific concepts as "primary process," "autism," "symbolic logic," and "private world." But if one returns to the model presented here and considers the early symptoms of schizophrenia, these preoccupations can be seen as attempts to reorganize a world of experience that has lost its meaning and continuity. A decay in the ability to interpret context and accompanying perplexity and arousal leads the schizophrenic on a search for relatedness. The patient will scan his or her environment for cues and symbols that can be woven together to remake an organized whole. For example, early on a schizophrenic may notice the coincidence of the passing of three items—the number three, the bosomlike appearance of a 3, and his own sexual feelings—and try to relate them to one another, to derive a meaning or greater significance. Later, if chronicity ensues, this individual may elaborate this into a more comprehensive private logic. The purpose is still to organize his perceptions and achieve some transactional predictability. This kind of struggle is not surprisingly laced with primitive thinking and strong emotions.

Often, the content of such a private system is expressed as a preoccupation with such polar values as love/hate, good/bad, right/wrong, freedom/control, and so on. This polarity can be understood as an attempt to establish stability and predictability by categorizing experience along fundamental value dimensions derived from earlier developmental stages. The child establishes order and predictability in a similar, if less verbal fashion. Figure 2-1 on pages 34, 35 is an excerpt from the notebook of a university student who developed schizophrenia.

Case Example

The patient, a 40-year-old housewife who had become silent and withdrawn during a controlled fight with her husband at the dinner table, became increasingly confused, perplexed, agitated, and thought-disordered over the next two weeks. Now she sat in an interview with the psychiatrist, a packet of sugar in one hand and a packet of nuts in the other, shifting them from hand to hand, seeming to weigh them. "It's just a matter of balancing protein and carbohydrate," she said to the examiner.

Life-skill and social-skill deficits. In the past, deficits in the area of life skills (handling money, cooking, shopping, catching buses) and social

6 a.m., Thursday — January 17,

world + breath = life

∴ life = species + matter

⇔ species = male + female

⇔ matter = species + breath

1. breath →
2. female ⇝
3. life →
4. male ⇝
5. matter →
6. world ⇝

January 17,
9 a.m.

Is it a terrible thing to tell the household?
After all, am I really too young?
No, I'm old and do I feel it:
Is everything really for you,
If so, than either forget it now for ever and ever.
I think I love you:
What do you think?
What is strength and what is weakness.
Strength is seen in a man
And acknowledged in a woman;
Weakness, delicateness is seen in a woman
And known in a man.
The household is terrible, 9:07 a.m
And it is only this one,
By my spiritual knowledge, I see:
Do you see?
Do you understand, or is this a flashback of torture.

Figure 2-1.

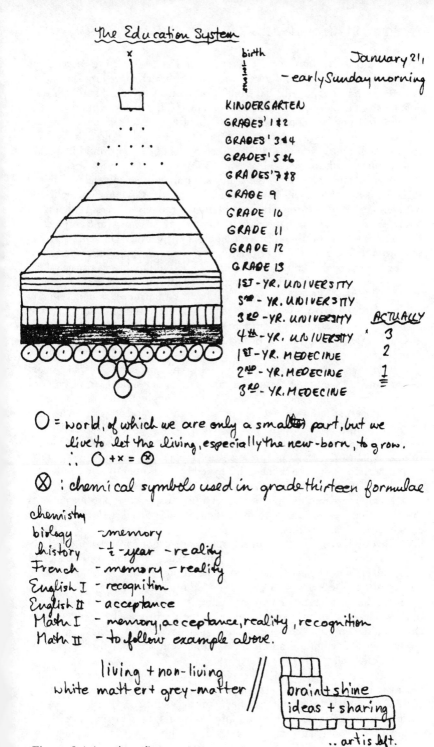

The Education System

birth

January 21,
— early Sunday morning

KINDERGARTEN
GRADES' 1 & 2
GRADES' 3 & 4
GRADES' 5 & 6
GRADES' 7 & 8
GRADE 9
GRADE 10
GRADE 11
GRADE 12
GRADE 13
1ST - YR. UNIVERSITY
2ND - YR. UNIVERSITY
3RD - YR. UNIVERSITY   ACTUALLY
4TH - YR. UNIVERSITY   3
1ST - YR. MEDECINE   2
2ND - YR. MEDECINE   1
3RD - YR. MEDECINE

$\bigcirc$ = world, of which we are only a small part, but we
live to let the living, especially the new-born, to grow.
∴ $\bigcirc + x = \otimes$

$\otimes$: chemical symbols used in grade thirteen formulae

chemistry
biology   — memory
history   — $\frac{1}{2}$ - year — reality
French   — memory — reality
English I   — recognition
English II — acceptance
Math I   — memory, acceptance, reality, recognition
Math II   — to follow example above.

living + non-living   //   brain + shine
white matter + grey-matter //   ideas + sharing

.. art is left.

Figure 2-1 (continued).

35

skills have received only cursory attention in the assessment of psychiatric patients. An underlying pathology was deemed much more important. Yet most schizophrenic patients have major problems with social and life skills, and it is often these problems, rather than the first-rank symptoms, that prohibit independent community life (Paul, 1969). There is yet no uniform and comprehensive description of those life and social skills required for independent living (Phillips, 1978). Such a list, of course, would be highly dependent on culture, social class, and values.

It is certain, however, that a large number of social skills or subtle social behaviors are essential for normal independent living. Schizophrenic patients are often deficient in these. This is probably the result of several interrelated factors: the primary deficit, compensatory and protective retreat and withdrawal, and environmental deprivation. The schizophrenic patient is deficient in the very building blocks that would otherwise allow him or her to develop adult social skills. These building blocks consist of the cueing and signaling of primarily nonverbal communication, which depend in turn on the ability to interpret context. Futhermore, a decay in the ability to interpret context leads the schizophrenic to remain in or retreat to preadult role relationships, a retreat reinforced to varying degrees by anxious parents, paternalistic professionals, and confining, limited institutions.

In extreme situations, "these patients do not engage in, or make social interactions as we know them; they use few or no signs [verbal or nonverbal] toward one another; they have no explicit leadership that is acknowledged or followed; they do not cooperate, trade off, or barter; they do not pick up from or renew an interaction with another" (Orford, 1976). Thus, to some extent, social-skill deficits are a product of the disease itself; to a greater extent they are the result of secondary reaction over a long period of time. This statement is illustrated by a number of programs, pioneered by Clark (1974) and Pasamanick (1967) among others, that have successfully improved the functioning of hundreds of schizophrenic patients through concerted efforts to improve their life and social skills and thereby enrich their environments.

Chronicity. Prognosis and chronicity are major concerns in the study of schizophrenia. They are often used in making the diagnosis itself, and many investigators have attempted to separate groups of schizophrenic patients into categories with prognostic significance (Myers, 1978). Still, the most that can be stated with assurance at this point is that some schizophrenics have good outcomes, others remain chronically disabled, and chronic illness remains chronic. That is, patients who have lengthy premorbid histories of symptoms and marginal functioning tend to do poorly postmorbidly as well.

Many factors may confer chronicity on a schizophrenic patient. If the primary deficit is severe, if it has been slow developing, if it appears at an early age, and if treatment has been unsuccessful for whatever reason, chronicity may develop. It is then more likely that the schizophrenic's idiosyncratic, personal, autistic interpretations of his or her environment will be well-established from habit, reinforcement, and memory.

Prognostication on the basis of severity of symptoms is unreliable. In fact, the more acutely ill schizophrenic patient often fares better than someone with a long-standing subacute illness.

The Elgin scale (Wittman, 1941), Phillips scale (1953), and other methods of separating process schizophrenia (bad prognosis) from reactive schizophrenia (good prognosis) include many developmental and social factors. As Strauss, Bokes, and Carpenter (1977, 1978a, 1978b) point out, however, these are the same factors that infer poor prognosis with any major illness. This last observation has far-reaching consequences. It implies that, rather than using developmental and social deficits as markers for assigning poor prognosis, clinicians should focus comprehensive rehabilitative efforts on them and begin to develop prognostic models related to patients' responses to these interventions. This is not a new concept for some areas of rehabilitative medicine; unfortunately, psychiatry is often as guilty as the rest of medicine in ignoring developmental and social factors in treatment and rehabilitation. Still, schizophrenia does pose a special problem, with its "poverty syndrome," "amotivation," and "avolition." Within the context of the model presented here, however, these latter progenitors of chronicity can be viewed as protective, compensatory mechanisms brought to bear on the underlying threat of disorganization.

Chronicity, then, is the consequence of an interplay, over time, of the central deficit itself, compensatory and restitutive mechanisms, extrinsic social and developmental factors, institutional environments, and, of course, community intolerance. Because so many factors are involved and because some of these may be modified by programs of treatment and rehabilitation, clinicians should remain reluctant to prophesy poor prognosis.

CONCLUSION

The syndrome of schizophrenia is a complex admixture of intrinsic symptoms, secondary symptoms, compensatory and restitutive behaviors, and extrinsic factors. The developmental pathway to this condition can be represented by the diagram in Figure 2-2.

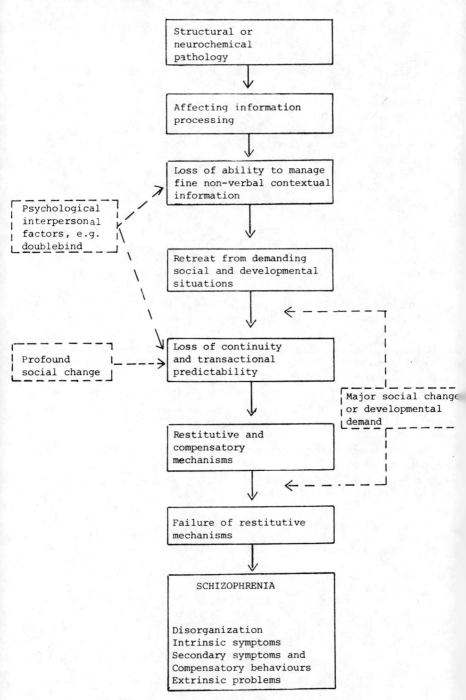

Figure 2-2: Developmental Pathway of Schizophrenia.

Chapter 3

CONVEYANCE INTO PATIENTHOOD

So I set sail for the northern skies and, trying very hard to balance myself on one leg, ran into a flamingo hunter.

— anonymous patient

The Definitional Process

In the previous chapter, a hypothesis was proposed describing the manner in which an individual might develop schizophrenia. This chapter will focus on the way in which the individual becomes a patient. Conveyance into patienthood is a complex process. The presence of disease is only one of many factors that determines when and how this might happen.

The personality of the individual and the existence of some kind of deviant behavior both play an important role in the evolution of the individual's patienthood state. In addition, two broad categories of factors influence help-seeking behavior and the manner in which a particular behavior or experience becomes defined as illness. They are (1) the large social context, including religion, social class, prevalent social values, and economics, and (2) family and small-group processes. The first category, the larger social context, is of particular interest to sociologists, health-care planners, and epidemiologists. These factors were closely examined in the works of Cumming and Cumming (1957), Dohrenwend and Dohrenwend (1974), Mechanic and Volkart (1967), and Volkart (1961), and in a collection of studies and essays to be found in Spitzer and Denzin's book, *The Mental Patient: Studies in the Sociology of Deviance* (1968). The therapist, though probably unable to influence these factors, should be aware that they operate on him or her, as well as on the patient. The therapist's perceptions of the presence of illness and the manner of participation in conveying the individual into patienthood will be influenced by issues related to the larger social context: economics, institutional values and beliefs, as well as both his or her own and the prospective patient's ethnicity and social class. The clinician, the individual, and the individual's ecological group (in most cases consisting primarily of family members) participate together in the process of defining an individual as being ill. The extent of awareness of the nonmedical factors influencing this process determines the extent to which the clinician will be able to avoid and resist misuse of illness definitions, patienthood, and institutionalization. The manner in which illness is discussed and patienthood proposed should be sensitive to ethnic and social-class conceptions.

In examining the treatment and rehabilitation of schizophrenia, family and small-group processes are of primary concern to the clinician. These factors more directly and individually influence the course of the illness, the point at which institutional help is requested, and the eventual success or failure of the patient's return to the community. Family process is especially important since schizophrenia is a slowly unfolding illness, the primary symptoms of which directly affect interpersonal communication.

The point at which the individual can be objectively identified as "having an illness" or "being psychotic" and the point at which that individual's family define him or her as "sick" and seek help may be far removed from each other. Generally, the illness has been evolving for some time before the individual comes in contact with the psychiatric system. Since the deficit or illness is usually slow in developing, the individual's family has plenty of time to adjust to the changes in the young prepatient schizophrenic. They often accommodate to his or her idiosyncrasies more readily than they seek external help. The changes in the schizophrenic family member may be subtle, inconsistent, and ambiguous. The compensatory mechanisms adopted (restriction of communication patterns, regression to or impasse at childhood roles) will press the family to further accommodation. The roles and perceptions of family members will shift to accommodate the behavior of the member developing schizophrenia. Although communication patterns within the family will reflect this shift, organization and predictability can often still be maintained. It is only when this accommodation is threatened by new and sudden changes or when it affects external relationships (for example, at school or work) that the family is pressed to move toward illness definitions and to seek external help.

This change might be a worsening of symptoms or attempts on the part of the prospective patient to alter the relationship with parents. Both can serve to disrupt the family equilibrium and send parents seeking external solutions. It is not necessarily a change in the schizophrenic member of the family that precipitates help-seeking behavior. A change in another family member (illness, sibling marriage, father's retirement) that disrupts the family equilibrium may send the family for outside help.

The remainder of this chapter will explore more fully the role of the family in the conveyance of an individual into patienthood.

The Family as System

A family is a human group with a number of special role-related characteristics.* Those characteristics of interest here are historicity, reciprocal dependency of role relationships, tradition-bound roles and expectations, and a shared world view.

Historicity. Historicity refers to the molding of expectations among members of the group, created by a long, close association or shared experience. Parents, for example, have long-range expectations for their child's behavior and development based on their association with the child, their relationship as spouses, and cultural and social influences.

Reciprocal dependency of role relationships. Key roles within the family are highly dependent on reciprocity or on the fulfillment of complementary roles by other family members. The congruent, satisfying exercise of the parent role, for example, is dependent upon an equally satisfactory fulfillment of the child role.

Tradition-bound roles and expectations. Some elements of familial roles and expectations prescribed by culture and tradition, though not always satisfying, are relatively immutable. When fulfillment of these roles is threatened by change in one family member, perception of that change may be determined by the imperative of satisfactory fulfillment of the roles. When the change brings about an actual disruption of the fulfillment of roles and expectations and of the maintenance of normative role-relationships, family members may collude on the development of a fictitious perception of themselves. This may entail ignoring conflicting information and isolating themselves from their community.

A shared world view. A shared world view (cognitive set or apperceptive mass) simplifies communication. It provides the family with a matrix for consensual validation, shared scripts, and predictable behavioral patterns. It also permits the kind of easy, simplified, and effective non-verbal signaling that exists within families.

Response to Change

These role-related characteristics are especially important in understanding how the family group confronts a crisis within its ranks. When the family member developing schizophrenia manifests a deviant behavior, though this change is discerned by family members, they will quickly subordinate their perception in favor of long-standing assumptions ("Bill's just not been himself this month"). Temporary aberrations will be ignored or overlooked with an expectation for an imminent return to the status quo.

A change in one individual threatens satisfactory fulfillment of the roles and functions of other family members. One of the parental functions threatened is the task of seeing that the child develops in a healthy,

---

*For a more detailed background and description of role theory, the reader is referred to Deutsh and Kraus (1965), Goffman (1959), Mead (1935), and Merton (1968).

normative fashion. Long before parents admit failure and seek external help for a behavioral change in their child, they will readjust their own behavior to regain reciprocity. If reciprocity cannot be regained in fact, it may be in fiction. This latter state probably overlaps with what Wynne, Ryckoff, and Day (1958) referred to as "pseudomutuality," the creation of a fiction to maintain reciprocity in role relationships and thereby maintain some continuity and predictability within the family system. The parents might profess to having a mutually satisfying relationship with no conflict, but appear to do so at the expense of ignoring the idiosyncracies of the schizophrenic family member and the particular sacrifices one parent might be making to accommodate them.

Those outside the family or immediate group system do not generally experience equivalent difficulty in recognizing that an individual is in crisis or in need of help. A neighbor or law enforcement officer will not have long-standing behavioral expectations of the particular individual. He or she will thus be quick to diagnose a human predicament. While perhaps uncertain regarding the status quo ("Has this person always been like this?"), he or she will seek external aid or at least acknowledge the need ("He should see a psychiatrist"), without hesitation, since to do so does not threaten fulfillment of his or her own role assumptions and expectations.

People do change, and family members do adjust to these changes. Role relationships can alter to satisfy changing needs; reciprocity and predictability can be restored without recourse to fiction. Such changes require signaling systems and information transfer. Sudden behavioral change without explanation is difficult for a family to integrate. A slow change (growing up, aging), accompanied by much transfer of information, can be accommodated.

As discussed in the previous chapter, this information will be contained in two basic forms: verbal and nonverbal. While active verbal content will contain information helpful in adapting to changing role relationships, nonverbal information is paramount. It is the nonverbal signaling devices, modifiers, and cues that manage and alter the basic parameters of relationships. If verbal and nonverbal messages lack congruency, the nonverbal messages will preside. They constitute the signaling system announcing changing needs and roles, and this signaling normally ensures a return to predictability and shared planning.

When communication signals are consistent, family members can develop and maintain shared and predictable patterns for interaction. When signals are continuously changing and conflicting, the family will fail to develop shared goals and patterns. Within the family group of an adolescent, for example, the trial-and-error nature of his or her role playing within the family creates inconsistent messages that cannot be integrated into a shared script.

When nonverbal messages cannot be integrated into a consistent, predictable pattern, verbal messages may be employed to maintain a fictive mutuality. The clinician encountering such a family will note the discrepancy between the verbal and nonverbal messages or gross behaviors.

If one family member is schizophrenic, the clinician may view this discrepancy as mad-making. One may perceive the pseudomutality as causative. While pseudomutuality might in fact be counterproductive and is certainly stressful to an adolescent in search of absolute truth, it is probably not a cause of schizophrenic psychosis. Rather, pseudomutuality may be the product of a family organism striving to regain continuity, predictability, and organization in the face of a seemingly insoluble predicament. In short, it may be simply an adaptive mechanism.

It is being suggested, then, that the central features of a family group are historicity, reciprocal dependency of role relationships, tradition-bound roles and expectations, and a shared world view. Change within the family is mediated primarily through nonverbal behavior, while verbal content may serve to maintain a real or fictive mutuality. A family facing change strives to regain organization, continuity, and predictability. If the change is slow in developing, internal accommodation may be possible. If the change is sudden, emergency compensatory measures may appear.

Schizophrenia and the Family

In this context is placed the young person developing schizophrenia. Initial changes in this individual, including adoption of one or more of the compensatory mechanisms listed in the previous chapter, may be gradual. The family will accommodate to these changes. In fact, one of the compensatory mechanisms that the subject may bring into play is a general restriction of communication patterns. He or she will retain the signals and display the nonverbal cues consistent with earlier years. In this situation, parents need only respond in kind to retain order. They will not have to make the major adjustments that they would otherwise have had to make for a growing adolescent. On the other hand, the subject will have trouble interpreting any signaling for change offered by the parents, that is, as she or he grows older and bigger, parents' expectations and therefore their communication to the subject may tentatively change. The young schizophrenic, unable to comprehend these signals and manage these changes, will resist them. For this family, developmental progress will be sacrificed for script consistency, organization, and predictability.

Over time, the schizophrenic member may adopt a particular stereotyped and impoverished role to which the family will adjust. This may then become the status quo. When the subject reports subjective experiences inconsistent with the family's shared apperceptions, family members can either choose to not hear (maintaining a fictive mutuality) or assign the subject a temporarily explanatory role (e.g., "You haven't been getting enough sleep"). Family members will attempt to fit the odd behaviors or reported experiences of the schizophrenic member into their own consistent apperceptions. This may entail some rather farfetched interpretations or direct perceptual distortion of the experience.

If and when this adaptive mechanism fails, they may draw on the assignment of a role sanctioned by larger society. The explanation for the subject's behavior may then become that he or she is bad or sad or sick or lazy. He or she may be assigned these roles on a temporary basis with an expectation of returning to the status quo. If the behavior persists, the family moves to crisis. They are confronted by a predicament they cannot resolve or avoid. It is then that they are forced to seek external help.

It is well to note here that if there has been previous extensive accommodation to the subject's regressed and impoverished behavior, the crisis may be precipitated by behavior another family would perceive as perfectly healthy. The 24-year-old filling the role of a rather dull 15 year old for a number of years may suddenly and "quite out of character" announce that he or she is leaving home. This may throw the family into as much turmoil as a reported hallucination. In addition, the subject is unable to interpret the messages coming from others that would otherwise have given clues to "what is expected of me;" that is, the subject is unable to respond to the parents' attempts to help her or him fit in.

Help Seeking

When the predicament is such that the family looks for assistance, the help they seek will depend on their tentative definition of the problem. Thus, if they approach a health institution, they are already considering the problem in illness terms and they are making application for official confirmation of the sick role. If the family has opted for an illness definition for their predicament, they must justify this solution by using illness language. To do this they may need to exaggerate some events and distort others. This is not conscious manipulation but rather a psychological adaptive mechanism common to all of us (e.g., the family may report an overturned chair and profanity as "He's been violent, Doctor; something has to be done").

At this point there is a danger that a variety of counterproductive definitions of the problem may become fixed and that the subject may be extruded from the family ("He's no good—always has been no good" or "It all boils down to laziness"). As discussed in later chapters, the family at this point requires assistance in settling on a serviceable definition of the problem and legitimizing their help-seeking behavior.

As noted earlier, the particular family structure, social class, and cultural values will have enormous influence over the processes described above. A rigid family may move to extrusion of the subject rather quickly. A chaotic family may initially tolerate a great deal of deviance but ultimately fail to provide a supportive, accommodating matrix. When the parents' relationship with each other is relatively empty, one or both parents may over-accommodate to the subject's regression; that is, the schizophrenic child may inadvertently fill a parental need that would be satisfied by the marital partner in a healthier marriage. In turn, the parents' behavior may reinforce regression, and a feedback loop may be established.

When the parents' relationship requires a foil or scapegoat, the schizophrenic child will be a natural choice. The interplay of the developing schizophrenia of one member and the "neurotic" problems (even minor problems) of other members over time might easily produce those disturbing family dynamics that many clinicians have come to view as schizophrenogenic. Of course, the more fundamental the disturbance in the spouses' relationship, the more schizophrenogenic the whole situation will seem—and the more difficult the tasks of treatment and rehabilitation will become.

Case Example

The boy, Harvey, was 24 years old. He lived with his mother and father in a comfortable ranch-style home in a middle-class suburb. He had one older brother who had moved to another city with a wife and two children. Until recently Harvey had been employed as a part-time helper in a one-man sign painting shop. The old man who ran the shop was a friend of the family, but the day came when he could no longer afford to pay Harvey the minimum wage for what were essentially housekeeping activities.

Harvey had a bedroom off the kitchen in his parents' home. It was small, white, and plain. No pictures hung on the walls. A big box of electronic and *Popular Mechanics* magazines sat beside the bedside table and lamp. His clothing, scattered about the room, consisted of the kind of wardrobe one would expect to find in the room of a socially inhibited 16-year-old.

In the large, clean basement of their home, Harvey's train set, a car-racing set, more magazines, and several electronics projects lay next to his mother's ironing board, washer and dryer, and sewing machine.

When Harvey was admitted to hospital, he proved to have above average intelligence on the WAIS. Yet in interviews he sat with head down, restlessly shuffling his feet and chewing his fingernails. He offered nothing spontaneously and answered most questions with short phrases or single words. There was a praecox feeling about him, and his answers to many questions seemed a little off the point. In the content of his speech there were hints of bizarre interpretations and abnormal experiences. During some tense moments a look of suppressed rage would pass over his face—and his words would become short and clipped. Virtually all his feelings, however, were denied. He was 6 foot 2 and weighed over 200 pounds.

His father was the manager of a small dry goods firm; his mother did volunteer work and looked after the house. Over the years the family had isolated themselves and had few friends. The father bowled and tended the garden; the mother looked after Harvey.

Harvey's illness could be traced back to his late teens. He began to fail in school and withdraw from any non-family activities. He had never dated, and he seemed to lose contact with any male friends he might have had. His interests shrank and he became, for the most part, noncommunicative.

Years later, family and conjoint interviews revealed that the parents' relationship changed at this time as well. Sexual activity ceased, friends were lost, the parents became emotionally estranged from one another; and an aura of mild hostility persisted. The father began to see his wife as being "a silly woman who viewed the world through rose-colored glasses," while the mother saw her husband as being overanxious and too concerned about problems at work. For a few years the father tried to encourage Harvey to go out, develop interests and find employment. Later he regretted a decision not to buy a chicken farm because he remembered that Harvey had once been happy and spontaneous when looking after animals. Harvey's father finally gave in to his mother's pleas to "leave the boy alone," although he did manage to attain part-time work in a sign shop for his son before he gave up.

The father withdrew further into his work, his bowling, and his gardening. He left the mother to deal with Harvey, and mother and son developed a simple, restricted, and comfortable pattern. Harvey played with his electronic toys and read his magazines alongside his mother while she did her housework.

Still, when Harvey was admitted to hospital at age 24, his parents denied any problems in their relationship and continued to deny problems through several family therapy sessions.

The events leading to Harvey's admission to hospital were rather idiosyncratic: since losing his part-time job, Harvey had become increasingly underfoot at home. He appeared moody and somewhat unpredictable to his parents. In the few weeks prior to this admission, Harvey's father withdrew further from the situation, proclaiming that half the boy's problem was the way his mother mollycoddled him.

One night, after the three had completed dinner with the radio playing quietly in the background, one of the mother's favorite songs came on the air. She turned the radio up and asked Harvey to dance. Whether she first asked her husband to dance is not known. Harvey reluctantly accepted the invitation and the two fox-trotted about the living room.

Suddenly Harvey's manner changed. His face contorted with rage, and he roughly shoved his mother away. She landed flat on her back on the living room couch. While stammering some expletives, Harvey moved his hands about in a threatening manner. His mother grabbed her coat and purse and fled the house. She went not to a neighbor's house but directly to a motel. From the motel she called home and told her husband that she wasn't coming back until something was done about her son. Harvey had by now retreated into his bedroom.

The father called the hospital and was put through to the newly established community psychiatry service. He told the intake worker that his son was violent and mentally ill and had to be put in hospital. A home visit was arranged for the next day. The father would be there but he didn't think his wife was coming home that night.

The next day a psychiatrist visited the home. Harvey's father was waiting in the kitchen, impatient to get back to work, while Harvey sat alone in this bedroom. The psychiatrist pieced the story together from the father, who seemed now undecided whether to support this wife or his son. The phone rang. It turned out to be the mother, who wanted to speak to both her husband and her son. To her son on the phone she appeared to tell him that he needed help and that he should go along with whatever the doctor decided. To her husband she reiterated that she was afraid of her son and was not coming home until Harvey was no longer in the house.

The psychiatrist had a long talk with Harvey in the boy's bedroom and, although feeling that the major problem at the moment was the mother's provocative behavior and over-reaction to her son's anger, he persuaded the boy to enter hospital. Whatever the source of the present crisis, the boy's situation warranted a thorough investigation. It took a fair amount of patience and reassurance to get Harvey to accept hospitalization.

Harvey stayed in hospital a short time—just long enough to cool the current crisis, try him on neuroleptic medication, and establish a contract for family therapy. In hospital Harvey was compliant with ward activities, medication, and occupational therapy programs. On discharge, however, he refused any rehabilitation programs. Neither neuroleptic medication nor family therapy seemed to produce any changes in Harvey's symptoms or his relationship with his parents. Active therapy was discontinued in favor of a supportive relationship and maintenance program. Two years after his hospitalization, Harvey agreed to enter a structured social and vocational rehabilitation program. This program consisted of six months of inpatient care using principally token-economy techniques. This was followed by placement in supervised apartment living and a sheltered workshop. Harvey stayed at his apartment during the weekdays and returned to his parents' home for weekends. His mental status and his communication skills remained about the same as before admission, but he had learned some instrumental skills necessary for partially independent living.

One year further on (with Harvey home only on weekends) the father arrived at retirement age. He became depressed and was referred to the psychiatrist who had originally admitted his son to hospital. Harvey's father had cataracts and a mild heart condition. He was clearly troubled and depressed but denied most affect. He claimed to look forward to his retirement, but he didn't want to spend it with his wife. They no longer had anything in common. She was a "thoughtless, empty-headed woman who had never helped him with Harvey." He talked about his earlier attempts to make something of his son and regretted his failures.

When he was interviewed with his wife, his anger was palpable. He wouldn't look at her. Though reluctant to talk of sexual matters, they angrily agreed that there had been nothing between them for about ten years. They dated this roughly to the time at which Harvey had become a problem. The wife pointed out that, when her husband retired, they would have to sell their house and rent a small apartment. They probably wouldn't be able to have Harvey home for weekends anymore.

Several conjoint sessions brought about a truce but no resolution of their conflict. The wife decided at this point that the problem was her husband's and she would no longer attend the sessions. Besides, they had both been very uncomfortable examining their own relationship. They despaired over their son's chronic illness (the father expressing the affect, the mother offering homilies), but they seemed to have little else holding them together or diffusing their hostility now that Harvey had achieved some independence.

Alone, the father could discuss the issues of impending retirement and reminisce about the past, but he denied most of his feelings and shunted aside the therapist's attempts to be empathic. He seemed to have little left but his dignity and the memories of his work. In the end he improved on tricyclic medication and decided to continue on at his job as a part-time consultant ("They need someone to show the new fellows the ropes").

A year later Harvey was still attending the sheltered workshop, living in his apartment weekdays and returning home on weekends. He had a few friends (other patients from the hospital), and he seemed less vulnerable to his parents' deficits and ambiguities.

Conclusion

In summary, then, the nature of a developing schizophrenic psychosis sets the stage for a great variety of family reactions including extensive accommodation at one extreme and extrusion at the other. The process by which the schizophrenic member of this family becomes defined as mentally or psychiatrically ill is very complex. The timing of this process and the particular symptoms initiating it vary from family to family and culture to culture. When a family does seek medical or psychiatric help for one of its members, the family can be considered to be in a state of crisis. Much of their behavior may be viewed as adaptive rather than psychopathological.

Part II

FRAMEWORK FOR INTERVENTION

Chapter 4

MODELS OF ILLNESS AND RECOVERY

I can really point this out to you now: My illness is deeply rooted; the effect it seems to boil down to is that I get very, very anxious— anxious, I guess, anxious.

— anonymous patient

Introduction

The description of the way an individual develops schizophrenia, outlined in Chapters 1 to 3, drew from a number of conceptual domains. These can be grouped and categorized under the headings of Medical Model, Social Model, Adaptational Model, and Developmental Model. The term "model" is used rather loosely here. It would be more accurate to say that concepts were drawn from medical, social, adaptational, and developmental perspectives. These same perspectives constitute a suprastructure for the treatment and rehabilitation of people with schizophrenia, but for this purpose emphasis must be shifted and concepts more carefully defined. In the following chapter, these four perspectives are explored. Though the term "model" has recently gained wide currency, it should be remembered that none of these "models" constitutes a unified theory. Chapters 7 through 12 describe the application of these models while chapters 4, 5, and 6 address theoretical considerations.

Medical Model

In understanding the application of the medical model to any human problem, it is important to distinguish between the disease concept and its social component.

Disease Concept

Advocates of the medical model rightly point to the incredible advances brought about in recent history by application of disease theory: the careful description and categorization of symptoms, the recognition of clusters of symptoms, and, from this, the description of syndromes. The disease afflicting one person can then be compared to that afflicting another. The notion that a given disease is not unique is in itself comforting. When the same syndrome has been described in a number of cases, its pathogenesis and natural history can be studied. From this—often long before etiology is discovered—methods of treatment and prevention can be systematically developed and tested.

The disease concept is most valid and effective when the syndrome can be described and defined in biological terms. Even when most of the symptoms making up a given syndrome are subjective experiences and descriptions of behavior, the disease concept carries with it an assumption of underlying biological disturbance. When the description of "symptoms" is further removed from biological concerns (i.e., to interpersonal and social phenomena), the disease concept must be considered less valid and more problematic.

The application of the disease concept to schizophrenia in a clinical setting permits therapists to view symptoms in clusters, to assume an underlying pathological process, and to apply specific treatment to ameliorate this process. But the symptoms of schizophrenia range from biologic to social. Some may be primary symptoms (emanating directly from biologic processes), and some may be secondary (only indirectly related to the biologic processes or reactive to them). In the chronic phase of the illness, the symptoms that produce the most disability and are of greatest concern to clinicians are interpersonal and social impairments, for which the disease concept has little usefulness.

Thus, for the pragmatic concern of treating a patient suffering from schizophrenia, the disease concept must be preeminent in the early (acute) phases but not considered a complete explanation for all behavior. For the treatment and management of secondary phenomena and later phases of the illness, the disease concept should be partially replaced by other models. It is not helpful to consider social isolation and restriction of communication patterns as symptoms of disease. If one considers instead that these phenomena are protective and adaptive, then attempts to alter them can be more productive.

While the disease concept has traditionally dominated treatment planning, it is being suggested that of all the behaviors and subjective experiences of schizophrenic patients, only some should be explained and treated from this perspective. Others are much better understood in developmental, social, and adaptational terms.

Social Component

The disease concept is usually applied within a particular social context. Some aspects of this context are in fact older and less ethnocentric than biological disease theory. This context is the particular social matrix within which a suffering person receives formal (professional) help from a socially designated caretaker or healer. In contemporary Western society this activity is often carried out in a designated institution. Even when engaged in outside the walls of such a physical institution, the activity is surrounded by institutionalized codes of behavior. This context constitutes the social component of the medical model. It is a phenomenon much studied (and criticized) by sociologists. The reason for emphasizing it over the next few pages and for considering it separately from the disease concept is that this context itself is a major determinant of clinicians' perceptions and patients' behavior.

Most societies have established mechanisms whereby the *sick role* may be conferred upon an individual by designated healers. In our culture a *social contract* is forged between the (now) patient and the physician representing society at large. As indicated in earlier chapters, becoming a patient is not the same phenomenon as having a disease. The subtle transactional rules, the privileges, and the obligations inherent in such a contract are known to all sensitive practitioners and patients alike. Parson (1951) suggested that the sick role constitutes the following privileges and obligations:

1. The individual's incapacity is thought to be beyond choice, and so he or she is *not held responsible* for it. Some curative process apart from his or her own motivation is necessary for recovery.
2. The patient's incapacity is grounds for *exemption from normal obligations*.
3. Being ill is thus being able to deviate legitimately. This legitimation is conditional, however, on the sufferer's recognition that to be ill is undesirable, something one assumes the *obligation to overcome*.
4. Insofar as the person cannot get well by him- or herself, the sufferer is therefore *expected to seek competent help* for the illness and to cooperate with healing attempts.

These privileges and obligations can be read as behavioral expectations incorporated into the social contract of the medical model.

On becoming a patient, one is no longer held responsible for one's incapacity and one may be exempted from such obligations as going to work or household duties. These are humane and efficacious privileges when conferred on someone suffering from an acute biological disturbance. They can be problematic when conferred on someone suffering from either minor disturbance, chronic illness, or behavioral problems. When the problems are minor, these privileges may actually increase the patient's incapacity and, over time, promote an exaggeration of the problem to account for the acceptance of the sick role. When the illness is chronic, such unbridled privileges may breed a decay in motivation and an expansion of incapacities. And when the problem is "bad," asocial, or nonproductive behavior, such conferred privileges may reduce the extent to which the individual assumes responsibility for him- or herself.

Schizophrenia is both an acute and a chronic illness. Its symptoms range from major cognitive impairment to minor eccentricities, including a number of asocial, antisocial, and/or simply nonconforming behaviors. Consequently, the social contract of the medical model provides a very useful and humane matrix for the treatment and care of some aspects of schizophrenia while being disadvantageous for others.

The excessive application of both the disease concept and the social component of the medical model to human problems has been justifiably criticized by Illich (1975), Rosenham (1973), Scheff (1968), and Szasz (1974). Szasz and Illich abhorred the extent to which human problems have been medicalized in Western society and the resulting abrogation of personal responsibility and, secondarily, the increase of such iatrogenic disease as diazepam addiction. Scheff and others focused on Parsons's fourth point ("the sufferer is expected to seek competent help and to cooperate. . . "). When the problem is behavioral, the sick role might be applied inappropriately and the person persuaded or forced to seek help for his or her behavior. Social control is then promoted in the guise of medical treatment.

Schizophrenics have suffered at least as much from the excesses of the medical model as other groups of people. Rosenham offered a good example of these excesses and an opportunity to clarify the distinction between the disease concept and the social component of the medical model. In his study, eight people pretending to suffer from existential hallucinations presented themselves to admitting physicians at eight different hospitals. Apart from their bogus hallucinations, they offered accurate accounts of their present mental state and personal histories. All were admitted to the hospital and all but one diagnosed as having schizophrenia. They had been instructed to tell the staff of the hospital on the second day of admission that they no longer hallucinated. Despite this, their length of hospitalization ranged from 7 to 52 days with an average stay of 19 days. Each person was finally discharged with the diagnosis of "schizophrenia, in remission."

This study is a powerful condemnation of something, but of what?

These subjects voluntarily presented themselves to health care facilities, and in so doing were making application to have their particular distress considered disease. It is not clear to what extent they also applied for sick roles. One suspects that while they did not make active application for the sick role (as many patients do), they did not put up much resistance either.

If the physicians fooled by this scam had been able to differentiate between the two aspects of the medical model, they might have fared better. They would then have been able to ask themselves, "Is the particular distress suffered (and reported) by this individual the result of a disease?" The answer should have been "possibly." This "symptom" might be the result of toxicity or a brain tumor—or an unlikely early sign of schizophrenia. The physician's task would then have been to offer the applicant a number of investigations and a period of observation to test the hypothesis. Both the observation and the investigation could have been conducted easily on an outpatient basis. Even if no specific disease was ever diagnosed, some medical treatment might produce relief from the "symptom" if it persisted and if it was distressing.

There was no reason at all to hospitalize these people during the investigation. Presumably they had homes of their own, and were functioning well in other respects. Being sent home with an appointment to attend a mental health clinic later that week would (or should) have produced the conclusion that no disease was present, no treatment warranted, and institutionalization of the sick role inappropriate. But they were hospitalized and thus committed to the full social contract of the medical model. The bureaucratized or institutional form of the medical contract requires that a label be attached (the disease be named) to legitimize the process, and so these patients had to be labeled "schizophrenic." Few other choices would justify the admission. The judgment of the physicians and the behaviors of the other staff were then influenced to an appalling degree by institutional requirements.

The social aspect of the medical model, at its best, can be a flexible, workable social contract between two people. When exercised in large bureaucratic institutions, it can become a thoughtless, unconsciously rigid process. In the above example, tentative application of the disease concept of the medical model would have been valid. Application of the full social contract of the medical model was inappropriate.

It is the thoughtless application of the latter concept and the operationalization of it through a rigid bureaucratic structure that deserve condemnation. Perhaps if the health-care system in the study had not been so dominantly bed-oriented, such an absurd response to these eight people would not have occurred. Unfortunately, the structure of our social systems guides our perceptions and constrains our behavior. The eight admitting physicians did not understand this when they exercised their clinical judgment.

For most schizophrenic patients, however, at least temporary entry into the social contract of the medical model can be beneficial. As long as the patient remains in treatment and/or is receiving medication, at least a modified medical model is indicated. Ideally, the social contract should change through the phases of treatment and rehabilitation in the direction of fewer sick role privileges and increased responsibility assumed by the patient.

One of the fundamental problems for people suffering from schizophrenia is a deficit in their ability to interpret or comprehend interpersonal relationships. Put another way, one might say that they have difficulty forging and participating in complex social contracts. For the acute schizophrenic, the medical model offers a relatively simple, traditional, and possibly previously experienced social contract. Where he or she can find no continuity or predictability in other relationships, these might be found in the relationships subsumed within the medical model. The rules are relatively straightforward; the paradigm is close to parent-child, and clear symbols abound.

In summary, then, it is being suggested that the social aspect of the medical model is an inescapable reality, that it is in fact humane and efficacious when applied to some aspects of schizophrenia, and that it should be employed judiciously and flexibly. A major task for the therapist is to help the patient adjust to the appropriate portions of such a social contract and to overcome or avoid excessive application of the rest.

Adaptational Model

A number of theories (e.g., Sandor Rado's adaptational dynamics) and schools of therapy (most notably crisis intervention) are based on principles of adaptation. These theories view abnormal behaviors not as symptoms or direct products of disease but rather as responses to insult. These responses are adaptational in that they act to relieve the insult and return the organism to a level of homeostatic organization.

The principle of homeostasis has been fundamental to the development of modern medicine since its introduction by Claude Bernard. The tendency for the organism to maintain within itself certain constant conditions to sustain life is a physiological concept that underlies most theories of human behavior. Crisis theory returned to this preexisting idea and expanded it to explain abnormal behavior. Crisis intervention techniques are based on the assumption that people strive for a homeostatic, integrated state, external conditions permitting.

The original crisis therapists would simply provide a supportive matrix and supplies (of information, empathy, regard, understanding, time, and energy) that would allow the organism to return to a homeostatic (normal) state. For some clients it worked; for others it failed. For the therapists it might have seemed as if some human organisms perversely strove for a state of disequilibrium. Nonetheless, the principle probably holds. The error here, a major problem with crisis intervention, is the inaccurate assumption that homeostasis and equilibrium can be equated with behavioral concepts of normality. For some people homeostasis might in fact be achieved with abnormal behavior and/or a continuing or intermittent reliance on health-care professionals.

This becomes more understandable when one moves from the concept of homeostasis to the broader concept of organization. It has been observed in a number of disciplines that a tendency to organization is part of the basic life force balance (rather than the more two-dimensional and physiological concept of homeostasis). That is, the fundamental guiding principle involves expending energy at all levels of structure in an attempt to maintain organization against inevitable personal and universal entropy. From the molecular to the social levels, energy is expended to maintain the organization. At the level of unconscious cognitive and mental organization, the guiding principle of organization is more primary than pleasure. At a conscious personal, familial, and social level, people strive to maintain order, consistency, and predictability.

It might also be suggested that when order is threatened at a number of levels (e.g., mental and social), the lower level (mental) assumes prime importance. The principle of organization will favor the lower level when the organization (or reorganization) of one can be achieved only at the expense of another. Put another way, when some insult threatens both mental and social organization, the organism will strive first to compensate for (reorganize) the disordered mental processes. The compensatory (adaptive) mechanisms required may lead to some decrease of social integration. Social function will be sacrificed in favor of mental organization.

A similar principle can be observed with physical illness. When the body compensates for injury or disease to its physiological level of organization, it may at times sacrifice mental organization. In an episode of hypotension and subsequent anoxia, consciousness may be sacrificed and the body subsequently assumes a prone position. In this position normal blood pressure is restored.

Symptoms of schizophrenia occur in the higher levels of organization (cognitive, interpersonal, and social), but it is assumed that deficits exist at lower levels as well. The adaptational model provides a way of understanding some of these individual symptoms and how they might be related to one another. The compensatory or restitutive symptoms described earlier could be said to be maladaptive at a social level. They can be seen as the sacrifice of a higher level of organization to regain organization (consistency and predictability) at lower levels. Thus, restrictive communication patterns limit social integration but restore order at cognitive, communicative, and simple interpersonal levels. As pointed out earlier, many of the major symptoms of schizophrenia can be viewed as ways in which the organism compensates for underlying insult. For therapists, the value of this model is fourfold: helping explain the manner in which symptoms at different levels of organization might be related, paying heed to the restitutive and adaptive strivings within the patient; suggesting that the therapist should view some behaviors as adaptive that have previously been labeled psychopathological; and providing an alternate goal for therapeutic interventions: adaptation rather than cure.

Social Model

There are several theories and models subsumed under this heading. The word "social" tends to be used as a catchall for the analysis of interpersonal phenomena, group behavior, rehabilitation issues, and societal structure. Each of these areas is really a discipline unto itself. The relationship of social phenomena to individual psychology is a further area of study. Meadian psychology and Sullivanian psychiatry attempt to integrate social concepts with the development of self. Social breakdown theory examines the manner in which social institutions affect individual behavior.

Each of these models seems relevant, at different times, to the task of understanding schizophrenia. Those concepts, ideas, and observations that appear to have special value in the psychotherapeutic management of schizophrenia will be encompassed under the social model of the treatment framework being presented here. They are: structural role theory, dynamic role theory, social breakdown theory, and social-skills concepts.

Structural Role Theory

Structural roles have already been discussed under the medical model. The concepts of the patient role, the sick role, and patient careers have been drawn from sociological literature. The importance of these phenomena is debated by psychiatrists. The implication in the sociological literature is that a schizophrenic's symptoms are determined more by the demands of the role he or she has assumed (and been assigned) than by any intrinsic disorder: behavior is transactional currency developed to maintain his or her position. Perceptions of the behavior on the part of clinicians are influenced by assumptions about the behavior that *ought* to be exhibited by someone who is sick.

There is validity to this extreme position in some cases. With some old, chronic patients (sometimes referred to as "career patients") it can be very difficult to tell if the reported symptom or the observed behavior has intrinsic origin or whether it is now learned and adaptive, designed to maintain the status quo of privilege and dependency (Geller, 1980). In other cases this would be a harsh judgment.

Nonetheless, role theory has a definite contribution to make to the understanding and treatment of schizophrenia. Becoming a patient, being a patient, being sick, and being handicapped are subject to social definitions. These definitions do influence the course of the illness, the recovery process, and both the patient's and the therapist's attitudes. There are times, as mentioned before, when the sick role and its contract with society are most appropriate and times when they are not. Furthermore, there is a tendency to assign the sick role in all-or-nothing terms; someone considered sick is considered totally nonfunctional. This mistake is made by staff and relatives alike. The patient is seen as either mad or bad. If bad, normative social expectations will be applied. If mad, no expectations are warranted: the schizophrenic patient, like the rest of us, is usually a little of both.

The therapeutic task is not to blindly disavow the sick role but to help the patient manage and modify it. The therapist will assist the patient in adapting to parts of it through the different phases of recovery. Other aspects should be entirely discarded from the social contract.

Dynamic Role Theory

A derivative of structural role theory and ultimately of Meadian psychology is the ongoing study of roles as tentative interactional patterns (rules and rituals) that unfold in any interpersonal relationship (Turner, 1962). Here interactional patterns are seen as being guided by a principle of relationship management. Behavior, especially nonverbal communication, is molded by a moment-to-moment feedback system. The individuals encountering one another strive to develop a communication pattern that will permit reciprocity of function with the fewest surprises. Goffman (1959) would take this idea further and suggest that psychiatric symptoms are identified when one participant fails to fulfill this obligatory interactional ritual. At that level of analysis this observation has validity, especially in the context of an overriding assumptive world. On the street some-

one who does not respond to the greeting "Hello" may be viewed as preoccupied, stuck-up, or deaf. If his or her response is exuberant (different tone
and quantity than the original greeting—not symmetrical), the response
may be, "I wonder what she's so pleased about."

In the psychiatric context, the former instance is liable to be taken as
evidence of depression or withdrawal, the latter instance as evidence of
hypomania. The psychiatric context provides ready-made explanations for
deviant interactional events (witness the nurse's note in Rosenham's study:
"The patient is engaging in writing behavior"). Such easy responses to or
interpretations of disturbed interactional rituals may be grossly unfair and
misleading. Therapists need to keep in mind the extent to which we all
value symmetry and reciprocity in our day-to-day relationships and the
extent to which we need explanations for any disturbance in the expected
pattern.

On the other hand, these are the very communicative processes with
which the schizophrenic patient has most difficulty. His or her inability to
process the moment-to-moment nonverbal cues necessary to manage interpersonal relationships will lead to many spoiled encounters. These encounters constitute a high source of stress, and many schizophrenic patients
retreat from them, while others self-destructively engage in, misinterpret,
and mismanage them. He or she may need direct help, counseling, and
explanation in the management of any new interpersonal encounter.

A definition of self arises from each encounter, and this definition is
reinforced by repetition. Spoiled encounters imply worthlessness or failure.
Acquiescence to a simple role (the sick role) reduces the complexity of such
an encounter and reduces the possibility of spoiling. The patient's relationship with his or her therapist is another relationship to be managed and
another relationship with the possibility of spoilage and/or implications for
self-definition. The transaction will occur primarily at a nonverbal level
and will include the structure and context of the meeting itself; it will determine the role assumed by the patient, on a moment-to-moment basis, and
it will ultimately affect the patient's sense of self. The management of this
relationship, then, quite apart from content, is a major task for the therapist. One's manner and the context of the meetings will convey to the
patient cues for his or her behavior. As much as they can be, these cues
should be consciously designed to enhance the position assumed by the
patient. In this way the sick role can be managed and healthier roles and
behaviors encouraged.

Social Breakdown Theory

Concepts of social integration, social support systems, and social relatedness are all relevant to the understanding and treatment of schizophrenia. Specifically, the schizophrenic person is especially vulnerable to
social breakdown in the manner described by Gruenberg (1967) and Wing
(1962). In the original explanation of social breakdown, psychiatric institutions received most of the blame. Certainly large "total institutions" have
played a major role in the production of impoverished, passive, restricted

mental patients with little capacity or will to lead independent lives. Yet schizophrenic patients are vulnerable to social breakdown in boarding houses and family homes as well. Over time their tendency to retreat from experience and expectations they cannot manage, into impoverished environments (partly of their own making), can produce social breakdown anywhere. Spontaneity dies, initiative is stifled, information is blocked, behaviors become simple and ritualistic, and eccentricities emerge without benefit of corrective feedback. The person's relationship with the outside world breaks down and he or she retreats further into a private universe.

Social-Skills Concepts

Long before this bleak picture might develop, the young schizophrenic is often found to be woefully lacking in social skills. There are four major components to most definitions of social skills (Wallace et al., 1980):

1. The patient's internal state: feelings, attitudes, and perceptions of the interpersonal context
2. The topography of the patient's behaviors: the rate of behaviors such as eye contact, hand gestures, body posture, speech disfluencies, voice volume, and latency of verbal response
3. The outcome of the interaction as reflected in the achievement of the patient's goals
4. The outcome of the interaction as reflected in the attitudes, feelings, behaviors, and goals of the other participant(s)

Deficits in social skills may be partly a result of the schizophrenic's fundamental difficulty in interpreting context, managing relationships, and thus learning social skills. They may exist partly as a result of a retreat from new situations, acquisition of a sick role, and possibly long periods of time spent hospitalized or convalescent.

Naturally, a number of interpersonal difficulties can be seen to emanate directly from absent or distorted social skills. The important point here is for the therapist to not assume that the patient has or can easily acquire any particular social skill. Nor should deficits in social skills be interpreted as unalterable conditions of the illness. The schizophrenic patient will usually require special assistance in increasing social-skill competency. The approach to these problems should be educational rather than exploratory, with a focus on breaking down the elements of a particular skill into several manageable units for teaching, modeling, rehearsal, and reinforcement. Thus, for example, it will be more useful to view the factor that prevents a young "recovered" schizophrenic male from asking a woman for a date as simple lack of skill and know-how rather than psychological conflict or latent homosexuality.

In the latter phases of treatment and recovery the social model assumes more importance. Here the goal of treatment and rehabilitation is to return the patient to optimal social functioning. The presence or absence of individual symptoms is important only to the extent that they interfere with this task or cause the patient distress.

Developmental Model

Concepts of development, genesis, and epigenesis find their way into most theories of human behavior. Still, it is only recently that these processes have been studied. It was once assumed that a child was simply a small adult, that an adolescent was simply an adult waiting for a vocation, and that an adult was the same adult at 30 and 60 years of age.

The discovery that the child, like the adult, is a sexual being, but that the mode of sexuality passes through a number of phases on its journey to adult expression, was the first of a long series of developmental revelations. Now we know that each dimension of human personality (perceptual, cognitive, affective, sexual, interactional, social) develops through phases and transitions from birth to death. On the whole, these passages unfold interacting with the environment. While human beings may be programmed to acquire certain social relationships in adulthood, their ability to do this successfully depends to some extent on their play as children. (See Munsinger, 1971, for a comprehensive review of child development.) The processes are complex and interdependent. There is at once an inevitability and a cultural relativism about them.

Some theories of schizophrenia have relied heavily on concepts of development (Kubie, 1967; Semrad, 1966). Most notable is the hypothesis that a schizophrenic psychosis is a response to a developmental impasse: The individual confronting a transition he or she must make but cannot (because of other psychological disturbances) chooses the alternative path to psychosis (Bowers, 1974). On the other hand, developmental issues are conspicuously absent in the writings of otherwise thorough investigators. Often, the schizophrenic's difficulty with social stress and quarrelsome families is highlighted, but the extent to which these difficulties might emanate from developmental conflict is only briefly alluded to.

From the stated hypothesis of this book, it should be clear that the potential schizophrenic will have great difficulty managing developmental transitions insofar as they entail changing interpersonal and social relationships. The importance of considering these problems as developmental as well as social lies in the acknowledgment of *developmental press*. Retreat from new social situations, such as dating, might be more adaptive for the young schizophrenic if he were not being pressed to move on, from both internal imperatives and external directives.

The developmental transition most important to the potential schizophrenic is that through adolescence into young adulthood. This is the age at which schizophrenia most often develops and these are the issues with which the schizophrenic patient has most difficulty. Will (1974) noted this struggle with his schizophrenic patients in describing the many developmental issues and tasks that someone of this age faces as follows:

1. The forming, outside the family of origin, of a human relationship of intimacy in which affection and respect can be recognized and expressed, self-revelation increased, and socially maladaptive autistic processes reduced

2. The refinement of juvenile group skills (such as competitions, compromise, cooperation, and use of stereotypes) in the service of peer relationships marked by a lessening of envy and jealousy, and an increase in the ability to deal with problems of leadership and collaboration
3. A patterning of sexual behavior that has at least come into awareness and is dependable if not always satisfying
4. A further separation—emotionally and probably physically—from the family, accompanied by a change of role in the family
5. A revision—or reevaluation—of personal and family codes and values
6. A consideration of and steps toward a career or life-style
7. An adjustment to one's culture with knowing acceptance, compromise, and rebellion, or retreat, but without reliance on autism and egocentricity
8. The maintenance of social contact sufficient to provide minimal satisfactions (food, shelter, bodily contact, communication) and the continuance of a reliable and adequate sense of self-regard

Levinson et al. (1979) descriptively labeled this particular period of human development as the "novice" phase.

However these developmental issues are described and categorized, it is certain that they are complex and interdependent and manifest themselves in such social activities as dating, joining, bonding, moving away from home, getting a job, and finding a comfortable position in the matrix of society. To manage these developmental transitions and related social circumstances requires a learning process dependent on the ability to engage in new interpersonal relationships. The tools required are those information processing and moment-to-moment feedback systems that seem impaired with the schizophrenic. When he or she retreats from these growth experiences, developmental lacunae are formed. There is a vast difference between the manner in which a 17-year-old boy is expected to approach a girl and the heterosexual relationship of a 30-year-old man. The latter will remain unavailable unless, in some manner, the former has been achieved.

For the therapist, developmental concepts should be preeminent in the phase of treatment that will be described under the heading "Growth and Change" in Chapter 11. An accurate assessment of the patient's developmental status needs to be made. Those development issues that appear to form impasses from which the patient has retreated need special consideration. The extent to which the schizophrenic patient requires direct counseling, information, and practice in the tasks described by Will and others should not be underestimated. Furthermore, it can be assumed that each developmental task accomplished and stabilized in new social circumstances will reduce the possibility of relapse and chronicity.

Conclusion

None of the four models described is discrete or wholly explanatory. Each does, however, offer some heuristic value in the treatment, management, rehabilitation, and continuing care of schizophrenic patients. Each model assumes a different position of importance through the phases of psychosis and recovery. The application or utilization of one model in preference over another in the management of any particular problem should be determined by the goals of intervention rather than consistency of theory.

Other models and constructs (such as psychoanalysis and existentialism) are helpful in attempts to understand the person who has schizophrenia. The models chosen for this book are those that seem to offer the most help in understanding and intervening with schizophrenia itself, while those excluded address more general issues of human behavior. Psychoanalysis and existentialism, for example, probably tell us more about what it is to be human than about what it is to have schizophrenia. For this reason they have been left to the reader to add to the already complex formulation.

Some symptoms are clearly better understood and treated within the context of one model (e.g., contextual failure). Others can be explained by several models. The inability to shop for food may derive from unlearned or lost instrumental skills, cognitive deficits, an inability to manage the relationship of shopkeeper-customer, or hallucinations warning against such activity. Even first-rank symptoms may be better understood with the application of several models. A young convalescent schizophrenic attends a party or dance and then reports to his therapist that his voices have returned. This incident could be understood and approached as simply a symptom of illness and evidence of decompensation, and treated with neuroleptic medication (disease concept). The therapist might suggest that the patient return to hospital and/or stay home from work or school for a while (social component of medical model). On the other hand, the therapist might perceive this communication as evidence of distress in confronting a difficult developmental hurdle (developmental model) or a social situation for which he is not prepared (lack of necessary social skills). With a more chronic patient it is often helpful to view such a communication as simply the equivalent of a statement to the therapist that means, in effect, "Don't forget I'm sick" or "Don't expect too much from me" (adaptational retreat to the sick role).

From this example it can be seen that, at different times, in different contexts, a given symptom may be most usefully understood within the parameters of each of the models listed above. The choice of model, and thus of response, should rightly depend on the ultimate management and treatment goals of optimal social functioning and freedom from suffering (as opposed to the eradication of symptoms).

Chapter 5

PHASES OF ILLNESS AND RECOVERY

I say to myself sometimes: Now you have to start with everything because you haven't started with anything before.
— **anonymous patient**

In order to intervene effectively during the acute psychosis and period of recovery, timing must be a major consideration. An ill-timed intervention can be worse than none at all. The timing of interventions should take into account: the individual patient's psychological reactions to the illness, the natural history and process of recovery of the illness, and the context of patienthood. A number of authors, briefly reviewed over the next few pages, have conceptualized the process of recovery in distinct phases. Some have attempted to delineate the patient's psychological reactions to the illness. Others have focused on the natural history of the illness and the internal process of ego reintegration.

Reactions to Illness

Mayer-Gross (1920) defined four ways in which an individual may respond to a psychotic experience: denial of the future or despair; creation of a new life after the illness; denial of the psychotic experience itself; and a melting of the illness into a continuous set of life values.

Semrad and Zaslow (1964) suggested that successful treatment requires that the patient acknowledge the importance of his or her psychosis, bear its painful aspects, and place the effects and ideas of the psychosis into perspective and continuity with his or her past. More recently, Jeffries (1977) commented on the patient's reaction to illness and the consequences of the experience of being psychotic. He compared the experience of psychosis to other major traumas and concluded that many symptoms of

64

schizophrenia can be likened to posttraumatic neurosis (see "Poverty Syndrome," Chapter 9).

Many liaison psychiatrists offered their colleagues a great deal of help in discerning and managing the natural psychological reactions to major medical illnesses. Kimball, Schmale, and Bernstein (1979), among others, cogently described the reaction to major illness in phases: acute, convalescent, rehabilitative, and chronic. Delineated in each of these phases were responses to illness and subsequent tasks of therapy. It is ironic that while such considerations are gaining currency in other medical specialties, they are often ignored in psychiatry. The notion seems to exist that recovering from a major mental illness is totally different from recovering from a myocardial infarction. Although responses to major medical illnesses are being described in detail using such concepts as anxiety, denial, bargaining, anger, depression and adaptation/acceptance, these notions are seldom applied to the major mental illnesses. It seems to be assumed that with schizophrenia, the psychological reactions are an intrinsic component of the illness. Amotivation, lack of insight, anhedonia, denial, overcompensation, grandiosity, isolation, noncompliance, avolition, depression, anger, and control struggles are often considered part of schizophrenia rather than reactions to it. Despite any truth to the argument that schizophrenia affects the mind and therefore the psychological reactions of schizophrenics cannot be trusted, it does seem that a great deal of inadequate psychosocial treatment has been justified by it.

When these phenomena are considered secondary rather than primary aspects of schizophrenia, then psychosocial programs can be instituted to modify them. Denial and overcompensation may be necessary, though one hopes temporary, reactions to a major insult. Amotivation, avolition, and isolation may be protective devices, while anger, lack of insight, and control struggles may constitute a form of bargaining.

The pattern of psychological response to psychosis is not clearly sequential, but, realistically, neither is the pattern of response to physical illness and death. The responses of people suffering from schizophrenia, like the responses of people with terminal illness, are understandable when one considers the degree of insult, the extent of loss, and, with psychosis, the fear of recurrence.

Process of Recovery

Many authors have described the process of becoming psychotic. A few have attempted to describe the process of recovery. Docherty suggested that recovery follows the same phases as becoming psychotic but in reverse: the psychotic moves (1) from a state of disorganization to greater organization with some disinhibition, to (2) increasing inhibition, and then (3) returns to a state of restricted consciousness. This last phase would coincide with the poverty syndrome or postpsychotic depression (see Chapter 9). Similarly, Donlon and Blacker (1973) proposed the following stages of reintegration:

Stage I: Psychic disorganization and relief from subjective pain

Stage II: Panic and horror! The appearance of primitive fantasies and images

Stage III: Depression and the intensification of psychological defenses

Stage IV: Denial and anxiety

Several authors (McGlashan, Levy, Carpenter, Docherty, and Siris, 1975; Levy et al., 1975 and 1976) described two distinct styles of recovery: integration and sealing over. These styles can be considered polar extremes at either end of a continuum of ways postpsychotic patients manage their recent experiences. This is a valuable concept and will be elaborated upon in later chapters.

One may observe and describe the process of recovery within as many parameters as one might describe the process of becoming psychotic. Individual biases will determine whether or not one focuses on subjective reporting of internal state, objective description of symptoms, inferences about ego integration from these symptoms, or improvements in communication and social skills. To follow is a description of the process of recovery based on the model developed in Chapters 1 and 2. There are definite similarities with the descriptions already presented (Docherty et al., 1978; Donlon and Blacker, 1973) but the emphasis is distinctly different.

When the psychotic schizophrenic is hospitalized and treated with neuroleptic medication, one of the first symptoms to show improvement is *textual failure*. This improvement is followed by a diminution of the praecox experience due, probably, to some improvement of the patient's ability to accurately interpret context. Accompanying this is an improvement in simple interpersonal communication and basic social skills.

Before an actual reduction of abnormal subjective experiences (e.g., auditory and tactile hallucinations) occurs, these experiences become less influential. The patient reports their existence but is no longer preoccupied with them. He or she can be distracted from hallucinations to engage in other more reality-based activities. These experiences seem to diminish, become less frequent, are less pervasive, and slowly recede into memory. (Of course, improvement may halt at any of these points, depending on the severity of illness and premorbid status.)

With the reduction of hallucinations and ideas of reference, the patient's earlier restitutive and compensatory mechanisms may emerge. This is the point at which *style* of recovery is determined. The patient may withdraw, isolate him- or herself, and severely restrict communication patterns—behavior that may develop into a postpsychotic depression and/or a state of chronic social impoverishment. Some patients, compliant and reasonable up until this point, may revert to chaotic searching. They leave the hospital against medical advice and search for meaning and continuity in travel, religion, diets, and fringe groups. Others may find a single truth and adopt its accompanying religious and social codes. Still others may return to their delusional beliefs, which they may or may not communicate to staff.

Those who recover past this point develop increasing skill in interpreting contextual information, and this skill in turn facilitates social integration. For full recovery, the patient must make some adaptations to his or her new position and, to some extent at least, learn to accept the illness. Finally, the experience of being psychotic and having an illness may be woven into the fabric of memory and the conceptualization of self. This might be considered a final stage of both social and internal reintegration.

The one dimension missing in all of these descriptions, however, is a consideration of *context*. If a model describing psychosis and recovery is to provide assistance in treatment decisions, it must take context into account.

The Context of Patienthood

In this sense context refers to the social milieu, (i.e., hospital, boarding home, rehabilitation setting) in which the illness and treatment are taking place and to the larger sociocultural environment. Clearly, these elements will influence the means and mode by which the patient may adapt to the illness and integrate his other experiences. Earlier it was suggested that the central deficit in the schizophrenias is a decay in the ability to interpret context. This is a specific use of the word "context," but it is clearly related to larger definitions.

As discussed before, there are three elements of context with which the schizophrenic might have problems, and which normally provide meaning and continuity for verbal exchanges: Extratextual referents; static situational variables (formal role relationships); and changing situational variables (ongoing relationship management).

Difficulty with these aspects of communication can, through the process described in Chapters 1 and 2, lead the individual to a schizophrenic psychosis and hospitalization. The impairment is manifested around such new or anticipated relationships as those found in dating, becoming a university student, or entering the working world.

When the prospective patient becomes psychotic and enters a hospital, admission itself presents a new context—another new set of relationships with which he or she is asked to cope. Unfortunately, an inability to master developmental transition and new social situations places the patient squarely within a very new and confusing situation. The context of treatment in this instance, more than with any physical illness, will have a profound effect on the patient's responses. A particular kind of approach will be required to help the patient organize the contextual information necessary to understand his or her situation.

There is further consideration of context to be made. Laing (1967), David L. Rosenham (1973), Scheff (1963), and others suggested that the context is the illness. "Schizophrenia is a myth." They proposed the following process: Deviant behavior is labeled, perceptions thereby changed, social sanctions and attitudes unleashed, and a whole treatment industry developed to mediate the sanctions, contain the deviancy, and assuage the communal guilt. They are certainly mistaken in their exaggerated and polemic claims, if not in their criticisms of the excesses of the medical model.

Schizophrenia as a "thing" may be a myth, but the concept of schizophrenia is not. This label is a convention that refers to a group of behaviors, experiences, and attributed feelings that, as Murphy (1976) demonstrated, are remarkably similar in diverse cultures. The Yorubas and the Inuit do not have a word "schizophrenia," but they do recognize the same constellation of symptoms and consider them abnormal. There are also remarkable similarities in the way they distinguish the normalcy of isolated symptoms (such as the short-lived hallucinations of the recently bereaved) from the full syndrome.

The problem is that the ongoing argument concerning the validity of labeling theory obscures the fact that social definitions of illness do exist and that these social definitions fashion our attitudes and actions. Furthermore, labeling someone schizophrenic may not make the person schizophrenic, but over time he or she will internalize this social definition. This does not mean that one should avoid the word. In a media-saturated culture such as ours, one of the first thoughts that comes to the mind of someone losing grasp on continuity and meaning is, "Am I losing my mind?", "Am I developing schizophrenia?", or "Am I a schizophrenic?" The assignment of the diagnosis of schizophrenia, if sensitively handled, can provide a framework within which the patient may begin to work on understanding what is happening.

It is not use of the label itself that has the profound effect. The instinct to name and to categorize is deep-rooted, and if this particular kind of deviance were not called schizophrenia, it would surely be called something else. It is the way in which people behave toward this person that will have a profound effect. The word "schizophrenia" itself is rather benign compared to the various alternate forms of incarceration and ostracism.

The context of treatment and rehabilitation carries implications for self-definition. The locked ward, the bubble room, restricted "privileges," loss of power and dignity, the imposition of a sick role, the fostering of pessimism, the decay of responsibility for self are all aspects of the context of treatment that can be powerful determinants of the way an individual will learn to define him- or herself. This is the context rightly criticized by sociologists and social psychologists as constituting a self-fulfilling prophecy. Their criticisms must be acknowledged without overresponding and discarding the disease concept. For the clinician, all treatment and rehabilitation decisions should consider the impact of context. A major task for the therapist is to provide a health-promoting context when possible and to help ameliorate the more negative experiences of the patient. The person recovering from schizophrenia is doing so in a context that will shower him or her with many varied and sometimes malignant definitions of self and illness. He or she must be helped to modify such definitions.

	Crisis and Transition	Beginning Reorganization	Superficial Recovery	Adaptation & Integration	Growth & Change	Continuing Care
Medical (disease)						
Medical (social)						
Adaptational						
Social						
Developmental						

Figure 5-1.

Conclusion

For the categorization of illness and recovery to have value in the conceptualization and implementation of treatment rehabilitation, it must take into account all three parameters discussed above: the process of recovery, psychological reactions to the illness, and the context of patienthood. These three parameters have been integrated into six phases of illness and recovery: (1) Crisis and transition, (2) Beginning reorganization, (3) Superficial recovery, (4) Adaptation and integration, (5) Growth and change, and (6) Continuing care. Each of these phases provides the title for a chapter in Part III of this book. When the models discussed in Chapter 4 are considered in each of the phases, a grid or framework is formed (Figure 5-1). This framework can be utilized to plan interventions in a phase-governed, goal-oriented fashion.

Chapter 6

TASKS OF TREATMENT
REHABILITATION AND

What do you need social skills for when you're in touch with the universe?

— anonymous patient

Effective treatment and rehabilitation plans are derived from a combination of psychotherapeutic and sociotherapeutic approaches. They therefore usually necessitate a team approach and the utilization of ancillary services. Unfortunately, the creation of comprehensive, pluralistic rehabilitation programs is often hampered by the following professional liabilities: polarized avowals about the relative efficacy of biological versus psychosocial treatment methods and rigid, limiting definitions of psychotherapy

Biological and Psychosocial Treatment

Philip May (1976b) claimed that only a lingering few still believe that "drugs have no place in the treatment of schizophrenia and that they are incompatible with psychotherapy and psychosocial methods." Perhaps there are also relatively few psychiatrists who ignore psychosocial considerations and treat schizophrenia with physical methods alone. The merging of biological and psychosocial perspectives in the the treatment of schizophrenia is remarkably recent, however, and often remains poorly conceptualized. When, in 1960, controlled research was taking place regarding the usefulness of individual psychotherapy as a treatment for schizophrenic patients, "it was regarded as unethical for a control group not to receive psychotherapy, but by 1968 it was considered unethical to give a control group in another study psychotherapy alone" (Mosher and Keith, 1980).

From an unfailing faith in psychological methods not so many years ago, psychiatry has rapidly shifted to an infatuation with the biological perspective. This shift has been justifiably supported both by the tremendous success of neuroleptic medication and by the need of the psychiatric profession to become more clearly defined as a medical specialty. Furthermore, the current explosion in brain-behavior research is stimulating unrealistic hope for simple biological solutions to complex problems.

In reality, neuroleptic medication is highly effective in the treatment of acute schizophrenia (with some exceptions) and very effective in the prevention of relapse (with more exceptions). Psychosocial treatments enhance the efficacy of medication and, in aftercare programs, prevent relapse, diminish morbidity, and improve social and vocational status (Gunderson 1977; Hogarty, Goldberg, and Schooler, 1974, Pasamanick et al., 1967; Stein, Test, and Marx, 1975, 1980). Nonetheless, with notable exceptions, psychosocial treatment continues to be applied in the wrong place, at the wrong time in the history of the illness, and in a very limited fashion. Clinical staff efforts and research are concentrated at the inpatient phase of treatment, where psychosocial interventions have been shown to be the least effective.

Psychotherapy

Psychotherapy, narrowly defined, has limited value in the treatment of schizophrenia. When psychotherapy is confined to a weekly interpersonal contact in which the roles of the participants are governed by psychoanalytic tradition and the content of each session is only exploratory, historical, and interpretive, it can be of value only to very well-integrated clients. Even then it tends to address generic existential problems more reliably than the illness-related problems of schizophrenic patients.

Theory and methodology are related but separate concerns. Generally speaking, the methods of each school of therapy reflect certain predominant theories of human behavior, but these same theories can be employed in completely different manners. Psychoanalytic theory is usually applied in psychoanalytic therapy, which implies a methodology consisting of a passive therapeutic stance, limited activity on the part of the therapist, a commitment to seek understanding on the part of the patient, and attention paid primarily to historical matters and transference issues. While this methodology is of little use in the treatment and rehabilitation of schizophrenia, the concepts embodied in psychoanalytic theory are. These concepts can be utilized in a different manner from that prescribed by psychoanalysis. Transference, for example, can be managed rather than interpreted. A therapist of the same sex may (and often should) be chosen to work with a young schizophrenic. He or she may choose a particular length of encounter and physical structure to decrease any distortions the patient may have about the relationship. On detecting a distortion, he or she may actively clarify the realities of the relationship rather than comment on transference.

Strict adherence to one or another methodology can prevent the development of flexible, coherent treatment plans based on a rational integration of relevant perspectives. Unfortunately, as Havens (1973) noted "psychiatric schools institutionalize themselves to protect and teach their theories and methods." Havens went on to make an eloquent plea for a pluralistic psychiatry, suggesting that *eclecticism* lacks integration and, at worst, implies a scattered approach to human problems. *Pluralism* implies a more conceptually integrated approach, drawing the best from each school while taking into account the time and context in which it might be most effective.

Though effective treatment plans borrow from a number of psycho- and sociotherapeutic methods, when applied in pure form without regard to context or the nature of the problem being addressed, they can be ineffectual and sometimes harmful. There are concepts and methodologies stemming from family-system theory, for example, that are very useful in the rehabilitation of a patient recovering from schizophrenia. However, when family-process theory is applied to a young psychotic and his or her parents, in undiluted form, it may increase disorganization in the patient, engender guilt in the parents, and preclude a working alliance.

The psychotherapies tend to be defined and taught as specific methodologies accompanied by theory, with little attention paid to the type of problem brought by the client/patient. While these specific methodologies (e.g., psychoanalytic psychotherapy and family-system therapy) have little to offer the treatment of schizophrenia, psychotherapy more broadly defined, or psychotherapeutic management (May, 1976a), does.

There is ample evidence in the work of Frank (1971) and Marmor (1976) to convince us that along with features in common, there seem to be certain central procesess common to all psychotherapies. There is further evidence in the work of Strupp and Hadley (1979) that certain common, nonspecific, or interpersonal-relationship factors may be more important in terms of outcome than the technical operations stressed by each school of psychotherapy. Frank (1971) described these factors as follows:

Technical operations

1. An intense, emotionally charged confiding relationship with a helping person
2. A rationale or myth that includes an explanation of the cause of the patient's distress and indirectly strengthens the patient's confidence in the therapist
3. Provision of new information concerning the nature and sources of the patient's problems and possible alternative ways of dealing with them
4. Strengthening of the patient's expectations of help through the personal qualities of the therapist; arousal of hope
5. Provision of success experiences that further heighten the patient's hope and enhance his or her sense of mastery and interpersonal competence
6. Facilitation of emotional arousal

from this

to this

His work and the observations of others (e.g., Greben, 1977) provided a description of the central features of effective psychotherapy, which might be listed as follows: *Central features of effective psych. Therapy*

1. engendering hope
2. explaining or clarifying the problem
3. providing support
4. demonstrating warmth and positive regard
5. being congruent and responsive
6. allowing the expression of negative experiences or feelings
7. suggesting solutions, directions, or options
8. offering empathy
9. shaping behavior with positive and negative reinforcement

The important point made by all these investigations is that nonspecific factors are central to psychotherapeutic work with any patient or client, and blind adherence to a specific mode or technology of therapy may be very limiting, if not damaging.

Aside from establishing a good therapeutic alliance with a schizophrenic patient and being the kind of warm, empathetic, congruent, accepting person acknowledged as being therapeutic, what else might be helpful? Three elements need to be added in the treatment and management of schizophrenia: (1) phase-governed, goal-oriented interventions, (2) specific consideration of the important role of social and developmental issues, and (3) a theoretical/attitudinal stance that can be modified with the patient's progress.

Goal-Oriented Interventions

Within the framework proposed, specific psychotherapeutic issues are described as they relate to the specific needs and struggles of a recovering schizophrenic patient. The framework is designed to avoid the problems described earlier of engaging in polarization of biological versus psychosocial perspectives, and application of rigid psychotherapy concepts. The psychotherapeutic issues highlighted throughout the framework may be addressed by a variety of therapy methodologies, choice being determined by the context of the illness, the skills of the therapist, the resources of the patient, and the facilities and staff available. The goal of therapy is to help the patient resolve a given issue according to his or her own needs and abilities. It is important to a recovering schizophrenic patient, for example, to develop a role other than that of "the sick member of the family." There are subtleties to this issue, of course. The patient must accept a self-definition containing "having an illness" insofar as he or she is receiving medication and attending an outpatient clinic and insofar as vocational expectations may need to be tempered. But it is important that "illness" not become an all-pervasive definition of self.

This is a consistent issue among hospitalized and posthospitalized mental patients. Extreme resolutions at both ends of the continuum are common. Some patients respond with total denial of the existence of illness; others allow it to become a pervasive determinant of behavior and adopt a chronic sick role. Families, too, respond in related extremes. Each stance is often reinforced and socially sanctioned—the former by certain religious groups, some sociologists, and a few psychiatrists, the latter by overly anxious and paternalistic professionals.

Managing, perhaps compartmentalizing, the idea of "having an illness" is a complex, important task that must be addressed by a therapist wishing to facilitate rehabilitation or at least optimal adjustment. This issue can be discussed (in intellectual and even social-psychological terms) in individual psychotherapy sessions with a verbal patient; a less verbal patient might respond best to simple concern, suggestion, and advice. Greater or lesser degrees of uncovering and exploration may be used with yet another patient. The issue may be discussed in group therapy sessions, and it will be ever-present in family interviews. In some circumstances, the therapist may opt for referral to the local vocational rehabilitation center with very little discussion about roles and feelings. This latter action might fall under the rubric "social therapy" but, nonverbally, it addresses the same issue.

The social therapies can be incorporated in this process. They are in a sense merely the enactment of the same issues and solutions discussed in psychotherapy. Instead of talking about the need for friends and the development of trust, for example, the patient is placed in a discussion/activity group where these things might occur *in vivo*. Similarly, a sense of mastery and an improved self-esteem might be achieved by placement in a vocational rehabilitation program along with therapeutic discussions. Each of the tasks delineated in succeeding chapters might be realized through psychotherapy and/or sociotherapy.

These issues are central to the psychotherapeutic management and rehabilitation of a patient with schizophrenia. They can be addressed in individual, group, or family therapy, or in a variety of less verbal and more directive social interventions. The choice of methodology should be guided by consideration of the optimal outcome for the patient and not by adherence to a rigid concept of therapy.

Social and Developmental Issues

In the psycho-sociotherapy program, specific attention must be paid to the current social and developmental issues, as opposed to the traditional psychotherapeutic concerns of conflict and early history. The achievement of social competence is crucial to the rehabilitation of people afflicted by schizophrenia, and developmental change, insofar as it entails engaging in new relationships, is especially difficult.

There is no point in talking with a schizophrenic about relationships, motivation, conflict, and vocations unless he or she has the opportunity to develop and practice the necessary skills inherent in these issues. The gains of a long program of therapy outside social context (e.g., two years in a mental hospital) will generalize only minimally to the community situation upon discharge. Such a program might, in fact, simply promote a comfortable adjustment to institutional living.

Modified Attitudinal Stance

In most applications of psychotherapy in other situations, the roles of the two participants remain more or less consistent throughout. The responsibilities of the patient and the relative authority of the therapist do not change. In the treatment of schizophrenics over a long period of time, it is important that the therapist be able to modify his or her position. Initially, one will be quite directive; later on initiative and independence should be encouraged. Later still, when possible, the patient may be allowed to control medication and negotiate appointment intervals. Similarly, the conceptual preoccupations of the therapist should shift. Initially they must be predominantly medical, later moving to social and adaptational concerns and, lastly, to issues of development and growth.

Throughout this process the therapist must monitor distance from the patient—both affective and physical. Certainly one should be more engaged than the oft-caricatured psychoanalyst, but conversely, a Rogerian closeness can be very threatening. Both a passive, ambiguous stance and an excessive display of warmth, empathy, and regard can foster recoil and disorganization in a recovering schizophrenic (Seeman and Cole, 1977). The therapist should strike an active, directive, professional stance initially and modify this with increasing warmth and informality as the patient improves. In later phases of recovery the schizophrenic patient may be able to tolerate a more passive, nondirective approach. Always, the therapist should take special care to clarify contextual information and reduce ambiguities.

Part III

PSYCHOSOCIAL TREATMENT AND REHABILITATION

Chapter 7

PHASE ONE: CRISIS AND TRANSITION

He didn't know who we were. He was crying, my mother was going
nuts, and yelling and everything else—I could see my dad was going
nuts and I was just hanging in there not going nuts.
—**brother of patient**

Description

The transition referred to in the title of this chapter is the process of
acknowledging the presence of illness, seeking help, and becoming a
patient. The family has exhausted its resources trying to contain their predicament, and they now seek outside help. The family in this situation
shows a number of features often mistaken for intrinsic pathology. Some of
these features may be more usefully interpreted as responses to stress (Horowitz, 1974) or as generic features of an individual or family in crisis. Of all
the crisis theorists, Hansell (1976) most recently provided a refreshing and
useful perspective. He wrote of individuals in crisis, but his observations,
when applied to the reactions of family groups, still ring true.

Using Hansell's terminology, it can be said that the family in crisis
with a psychotic member will have a "fixed span of attention." Certainly
the history obtained by the interviewer at this point may be distorted and
selective. The famiy may focus on one specific event or symptom—for
example, a real or threatened episode of violence—and this will be presented as "the problem."

The reported threat of violence or distress may seem grossly exaggerated to the interviewer. When one tries to elicit details about the problem,
one may find them to be elusive or not amounting to more than profanity
and broken crockery. Should this distortion be viewed as family pathology
or even family conspiracy, as suggested by Laing (1964)? Certainly there

are instances when families conspire to have one of their number extruded and incarcerated. Many individual problems can be better understood as products of a disordered system. Nonetheless, when one family member is truly psychotic, it is usually more helpful to view the family's distorted communications as an adaptive response. The family is a small group in crisis attempting to contain or extrude a problem. Once the family decides to seek external help, they must also resolve the *cognitive dissonance*, that is, their perception and interpretation of events and behavior subtly shifts to support the decision made.

Introduced by Festinger (1957), cognitive dissonance is a term that refers to a psychological state resulting from confrontation with information that is inconsistent with one's attitude or opinion. In order to reduce the dissonance and achieve consonance, one adopts a new interpretation of the information. For the family of the schizophrenic, this may mean an extreme shifting of position from initially viewing the individual as lazy or "going through a stage" to stating that he or she is hopelessly sick and should be locked up.

The family and the prospective patient may also show a "loosening and widening" of affectional attachments (Hansell). It is well to remember that they are seeking help from a new source and have either exhausted or bypassed their natural network of helpers, caretakers, and problem solvers. Consequently, they are vulnerable to a self-imposed isolation and an excessive dependency on mental health workers.

The problem and its identification as an insoluble human predicament can throw the family into disarray. If it can be said that a family or ecological group has a sense of identity, a sense of position, and social membership, these might be threatened by the development of a psychosis. When the family is unable to cope with the crisis, fulfillment of the established roles of each member is threatened. Parents find they can no longer parent.

Hansell observed that an individual in distress exhibits "random access memory and magical thinking." It is useful to transpose this concept to the family: Typically, a family with a psychotic member will offer bits of irrelevant data to the interviewer suggesting rather farfetched etiological factors and explanations. This is not necessarily lack of sophistication or magical thinking; it is an intense human need for a hopeful explanation, and an adaptive response. Hansell and other crisis theorists suggested that "individuals in distress send signals of distress." The point of this rather tautological observation is that some clinical findings may be more usefully interpreted as generic signals of distress than as symptoms of illness. When this concept is applied to the family of an acute schizophrenic, one can view their conflicted, ambivalent, confusing, and sometimes bizarre behavior as signs of stress rather than schizophrenogenesis.

Thus, in this phase of crisis and transition, there is *an individual* who is psychotic and in crisis and *a family* in crisis. The context of this situation is the first contact with an outpatient clinic or emergency service and a psychiatric inpatient unit. In this phase, the normal social network has failed and the family, by virtue of having brought the individual to the hospital, has defined the problem as one of illness.

Dominant Model

In this phase of illness and treatment the medical model retains a paramount position. One may argue for it on the basis of efficacy and humaneness as well as on the evidence that schizophrenia is, in fact, an illness. Two less obvious factors support this position as well.

The subject is perceived as "being sick" by his or her family and society. The family is making application for the assignment of a sick role. Their other options include abandonment and/or application to religious or correctional institutions. The sick role has hazards, but fewer than alternative solutions. The young schizophrenic is perplexed and frightened, struggling with the failure to understand what is happening and being unable to discern the expectations of others. Here the medical model provides a simple, traditional, time-honored context. The roles of doctor, nurse, and patient are probably within access of the young patient's understanding. These transactions are relatively simple and predictable, especially if they are carefully explained.

Similarly, the medical model can provide the family with a way of understanding their predicament, preferably one that will facilitate treatment and rehabilitation. The word "schizophrenia" should not be avoided. After all, the examiner has probably inquired of cases of mental illness in relatives, and the question of schizophrenia will be uppermost in the parents' minds. But it is important that the word itself be diffused with an explanation that at this point it essentially means no more than "breakdown" and does not necessarily imply a chronic state. (More about the use of the word "schizophrenia" will be described in the "Special Problems" section toward the end of this chapter.) An explanation of the investigations to be carried out, the approximate length of stay, the possible use of medication, and rehabilitation prospects is in order at this point. It is important to legitimize parents' conveyance of their child into psychiatric patienthood to minimize any guilt and conflict.

One need not attempt to convince the patient that he or she is "sick." The words the patient has used to describe his or her own distress can be repeated to reinforce the need for help. Despite the psychosis, meticulous care should be taken to introduce and explain any questions, investigations, activities, or treatments. In this connection social introductions, explanations and requests, and maintenance of basic etiquette are very important, not simply on humanitarian grounds, but also as a way of providing an understandable and orderly context.

At this crisis point families tend to want to pass their predicament onto health professionals and retreat in failure. They can be helped to assist the patient and remain involved with some of their burden alleviated.

Tasks and Interventions

Any person at the point of becoming a psychiatric patient is vulnerable to a loss of his or her normal attachments: social position, roles, and functions. He or she is susceptible to a permanent shift in self-concept. The young schizophrenic is especially vulnerable to this dispossession because social relationships are the very apparatus he or she is having trouble maintaining or achieving. In addition, society is generally all too ready to assign to this individual the permanent "spoiled" identity of the mentally ill. (Goffman, 1963). It is thus of crucial importance that the treatment team, in carrying out all other tasks and interventions, ensure that conveyance of the individual into the sick role is partial and/or temporary.

One of the principal tasks at the point of first contact with the individual is, of course, to make a diagnosis. Schizophrenia remains to some extent a diagnosis of exclusion. Psychosis of organic etiology must be considered first. The differentiation of "functional" psychoses is a secondary consideration. Even then, the practical question must be responsiveness to medication. Diagnostic implications for long-term management and prognosis can await a more complete assessment over time. This complex matter will be left to the many standard texts, except to point out that in this kind of situation, intervention cannot always wait on the diagnostic process. The interview assessment and other diagnostic investigations usually must be intertwined with management activity.

The principal psychotherapeutic management tasks of this first phase are described in the following.

Engage the patient. Engage the patient in treatment using the person's own words to describe his or her distress. He or she should not be expected to verbalize "I am sick," and may instead describe the experience as "feeling funny," "interference," "confusion," and so on.

Clarify experience and expectations. Explain the illness carefully to patient and family in clear and realistic terms with reference to expected length of stay, medications, rehabilitation requirements, and probable outcome. Often patients who appear reluctant to be hospitalized are told that they will be in for "a short time" or "a week or so." As the weeks in the hospital go by the patient understandably becomes angry at the earlier misrepresentation. Being clear about what you do know about the illness and its treatment (i.e., specifics regarding use of medication, inpatient treatment routines, conservative estimate of length of stay, and nature of rehabilitation options) will make it easier for the patient and the family to tolerate the less definable aspects of the situation.

Provide medical care. Family interviews during this stage can focus on assessment, diagnosis, family situation, some idea of family dynamics, and developmental issues without focusing blame or guilt.

Dampen anxiety and offer some control. Decrease excessive stimuli, give repeated reassurance, and respond to any reasonable request from the patient as a way of reinforcing healthy ego functioning.

Name/explain experiences when the patient is perplexed. Interpret upward; that is, depending on the skill and experience of the therapist, psychotic material produced by the patient can be translated actively by the therapist into a less frightening approximation of reality or a legitimized emotional state.

Patient:
Hey man, anything could happen, they're going to get me, I'm in a box.
Therapist:
You're very frightened, but this is a hospital; we're not going to lock you up, we're going to help you by . . . .

Obtain a limited developmental history. Obtain developmental history with the knowledge that some information will be distorted at this point. Parents should be interviewed for further information at a later stage.

Avoid engendering parental guilt. Any focus at this time on parental inadequacies or issues of separation will increase guilt and will make further work with the family difficult.

Offer specific roles (tasks) to family/parents. Family interviews should not be exploratory but rather focused on specific issues that might clarify diagnosis and aid this phase of management.

Note developmental and family issues of etiological significance. During this phase some developmental issues of etiological and rehabilitative significance may be vocalized by the patient. In general, these are best noted now but dealt with psychotherapeutically at a later stage. It is not helpful, for example, to encourage the patient's struggle for autonomy and independence until he or she has at least partially recovered.

Develop the relationship. One person should be assigned as primary therapist.

Acknowledge firm beliefs without colluding or confronting. Be meticulously honest, especially with a paranoid patient.

Use a consistent approach. The assessment has involved a thorough mental status examination, and a consistent psychotherapeutic approach to specific symptoms must be devised; for example, after eliciting a delusion the therapist should not inquire of it daily. The treatment team's interactions with the patient should be consistent with the therapist's.

Shape the patient's communications. Distract from symptoms and shape the patient's communications. It is important that the symptoms not be reinforced and also that they not be expected to disappear overnight.

Consider developmental-age-appropriate conflicts in the management plan. Hospitalization, socialization into the patient role, and the giving of medication should be modified to some extent by awareness of the control-dependency-autonomy issues prevalent at the patient's developmental stage. Consider the patient's response to the ward and to the treatment program as a function of developmental stage as well as of illness and/or denial of illness. One approach to hostile dependency and control issues is for the therapist to allow the patient some aspect of control and autonomy in life areas appropriate to his or her current level of functioning, such as planning his or her menu or choosing from two or three recreational activities, while still providing an external structure and control for other areas. A major task is the prevention of regression.

Monitor other relationships. Monitor all forms of stimuli encountered by the patient. Visits by staff, family, and friends should be controlled and monitored. Decisions with respect to who should visit and how often must be made by balancing the social disruption and isolation caused by nonvisiting against possible loss of credibility of the patient in the community if friends see him or her as bizarre and frightening.

Prevent further deterioration in role expectations. Arrange for visits in the near future. Family and friends should be encouraged to retain contact and reasonable expectations of the patient. In the medication transaction, staff should be careful not to increase the patient's regression and isolation by communicating the notion that he or she is a wholly passive/dependent object.

Prevent social network breakdown. Take action to ensure that the patient's position in school, job, and so on will not be lost during hospitalization. Negotiate this arrangement with the patient. Interview family and friends to decrease their fears, answer their questions, and ensure that their relationship with the patient does not break down.

Special Problems

Interviewing

The sensitivities and skills required for interviewing a psychotic patient alone or with his or her family are beyond the scope of this book—perhaps beyond the scope of any specific written work—but guidelines will be presented.

It is important that the therapist monitor physical and affective distance from the patient. It has been suggested that schizophrenics suffer from a basic "need-fear dilemma" (Burnham, Gladstone, and Gibson, 1969). This is an analytic inference based on observations of schizophrenic patients' conflicting need for close, dependent relationships and their tendency to distance themselves. The concept has universal appeal, and to a great extent describes one aspect of the human condition not wholly unique to schizophrenia. Still, schizophrenic patients do distance themselves to an inordinate degree. This behavior can be more usefully interpreted as a response to their inability to handle or manage the torrent of information exchanged in a close relationship. A few schizophrenics seem to overcompensate and, at least with health care professionals, establish what has been described as "sticky" relationships. This minority appear to be able to ignore their therapists' verbal and nonverbal cues of dismissal and forge intrusively ahead.

The psychotic patient is usually highly sensitive to both intrusions and rejections, though responses to these will seldom be direct. He or she may retreat, withdraw, become angry, or comment obliquely. One half of the normal monitoring feedback system (nonverbal signaling) enabling two people to manage their adjacent boundaries has broken down. Therefore it is up to the clinician/therapist to remain especially sensitive to this boundary. In part one may do so by clarifying context, honoring social etiquette, and simplifying communication. One must also be ready to understand some of the patient's thought-disordered statements as symbolic or metaphorical comments on their relationship.

The psychotic patient is sensitive to the mood and attitude of the examiner, although unable to clarify either in dialogue. It is important for interviewers to acknowledge their own fears and anxieties themselves (and in certain cases, to the patient) in order to diminish the effect they might have on the patient's behavior. Though anxious and perhaps frightened, they must approach the patient from a position of calm and confidence. This does not require heroics so much as sensitivity and well-considered milieu. This latter refers to the very simple caution of having help nearby, clear supervisory back-up, and an open, comfortable (calming) interviewing room. When possible, appointments with psychotic patients should be scheduled before 3 or 4 P.M. to ensure that colleagues are nearby and that the therapist has adequate emotional resources.

The secret, perhaps, of all therapists renowned for their work with psychotics is that they consistently assure predictability and meaning in their transactions with their patients. The patient is not left hanging in his or her perplexity. Beginning interviewers often accelerate the patient's anxiety and confusion by insensitive questioning (objective-descriptive school) or passivity (psychoanalytic school). Successful therapists explain the context and find meaning in the transactions. They include Rosen (1962), whose bizarre interventions at least had the effect of reducing communication to its simplest, primitive form. Others, such as Arieti (1955), Fromm-Reichmann (1952), Searles (1965), Sullivan (1962), and Will (1974), went to great lengths to find and clarify meaning in the productions of their patients. Their interpretations of schizophrenic communication at times may have been penetratingly insightful and at other times rather far-fetched. But content being less important than process, their committed and energetic efforts to clarify context, forge links with their patients, and establish meaning was central to the success of their work.

With this in mind, then, a therapist should engage a psychotic patient by meticulously explaining the context of the interview, the purpose of the interview, the role of the interviewer, and expectations of the patient. One should directly assist the patient in clarifying the patient's feelings and experiences, gently reinterpreting the patient's more bizarre comments in the direction of legitimized affect and shared perceptions. Having elicited mental status information, one should not dwell on it. Rather, one should focus in the interview on reality-based needs and events.

The permutations of this process are infinite. The therapist must, through experience, develop an individually effective style. But it is a good rule of thumb to remember that anything the psychotic patient says holds something relevant to the present situation. He or she is saying something meaningful, which if you can grasp the hidden meaning, can be responded to in a way that reduces his or her anxiety. Some examples follow.

Example One. A male patient is being interviewed on an inpatient unit by his therapist, who has brought along a medical student.

Patient:
My problem is that I can't get any privacy, they're always on my back.
Therapist:
You're right about the importance of privacy, and if you like I will ask the medical student to leave.

Example Two. A male patient is being interviewed in the emergency unit by a female interviewer. Because all other rooms are being used, the interview is taking place in a very small, enclosed space.

Patient:
Women are after me. They are closing in and sapping my juices.
Therapist:
It *is* very small and close in this room. Let's move out into the hall to talk.

Participant-observation. Communicating with the schizophrenic patient in the language Hill (1955) called "schizophrenese" and remaining an objective clinician is a difficult balance to maintain. The longer one communicates with a thought-disordered person—providing context, filling in gaps, interpreting symbols, and extracting order from disorder—the less one becomes aware of the other's strangeness. Indeed, working with a psychotic patient in this manner over a long period of time can lead a therapist to experience what has been most cogently described by Sullivan as, "Schizophrenics are not schizophrenic with me." For therapy this is good; for assessment it can be misleading.

On the other hand, when the process of objective assessment dominates, and the interview is limited to a mental status and social function inquiry, it can lead to a relatively sterile yet anxiety-provoking exchange. It can also miss the point: An accurate diagnosis is of little benefit if the patient is lost to treatment. One way of maintaining a good balance is to consciously and temporarily separate the processes. Quietly and privately consider against assessment parameters the information that has accumulated during an involved and active exchange in a few moments' reflection during or after the interview.

Talking with family members. Information necessary for diagnosis, or at least for the exclusion of a diagnosis of organic psychosis or affective disorder, must be gathered from family members. The initial interviews with a family should not contain a probing search for family psychopathology. At this point such a search will most often produce random, distorted, and misleading information. It will also reinforce the concern, albeit defended, that they, the parents, caused the problem. At this time it is beside the point whether or not parenting or lack of parenting contributed; the parents need help in their state of crisis to ensure that, together with the therapist, they can later contribute to their child's recovery and rehabilitation.

Unfortunately, even a medically oriented family inquiry can engender problems. Such an inquiry can, for example, support (or refute) the husband's certain knowledge that the madness flows from his wife's family and not his own. There may be a preexisting family myth (sometimes a reality) that has disturbed the family's harmony for years.

Case Example

One patient's mother mentioned to the interviewer that, knowing several of her close relatives had become psychotic and that she herself was prone to the occasional depression, she had purposely and consciously chosen her husband—the patient's father—as a stable, "rock solid" man whose genes might counteract her own. She discovered during her son's childhood, however, that her scheme had failed. He [her son] had the same skin texture and body odor as her own.

She assumed therefore that he also carried her genes for madness, and consequently she devoted an inordinate amount of time protecting him from stress.

Now, a family-process theorist could make a lot out of this mother's "confession" to the interviewer, while a geneticist might see the lady in question as a person of education, perception, and remarkable foresight.

During initial family interviews it is not important which viewpoint is more valid. At this time blame and guilt must be tempered. There will be plenty of time later on to determine more exactly the relationship this individual's problem has with relatives' illnesses. There will be time as well to explore ways of intervening in a mother-son relationship that has too few boundaries and too little individuation.

Even later, the therapist's goals should be not to unearth "the" cause of the schizophrenia but to find ways of modifying those family dynamics that might inhibit rehabilitation and the successful passage of developmental milestones. One might find, for example, that mother and son have an overly strong bond that constitutes a power base and excludes the father (Mishler and Waxler, 1968). This should be dealt with, not as a cause of schizophrenia, but rather as a family problem that may impede the son's separation from the mother and his growth into adulthood. In fact, the boy's illness can be used as an explanation to the parents of why the mother's overprotectiveness has developed. During the initial interview, however, these dynamics should be noted simply for future reference. At this time the parents need a simple explanation of what is happening, probably repeated at different times in different ways, and some direction in what to expect and what they can do to help.

The word "schizophrenia." To the lay person and many professionals as well, the word "schizophrenia" carries with it a host of images and inferences that go far beyond a "limited disease concept" (Wing, 1978). "Madness" conjures up metaphors ranging through religious, ethical, and moral concerns. Yet both "schizophrenia" and more generic concepts like "madness" or "mental breakdown" surely occur to both patient and family in much the same way that a man complaining to his doctor of a lump and weight loss is undoubtedly wondering about cancer.

In the latter situation a sensitive doctor, after examination, asks the patient what he thinks he may have or asks directly, "Are you worried about cancer?" When the patient answers honestly, expressing his fears and preoccupations, the doctor may explain the investigations he plans to make and the specific disease he is considering, albeit weighted in the most hopeful, optimistic direction. Similarly, the psychiatrist can ask the family what diagnosis they are thinking about. This question often brings forth concerns that their child has the same problems as Aunt Molly, who died in a mental hospital.

Unlike the lay word "cancer," which a physician can categorize into many different and discrete diseases, the word "schizophrenia" remains vague even within professional usage. The interviewer must face the complicated, educative task of discussing the concept of schizophrenia with a family in order to reduce any misconceptions they might have. One must explain, for example, that the acute breakdown of the patient may be unrelated to the chronic disease seen or imagined in mental hospital wards even though the terms "psychosis" and "schizophrenia" are used to describe both. The word "schizophrenia" can be spoken, but its inherent excessive connotations should be dispelled.

The family group needs hope, activity, and a sense of usefulness. They need a way of understanding what is happening that is optimistic but not unreasonable. They need to be prepared for the later period of convalescence and slow recovery. And, whenever possible, they need their questions answered.

Hospitalization: Voluntary and Involuntary

The topic of involuntary hospitalization is seldom addressed in a clinical book or, for that matter, discussed in medical school and residency training programs. Yet it is an action that symbolizes one of the major functions of psychiatrists, and it is the activity most scrutinized in the public eye. It constitutes legal enforcement of the social contract of the medical model. This function of psychiatry is rather disparagingly referred to by sociologists as "control of social deviance." More charitably and more accurately it could be described as the role of arbitrating between the needs and rights of individuals and the needs, rights, and demands of society. Inevitably, psychiatrists find themselves acting as arbiters between the rights of individuals and their social groups.

Many psychiatrists deny this; they see involuntary hospitalization as simply a clinical issue. They view it as a decision of clinical judgment based solely on a patient's distress, the presence of mental illness, and the likelihood of imminent disaster. Others see involuntary hospitalization as a strictly social action: essentially a political-legal action quite unrelated to the traditional concerns of medicine. They argue for the whole process being turned over to the judicial system, removing the power of commitment from physicians and placing it under the jurisdiction of citizens' boards and due legal process. The actual laws governing involuntary hospitalization vary from state to state and province to province, and in many communities are currently undergoing revision. The issues remain unresolved, the legislation unsatisfactory. They are unlikely ever to be resolved, because this problem encompasses so many philosophical and ethical questions and because, as alluded to earlier, it reflects the ever-shifting dynamic relationship between the individual and his or her society.

When a clinician in the emergency room is confronted by a psychotic, reluctant patient, an anxious family, and a stern police officer, and reaches for the shelf holding committal forms, he or she is making a decision that carries reverberations throughout the very structure of our society. It is no wonder that clinicians often prefer to view this decision as simply medical or a matter of following the established procedure. The hypothetical patient in this example, being considered for involuntary hospitalization, is likely schizophrenic. The occurrence of involuntary hospitalization is often a central and sometimes repetitive event in the life of a schizophrenic patient. As much as we would like to avoid the issue, then, it must be considered in any work on the treatment of schizophrenia. The concern here will not be with the intricacies of this major philosophical question. For this the reader is referred to Ennis and Siegel's *The Rights of Mental Patients* (1973), Kittrie's *The Right to Be Different* (1972), to Chodoff (1976) and to Roth (1979).

Whatever the laws and methods, involuntary hospitalization is a distressing event not soon forgotten by the patient or his or her community. Yet it is often a better, safer, and more humane act than all other options. It is the clinician's onerous task to ensure that involuntary hospitalization occurs as infrequently as possible and that any form of hospitalization be a constructive experience. This entails consideration of long-term as well as short-term goals, an awareness of the social pressures to incarcerate and/or extrude a deviant person, and a sensitivity to the experience of entering a hospital.

Social pressures. The decision to hospitalize and to hospitalize involuntarily is influenced by a variety of factors apart from clinical judgment and legal requirements (Bartolucci, Goodman, and Streiner, 1975). These factors include the age and experience of the mental health worker, his or her relationship with supervisors and the institution as a whole, and the explicit and implicit rules of conduct of the institution. The pressures brought to bear by the patient's family members, spouse, landlady, colleagues, other professionals, police, lawyers, and religious groups, and by the most recent experience the worker has had with suicide, scientologists, and civil libertarians are difficult to resist. Of further, even less palatable influence are the patient's sex, race, and social class.

When these influences are denied by the psychiatrist, they tend to carry more weight in one's decision. The psychiatrist claiming to make a decision on simply clinical factors, and claiming not to be influenced by social factors, is the very professional whose activities are most likely governed by social pressures. To acknowledge these pressures and influences is to find the means, when appropriate, to resist them. Then the decision to hospitalize involuntarily can be truly a clinical one, tempered with an arbitration between the rights of an individual and the rights of his or her (and the clinician's) society. In short, the decision should never be taken lightly or simplistically.

The experience of hospitalization. No matter how much we would wish it otherwise, the hospitalization of someone with schizophrenia is unlike any other. It is a difficult decision in the first place. For other illnesses people are hospitalized because the necessary treatment can be administered only in a hospital. For schizophrenia this is not always the case. Medications can be administered in the home (if not so effectively), home nursing care can be organized, and psychotherapeutic management can be offered daily in home and clinic, though the present organization of health care services often makes this impracticable (Stein, Test, and Marx, 1974; Stein and Test, 1980). Rather, hospitalization is chosen because of dangerousness, noncompliance, and exhausted resources.

To say the acutely psychotic individual may be ambivalent about hospitalization is a gross understatement. He or she is usually struggling to maintain some semblance of self-control and autonomy. The person's own disordered thinking is not apparent to him- or herself and the ensuing restitutive efforts to organize the chaos of the mind further remove the person from sharing the perceptions of an examiner. Still, the one thing the patient usually knows is that he or she might be in trouble or that others might think so, and that the mental hospital awaits. The asylum looms in myths and fantasies. Transferring acute care to the general hospitals has changed this picture somewhat, but not altogether. Whether it's "up the hill," Toronto's "999," Vancouver's Essondale, New York's Bellevue, or the "psych ward" in a modern community hospital, myths and fantasies still surround the locale of psychiatric treatment.

Nonetheless, the clinical decision is often made, and rightly, to hospitalize a schizophrenic patient. If he or she turns down the recommendation for voluntary hospitalization, involuntary hospitalization is considered. On the principle that voluntary hospitalization augurs better for most patients than involuntary hospitalization, the next few paragraphs are devoted to the problem of convincing an ambivalent patient to accept hospitalization.

Working toward voluntary admission. Despite the fact that family and friends have usually been instrumental in bringing the patient to the attention of health care professionals in the first place, they are often ignored in the decision to hospitalize. This is perceived as a doctor's decision and a contract between doctor and patient alone. In some instances this approach is best: The relationship between patient and family has become so tangled and painful that it is a humane act for the doctor to assume private responsibility for such a decision. At other times, though, family and friends can be brought in for a discussion with the patient on the pros and cons of hospitalization. The doctor can set the tone, explain as clearly as one knows them the options available, and engage the patient and family in shared decision making. If the patient balks at hospitalization, the family is there to tell him or her clearly (with the doctor's assistance) of the consequences. Family members may be exhausted and unable to care for the patient any longer, and this he or she can be told.

On the other hand, the family may relent. They may agree to take the patient home. At this time the physician is in a position to strike a contract with the patient and family to the effect that, for example, they try it at home, with medication as prescribed, for three more days and then meet at an agreed-upon time to review the situation.

This point is often missed by physicians. Once they have offered hospitalization, a refusal is viewed as being "against medical advice"; a control struggle ensues, and the doctor-patient relationship becomes soured. This impasse, however, can sometimes enhance the doctor-patient relationship if dealt with differently. When a patient offered hospitalization verbalizes, "No, I can make it on my own," he or she may be rallying strength and resolve. Before the person wasn't sure. Now, offered the refuge he or she feared and longed for, it isn't needed so badly. It is often wise for a physician to heed this thrust of self-reliance. In fact, when a physician respects the patient's right to make such a decision, an alliance can be formed that will make outpatient care or future voluntary hospitalization possible.

In negotiating with a patient to enter the hospital, it is well to remember that, though the patient might be aware of his or her own distress and vulnerability, he or she may not be willing to say, "I am sick" or want to hear, "You need help." He or she may be willing to accept hospitalization and accept help only if allowed the face-saving device of verbally denying this need. But the patient should not be tricked. It is a case not so much of colluding with his or her denial as simply not responding to it. It goes without saying that the process of hospitalization should contain none of the facets of the "stripping" process described so vividly in Goffman's *Asylums* (1961).

Case Example

A psychotic woman, a few days into hospitalization, symptoms still acute, announced that she was leaving the ward and going home. A ward nurse called her therapist to speak to her. On meeting with her therapist, the woman again announced that she was leaving, but added this time that she would go "after she had a little rest." The therapist sensed the woman's ambivalence about leaving, but could not talk her into staying. With her permission, he called in her children and a close neighbor who was looking after the home. With the assurances of her friend and children that things were being taken care of at home and with their expressions of concern regarding her well-being, the woman agreed to stay in hospital without further direct pressure from the hospital staff.

Hospitalization entails a transaction between patient and therapist. In this respect there are certain imperatives of dialogue to keep in mind. In common speech, "Would you like to come with me?" can really mean,

"Please come with me." We are not really inquiring of the person's prefer-
ences. For the psychotic, ambivalent patient, the former statement leaves
room for pondering. Not certain of the question, he or she might dwell on
the superfluous portion, "Would you like?" The latter statement, on the
other hand, is easier to interpret and more difficult to ignore.

One could describe on a continuum the various ways in which hospitalization can be broached with a patient. These would include the
following:

> "It has been very difficult for you these past few days; what would you
> think of coming into the hospital for a while?"

> "Maybe I can arrange a hospital bed for you if you think you need
> it."

> "I think you need to come into the hospital for a while."

> "I want you in the hospital for a few days; I'll make the
> arrangements."

> "You must come in the hospital. You're not managing outside."

> "I'm putting you in the hospital...doctor's orders."

> "If you don't come in now I'll have to sign a certificate and get the
> police to bring you in."

Each has its place. Where one statement may cause either equivocation or
outright refusal, another might lead to relieved acceptance. The response to
each will depend on the age, distress, and personality structure of the
patient, the context of the interview, and the quality of the doctor-patient
relationship.

When the statement is made is as important as *how* it is made. Generally it should come after some rapport has been established. The interview
can in fact follow a path that leads through assessment questions, explorations of current distress, status of coping, empathy offered, anxiety
reduced, fears of either being locked up or rejected alleviated...and then
the question of hospitalization is asked. In some cases the patient will
respond best to a clear recommendation; in other cases he or she will
respond best to options. It is important for the physician to retain a flexible
repertoire.

On some occasions the transaction can be quite complex, involving a
period of testing, bartering, and trust building. Throughout this process it
is important to protect the patient's dignity and sense of worth. The following is an example, described at length, that illustrates several principles.

Case Example

The patient, Mrs. C., was a Greek woman in her late forties. She had been hospitalized before and was now maintained on phenothiazines, twice-monthly outpatient
visits, and family benefits checks. She owned a small house where she lived with her
young son and 16-year-old daughter. Her husband had left her years before, and

whenever she became psychotic her very real grievances against men and the sub-servient position of women became entangled with elaborate delusions.

Now she had once again gone off her pills and stopped attending the outpatient department (OPD), perhaps in response to problems with support checks. The daughter called the therapist. Mother had been up wandering and shouting all night for three nights running. She no longer cooked or cleaned, and the daughter had taken over these duties. The son was frightened and stayed as long as possible each day after school at a friend's house. It was getting worse each day. Mother had smashed a glass ashtray against the wall and the pieces of glass lay there. She wouldn't let her daughter clean them up.

The nurse-therapist visited the home and talked with the daughter, but the mother wouldn't come downstairs. The next day the nurse went back with a psychiatrist in tow.

The daughter, a plump, soft-spoken girl, returned to watching television in the living room after letting the nurse and doctor into the hallway. Mrs. C. was upstairs but called down, "Is that you, Mary?" (the nurse's name). Informed that the doctor was here, she came downstairs.

The doctor was introduced. Mrs. C. spoke angrily to her daughter, talked in a confused manner about a number of irrelevant events, but offered tea and led the doctor and nurse to her kitchen.

While her guests sat at her kitchen table, Mrs. C. bustled about filling a kettle, plugging it in, and fetching cups and saucers. Each action was mannered and bizarre. The cups were wiped out with newspaper; some were rejected for being wrong size or type. They and the spoons were put on the table and taken off and put on again. All the while she talked of becoming the Queen. Soon she would be going to Ottawa to take over the government. This was spiced with references to the failures of men and the importance of women. When the kettle had boiled, she unplugged it and brought it to the table. Instead of pouring it, though, she passed it several times in circles above the head of the doctor. Briefly he imagined the painful splash of boiling water as Mrs. C. took revenge for all downtrodden women.

But she stopped and made the tea. Then she brought out a collection of clippings and scraps of paper she kept in a shoebox. Her explanation of these items made little sense. The doctor showed an interest in these items, and she warmed to him. Her attitude was at once hostile and flirtatious. She went on about being the queen, pausing only to let the doctor and nurse know that she wasn't going to take their pills.

The doctor suggested to her that in Canada it wasn't the queen who had power but rather the prime minister. She asked then if the doctor might become the prime minister. He responded that it might be a good idea; maybe he should go into politics and become prime minister.

They spoke in this vein for a while; then Mrs. C. let them know she wasn't coming to the hospital but she might take one of the pills that night. She punctuated this by deliberatley smashing a glass on the floor.

The doctor asked her if she would come to the clinic tomorrow to continue the conversation. She said she would; "You visit me in my house. I come to yours. Tomorrow. We talk as equals, eh?"

The daughter had remained in the living room watching TV. She hadn't wanted to participate. She was told of the appointment the next day, and she said she felt she could cope that night.

The next day Mrs. C. and her daughter arrived at the clinic. Mother had a large bunch of flowers in her hand which she had ripped from the flower beds of a city park. She played with these during the interview, shifting them from hand to hand. She was agitated, frightened, and thought-disordered. The nurse brought a vase for the flowers but Mrs. C. wouldn't put them down.

The doctor said something like, "Mary will take you up to the hospital now. You can take the flowers with you if you like. I'll get a coffee for you while we wait for a taxi."

The patient presented the doctor with one of the flowers, sipped her coffee, and, when the taxi arrived, went willingly with the nurse to the hospital.

Paranoia and the Threat of Violence

In considering psychotherapeutic management of paranoid conditions in the context of an acute psychotic episode, one's goals are limited to management rather than treatment. The recommendations that follow do not have as their objective the amelioration of the symptoms as much as the prevention of the many unhappy consequences that can stem from an encounter with a paranoid person.

In the acute phase of illness, delusions are unlikely to be "fixed." The more common clinical picture is one of fleeting, fluid, and unorganized misinterpretations, in search of an explanatory "context"; or a labile projective state in which cause, motivation, and explanation are imputed by the patient in a wide variety of events—including such innocent things as the interviewer's frown. When the mental health worker encounters a person in this state, a number of factors should be considered carefully before and during the interview: time/timing, honesty/trust, control/autonomy, and the assessment of risk.

Distance. When a therapist encounters a patient exhibiting either labile projective symptoms or fixed delusions, careful monitoring of interpersonal distance is important. This includes physical, affective, and content distance. The therapist's physical position should be neither threatening nor intrusive. In a labile situation, the therapist should sit low in a chair, taking a relatively passive position, and leave the patient clear access to the nearest door. Similarly, the therapist should modify any natural tendency to exude empathy and offer positive regard, presenting instead a more neutral, professional style. The therapist should not probe into areas the patient has clearly indicated he or she does not wish to discuss.

Time. Unlike the usual situation of a 5-, 10-, or 15-minute period of warming up at the beginning of the interview, it may take a much longer time (within the context of one interview) to reach the point where this patient can relax vigilance, establish a tenuous rapport with the interviewer, and disclose some personal information. When this point is reached with the paranoid patient, it should be handled gingerly and not seen as an opening to be exploited. The patient will probably withdraw trust at the end of the interview, and the process may need to be repeated during the next session.

Honesty. Honesty, without a doubt, must be a prominent characteristic of all psychotherapeutic encounters. But with the best of intentions, therapists do tend to offer unrealistic empathy, promote false promises, engender unwarranted hope and encouragement, and blur or downplay probable consequences of illness and treatment. With the paranoid patient who unceasingly scans for falsity or misrepresentation, it is essential that the therapist be meticulously honest.

Control. In many therapist-paranoid patient encounters, a control struggle is inevitable. Deleterious effects can be decreased by a therapist's allowing the patient the opportunity to question the competence of the therapist, location of the interview, instrumental aspects of the interview, and efficacy of therapy. The therapist should guard against being provoked into struggles over control and should be willing to discuss the above questions, and many others, from an open-minded point of view. A total rejection of the therapist by the patient will often constitute a test of the therapist's candor; acceptance of the patient's right to do this may allow him or her to return and engage in therapy.

Assessment of risk. During the initial assessment of a paranoid patient, it is incumbent upon the psychiatrist to assess the risk of dangerousness to self and/or others presented by the patient. Although the assessment of risk must continue throughout the therapy program, it is important that the therapist not become locked into an attitude of vigilance and surveillance. This can be managed by the therapist's separating the task of assessment from the task of therapy and, for example, taking one minute after the interview to consider information from the session against parameters of dangerousness and then to make the decision about risk independent of the psychotherapeutic encounter.

The interviewer must monitor his or her own affective responses and admit to any fright or provocation. It is well to remember that the patient is also frightened, although it is usually unwise to point this out. Such knowledge can help the interviewer ignore the patient's bluster and provocation and maintain a calming, stabilizing attitude.

In this connection there are some insights that cannot be verbalized but can be covertly and tacitly acknowledged. The paranoid patient may say, "There's nothing wrong with me. You're the sick one. I just came to check this place out and to tell you what I know. I'm the healer." It is usually pointless to try to make this patient say that he is sick. This would simply engender more denial and hostility, and perhaps fuel an adversary relationship. At the end of a good, honest encounter, however, this patient may agree to come into the hospital or return for another appointment all the while strenuously denying any illness. The paranoid and psychotic patient always has, somewhere in the back of the mind, a notion that something may be wrong with him or her and that help might be advantageous. This patient may be willing to act on this notion even while needing to defend against it verbally. If one can appeal to this awareness and this need without threatening his or her fragile autonomy and tenuous self-esteem, then an alliance may be formed.

The concept of "face" is important here: One can view the patient's protestations as conviction, delusion, or denial, but often an interactional analysis will be more fruitful. The patient may be willing to accept treatment so long as there's no need to experience or acknowledge supplication. He or she may be willing to walk with the worker to the ward if allowed to deny the need for treatment and to maintain at least the illusion of control and decision making. Here it is important, as mentioned in the section on hospitalization, that the therapist choose words and phrases that avoid the polarized debate of "You need help." "No, I don't."

The paranoid patient's behavior in an interview is often determined by a pervasive fear that the interviewer will assault his or her autonomy, undermine tenuous control, and, more simply, lock him or her up. Sensing this, the interviewer may provide reassurance that the patient will not lose freedom and nothing will be forced upon him or her. Words, however, may have little effect. The proof is in action. The examiner must be willing to let the patient decide the question of treatment himself or herself and be willing to let the patient go home today so that he or she might feel free to return tomorrow.

Specific Techniques

Some specific techniques are of value in the management of a paranoid patient. In "Crisis and Transition" and the second phase of "Beginning Reorganization" these include (1) Ignoring and avoiding delusional and hallucinatory material, (2) Interpreting upward, and (3) Direct interpretation.

Ignoring and Avoiding Delusional and Hallucinatory Material. The delusional material is elicited in the initial assessment and is not referred to by the therapist in any successive interviews. In the initial in-hospital treatment phase of an acutely psychotic individual who is being treated with neuroleptic medication, labile projective phenomena should diminish and fade away over a period of a few days to several weeks. It often seems, however, that in order for a patient to give up ideas that he or she has held to be true only a few days or weeks previously, he or she must be *allowed to forget them*. A way to save face must be offered during the process of changing his or her mind. Later, in the process of rehabilitation, the therapist and patient may want to discuss the "crazy ideas" the patient had when first admitted to the hospital, but in the tenuous period of reorganization, repeated inquiries into the nature and extent of the delusions serve rather to reinforce them and to engage the patient in an adversary relationship.

Interpreting upward. This technique implies active participation on the part of the therapist in the process of translating the patient's statements into ideas and feelings that offer more immediate and rational communication. The patient, with a haunted look in the eyes, expresses to the therapist, "They're after me." The therapist counters with, "You've very frightened today and feeling vulnerable." The patient may accept this empathic response, relax, and engage with the therapist in a discussion of issues and feelings rather than distorted beliefs. This approach seems most valuable in the management of a labile projective state in which the delusional material appears clearly related to an identifiable affective state or current experience.

Direct interpretation. This may have some value in labile projective states. It refers to the therapist's making a direct empathic interpretation of despair, failure, loss, isolation, or other defended affects in order to undermine the patient's projective and hostile defensive posture. It can be effective only when the defenses are already weakened, when some trust, if tentative, has been established, and when the therapist and the institution are prepared to respond to the patient's despair in a helpful and nonthreatening fashion. If these conditions are not present, the patient's response will likely be one of denial and anger.

While the second and third interventions appear similar, they are different in intent and quality. "Interpreting upward" refers to a very gentle molding of the patient's communications toward an acceptable and understandable interpretation of experience. The goal is to diminish anxiety and to forge an alliance. Direct interpretation assumes that the projective stance or delusional material is compensatory in nature, covering or defending against a morass of despair and confusion. Here the purpose of intervention is to sweep away the armor and reveal the pain. On occasion it works dramatically.

Case Example

The patient, a 37-year-old woman, left the ward on the second day of her admission and retreated to the main foyer of the hospital. Here she demanded her discharge. The therapist came down to see her and received an outburst of hostility. The woman swore and cursed, expounded on plots and intrigues, denounced the doctor and his hospital, and blamed her ex-husband for all her misfortune. After a time, most of her anger was spent, and her face took on an expression of brittle sadness.

The therapist said, slowly and intensely, "You're very sad about something."

The woman wept and later walked back to the ward with her therapist.

Chapter 8

PHASE TWO: BEGINNING REORGANIZATION

Recovery comes to the patient if the brain begins to function by trying to remember.

— anonymous patient

Description

Beginning reorganization refers to the period of beginning diminution of the more extreme symptoms and affect. Attending these, generally, is a decrease in the examiner's experience of praecox feeling and thought disorder. Basic social functioning improves in the individual, and the influence of abnormal subjective experiences, misperceptions, and delusions decreases.

There is a pattern to the reorganization of the psychotic mind. Perhaps the main contribution of neuroleptic medication is the acceleration of this reorganization. Medication does not seem to eradicate delusions, but rather provides the groundwork and facilitates the process whereby delusions can be given up. The reorganization is variable: Sometimes it is surprisingly rapid, stimulating clinicians to reconsider their diagnosis; sometimes it is painfully slow, raising the spectre of "process schizophrenia."

This reorganization is highly susceptible to environmental influences. Unfortunately, more is known about the negative influences than the positive ones. Detrimental factors include a disorganized or chaotic hospital ward or simply a ward where the administrative structure is unclear, the lines of communication blurred or impaired, and the decisions made at random. Unresolved and covert staff conflict, excess staff anxiety, and unclear ward norms, rules, and expectations are further negative influences. When staff members are anxious, confused, or unsupported in their activities, the patient, here a "dependent third," will experience the mood or tone and at times act upon it (Stanton and Schwartz, 1954).

Symptoms should not be expected to disappear immediately upon institution of neuroleptic medication. Recovery is a process and a progression. For most cases this progression can be described in the following manner. With the establishment of a nonthreatening environment and treatment with neuroleptics, the component of the patient's thought disorder that has been labeled "textual failure" will improve. The patient's utterances will be more cohesive and understandable. This improvement may be accompanied by a decrease in the patient's more grossly bizarre behavior or at least in those behaviors that were caused by the patient's fear and confusion. Some improvement in the patient's ability to accurately interpret context follows. He or she becomes more aware of and responsive to environmental cues, a change that will be experienced by the examiner as a diminution of the praecox feeling. The remaining progression has been described in Chapter 6.

As a reminder, it can be diagrammed as improvement in the following sequence of symptoms:

> textual failure
> grossly bizarre behaviors
> praecox experience
> contextual failure
> interpersonal communication and basic
>   social skills
> responsiveness to abnormal subjective experiences
> abnormal subjective experiences

This improvement may be followed by a reemergence of compensatory and restitutive mechanisms into one of three patterns:

1. Isolation, and restriction of communication patterns (poverty syndrome)
2. Chaotic searching and/or conversion (flight)
3. Assumption of stereotypical role for self, and projection of context (delusions)

Further improvement beyond these mechanisms involves increasing skill in interpreting context, adaptation, acceptance, and integration.

The patient's progression of recovery may halt with the reemergence of compensatory and restitutive mechanisms. He or she may slip into a poverty syndrome or be lost to treatment via flight and/or delusions. These may be more or less adaptive and more or less tenacious. The patient may be able to move past them to a healthier level of integration with time and sensitive psychosocial management. The extent to which this happens will depend on the extent to which these mechanisms have developed a life of their own, that is, the extent to which they have become established adaptive mechanisms.

In the beginning reorganization phase, then, the individual's symptoms are beginning to decrease. The situational context of this phase of illness and recovery is usually the admission ward of a general hospital, a private psychiatric hospital, or a public mental hospital. Many acute psychotic episodes can be managed in outpatient and home care with the same success rate and, at times, more rapid rehabilitation. Home management will be mentioned later in the chapter, but this phase will be for the most part addressed as if the patient were in hospital, since hospitalization of the psychotic patient is the more common practice.

Dominant Models

During this phase of psychosis and recovery, there is a slight shift in the roles the models play in guiding treatment interventions. The medical model still prevails in providing a central frame of reference for monitoring recovery parameters; however, the other models begin to assume positions of importance in planning treatment for the patient. The adaptational model provides a useful perspective for assessing the individual's ability to defend him- or herself adequately in adjusting to group and other ward activities. The social model will be used in planning the beginning social rehabilitation of the patient. The developmental model provides a focus for clarifying hospitalization and therapy goals with regard to the developmental stage of the patient and his or her premorbid relationship with family members.

Goals of Therapy

Many recommendations for the first phase hold throughout this second phase. The important point here is to consider the recovery a process, rather than expecting immediate alleviation of the full range of symptoms. It is equally important during this phase to settle on a consistent attitude regarding the abnormal experiences and preoccupations of the patient.

Despite the claims of R. D. Laing and others, there is no scientific evidence that psychosis can be good for you. Still, it is difficult to refute the claims of many therapists (e.g., Arieti, 1955) and a few patients that, in some individual cases, the patient's level of functioning or personality structure is improved following the psychosis. These instances should be seen not as a restructuring of personality or the gleaning of insight but rather as instances in which the psychosis and recovery have permitted, or even precipitated, passage through a developmental impasse.

On the whole, developmental blocks and social inhibitions are better addressed in therapy in the later phases of adaptation-integration and growth and change. While the patient is in the beginning reorganization phase, it is usually unwise to explore such issues as authority conflict with the father and dependency on mother. Nonetheless, psychoses sometimes reveal important and otherwise hidden affects and dynamics a skilled therapist can nudge toward healthy resolution without provoking further disorganization. There is no way at present to predict in which instances this might be the case.

There are some times when the full psychosis can be resolved with psychotherapeutic intervention alone. This phenomenon can be dramatic and long-remembered, but it is wrong to generalize widely from such experiences. These dramatic cures seem to happen when the patient's psychosis derives in part from a conflicted and perplexing relationship with a spouse or parent. To understand these situations, one needs to invoke a concept of vulnerability to schizophrenic breakdown within specific interpersonal conditions. Those interpersonal conditions would seem to contain the following features: intense or binding dependency; confused, masked, or ambiguous communication; and threat or hostility.

Rage seems to be the most disorganizing affect, especially when suppressed and when the patient cannot grasp the source, cause, or "context" of the feeling. It is consistent with the hypothesis of Chapters 1 and 2 that when the ability to interpret context is impaired, anger experienced could be especially anxiety-provoking and disorganizing. Below is further discussion of the case example used in a previous chapter concerning the woman who became preoccupied with the balance of carbohydrate and protein.

Case Example

This woman was intelligent, educated, and the mother of two children. She was quiet and unassuming; she generally denied conflict and floated through life seemingly oblivious to the personal and moral dilemmas that preoccupy much of the rest of humanity. This was in marked contrast to her husband, who weighed every matter ponderously, spoke as a habit through clenched teeth, and never felt satisfied with his own life. It was the husband who in fact was attending therapy for an "intractable depression."

One evening his wife became psychotic at the dinner table, during what seemed, in retrospect, a bitter, prolonged, and silent struggle. The husband, in indirect ways, principally through nonverbal communication, persistently derided, accused and negated his wife. (It turned out he was trying to decide whether or not to run off with his mistress.)

During the dinner in question, the wife began to talk in a bizarre, disconnected fashion. Her husband brought her to the hospital. Here they were interviewed together, the husband tense and controlled, the wife talking distractedly about sugar and protein while exchanging questioning glances with the therapist. During the course of the interview, she was helped to speak directly to her husband and he was helped to clarify his own communications. As the hour wore on, her statements to her husband became more directly angry and at the same time clearer. In the end, under the protective umbrella provided by the therapist, she revealed to her husband the extent of her rage, and the "thought disorder" peeled away.

Such cases are rare and should not be taken as license to engage in cavalier psychotherapeutic techniques with every psychotic patient. Rather, they imply simply that it is well to try to understand the psychosis while attempting to treat it. The decision regarding when to intervene with a direct psychotherapy method must be left, at the moment, to experience, sensitivity, and intuition. In most cases, psychotherapeutic management is a longer and far less dramatic process.

Psychotherapeutic Tasks

The principal psychotherapeutic management tasks for this phase can be listed as follows:

Monitor several recovery parameters. The ability to engage in simple social relationships and a relationship with the therapist may improve before concentration and other cognitive functioning.

Further assess the development of the illness.   As the family sees the patient improve, there is a greater chance of gaining accurate information about premorbid functioning.

Begin social rehabilitation.   Decrease the possibility of social breakdown by involving the patient in protected groups. Monitor visits by family and friends. Gradually step up entry into the milieu and social life of the ward. The therapist and other ward staff should have some expectations of the patient regarding self-care.

Clarify hospitalization and therapy goals.   The therapist should be developing clearer notions of the developmental stage of the patient and the premorbid relationship with family. The psychotic episode may allow the patient to pass through what had otherwise been a developmental impasse. If this appears to be so, the passage should be cautiously reinforced and assisted.

Reinforce healthy ego functioning.   The therapist can respond to the healthy components and communications of the patient, paying a great deal of attention to ordinary social etiquette and activities. Engagement in some interpreting upward might accompany a shift to a new balance between directing the patient and allowing him or her some initiating and decision-making. The therapist should monitor the patient's ability to defend him- or herself in group and other ward activities.

Name and explain the problems.   The task of helping patient and family adjust to the fact of illness and hospitalization is still paramount. In fact, the patient's disorganization during the first phase may have been so severe that the question did not even arise. Now, more clearly able to assess the situation, he or she should have many questions to ask. Again, the questions need to be answered even if not directly verbalized by the patient. Family members may have heard little of what was said to them during their crisis; therefore, it bears repeating. It may be only at this point that they can ask for clarification and express their own ideas and fears. Similarly, a more accurate premorbid history may be gathered now.

Special Problems and Issues

Rapid Neuroleptization

Rapid neuroleptization has recently become a popular form of treatment in many inpatient units (Lerner et al., 1979). The medications used have proved surprisingly safe, and larger doses seem to be utilized each year. This method has been a boon for the control of grossly disturbed or threatening behavior, but, in the majority of cases, it does not accelerate or improve recovery. When symptoms are going to respond to neuroleptic medication, they respond to less heroic regimens, with some rare and idiosyncratic exceptions. Symptoms do not resolve faster with heavy, early loading.

The behavioral-control advantage of rapid neuroleptization must be weighed against the possible consequences of increasing regression and promoting an adversary relationship between patient and staff. As one heavily sedated patient said, while unsuccessfully trying to raise himself from his mattress on the floor, and slurring his words with dry and thickened mouth, "Christ, now they've got me talking like a baby."

Rapid and heavy neuroleptization should be reserved for emergency and problem situations. The compliant schizophrenic patient will benefit more from a moderate neuroleptic regimen and some patience on the part of staff. In a few instances the psychosis may resolve without the aid of neuroleptics (Marder et al., 1979). In these instances it may be wise to ensure the patient a good night's sleep, but to otherwise withhold drugs.

Developmental Impasse

For many people, whether schizophrenic or otherwise afflicted, hospitalization or simply entering therapy constitutes the watershed of a developmental impasse. That is, therapy and/or hospitalization often occur at the point of a difficult life transition. The person "cannot" move forward; the present situation is intolerable and the past unattainable. Sometimes therapy and hospitalization are entered at this crisis point without the presence of a diagnosable illness. In these cases it is easier to recognize the impasse and facilitate its successful passage. Typical patients here include the teenager who "must" leave home and the elderly person who "can no longer take care of him- or herself." The crisis and turmoil lead to hospitalization, psychotherapy, or psychiatric consultation. The therapist recognizes the underlying transitional state and focuses efforts upon it.

When real illness is superimposed on developmental struggles, the transition state becomes obscured. The treatment team may concentrate its energies on eradicating the symptoms and returning the patient to the status quo. They may, through good management, return the patient to his or her level of premorbid functioning. Now they turn to the family in preparation for discharge and are surprised to hear, "He can't live with us any longer." Or, as is the case more often, they are greeted with an ambivalent response. It may appear as though the parents (siblings, sons and daughters, spouse) are unhappy to see the patient well again. Actually it is more likely that they had hoped he or she would not simply have become well, but would have changed or moved on developmentally. The issue is further complicated by guilt and the family's own dependency. The parents may have spent the last few years attending to their different son and protecting him from the realities of the outside world. They would dearly love to see him grow up and move on, but gradually, on their own terms, and to an environment at least as protective as their own.

These are issues to be dealt with more thoroughly in later phases, but their recognition is important here. The planning should start early. It is sufficiently difficult for any 23 year old to leave his or her family and move into a downtown boarding home or establish an apartment. It is much more problematic for a young schizophrenic. Furthermore, the physical move is only a symbol of a much more protracted developmental transition. How long does it take anyone to accomplish the tasks delineated by Otto Will? (000)

At this point and through later phases, the family's help can be enlisted to clarify the transition at hand and to prepare for it.

Ward Rules, the Giving of Medication, and Other Transactions

One need only scan the list of developmental tasks put forward by Will to see that life on a psychiatric ward may come in direct conflict with the needs and aspirations of a young adult. It is important to understand this in order not to provoke rebellion or flight. Excessively rigid rules, unreasonable regulations, and belittling transactions may provoke a rebellious response. In such a context a young patient struggling to reorganize, grow, and regain some sense of dignity, independence, and autonomy may not fare well. This person will be labeled, at best, uncooperative, and his or her other strengths will be quelled. A patient with a poor prognosis, frozen at earlier developmental levels, passive, unquestioning, and obedient, might be wrongly perceived as a good patient. His or her passivity, denial, and ultimate social breakdown will be reinforced.

On the other hand, a laissez-faire or confused structure will promote disorganization. Some compromise is required: a good human environment, but one in which the social structure is clear, simple, and explained to the patient. It is the task of the therapist and treatment team to assist the patient in comprehending contextual information. The expectations and rules should be communicated in a fashion that permits dignity and the preservation of self-respect; whatever can be reasonably negotiated, should be. The patient should be allowed choices, decisions, and initiative wherever possible.

Rules that are spelled out as absolute must carry with them negative sanctions the treatment team is willing to enforce. Put another way, if the rule cannot be enforced, it should not be declared. This applies to moment-to-moment transactions as well. There is no point in telling a patient he or she *must* do something unless you are prepared to follow through with the tacit "or else." It is often more useful for a therapist to examine his or her own need for control and obedience before issuing an ultimatum.

As mentioned earlier, there are imperatives of dialogue. The question, "When you took the pills, did you mean to kill yourself?", spoken to an angry adolescent, must engender the response, "Yes, of course I did!" The content of the transaction is guided by the unfolding dynamics of the immediate relationship. This relationship must be considered by the therapist to ensure a good resolution of the transaction about to occur and to evaluate its content. There are a number of ways, for example, of asking a patient to take medication. They range from, "Here are your pills, John. Check them to see I've got them right" (a neutral presentation with a suggestion to the patient that he take some responsibility in managing his own medication) to, "You swallow these pills or we'll put you back on the needle."

Each has its own imperative. The question. "Would you like to take your pill, John?" is really a strong suggestion. But the literal-minded patient is almost invited to respond with a "No, not really." This is not to advocate one syntax over another. Rather, it is to point out how the choices of language can invite particular responses and how these responses will in turn determine behavior.

Specific Techniques for Managing Paranoid Symptoms

The techniques discussed for the first phase can be carried through into the second and third. The beginning reorganization phase is a good time to consider behavior modification. Even if formal behavioral modification techniques are not used, the principles should be considered for general management. All aspects of the patient's improved functioning, social etiquette, participation, concern with and discussion of reality issues, and self-care can be positively reinforced. Regression to primitive thinking, isolation, the expression of delusional ideas, preoccupation with hallucinations, and other abnormal perceptions can be ignored if not negatively sanctioned. Direct negation of a delusional belief is not generally recommended, but one finds this approach actively used on some inpatient wards. It carries with it the danger of flight, hostile or aggressive response, shame, "stripping," and loss of dignity. It may increase the patient's underlying mistrust and endanger future therapy.

Home Management

For a number of reasons home care may be chosen over hospitalization for the treatment of acute psychosis: The patient may be unwilling to be hospitalized, his or her family may prefer outpatient care, or the patient may have responded poorly to hospitalizations in the past. Community-based care, with a focus on home management, can produce equivalent rates of symptom remission, improvement of some role performance, and reduction of psychosocial burden to the family (Fenton, Tessier, and Struening, 1979; Pasamanick et al., 1967; Stein, Test and Marx, 1975; Stein and Test, 1980). In addition, there is some evidence that, with home treatment or day-care programs, patients regain social roles earlier than they do if hospitalized.

The benefits of home treatment versus hospitalization must be balanced against the potential negative effects of each. Hospitalization may force formalization of the sick role in a way that results in stigma, temporary loss of contact with the community, and potential threat to the patient's job, family, and community tenure. In addition, hospitalization may result in an unnecessarily lengthy period of total patienthood. Effective hospital treatment is dependent on the availability of a good inpatient unit. Good home management, on the other hand, requires that the patient have family members or friends with whom he or she lives and that the patient and family or friends agree to a plan of home treatment. The family members or friends must also have the energy to make a commitment to support such a plan. The patient's symptoms must be amenable to treatment in the home environment. This excludes patients with active suicidal or homicidal tendencies. In addition, other psychotic symptoms must be contained to the extent that the patient will not lose face or permanently damage his or her public image through appearing crazy to friends and family.

When the home is the chosen treatment setting, it is especially important that the patient and participating family members or friends be actively included in the planning and implementation of treatment. The plan should be tailored to suit their needs and capabilities. Clinic staff should be prepared to work around their needs as well as those of the patient. For example, the mental health worker may plan his or her home visit for a time that will allow the mother to get out to do her shopping.

Over a long period of active treatment, comprehensive community management is not necessarily cheaper than basic institutional care (Stein and Test, 1980), however, home treatment of the acute illness is less expensive than admission to a general hospital. This consideration has become increasingly important with the rising cost of building and maintaining inpatient units.

The present organization of medical service favors hospital treatment. Full implementation of home care will require a reorganization of resources and the development of new skills. It also should be acknowledged that a treatment program without the natural boundaries of admissions, discharges, beds, and walls is more difficult to plan, implement, and manage than a hospital ward.

Chapter 9

PHASE THREE: SUPERFICIAL RECOVERY

I knew darn well I wasn't ready; I felt fine on the ward, but that's a closed environment in there.

— anonymous patient

Description

The context of this phase of recovery is generally still the protective environment of an inpatient ward. If treatment has been taking place with the patient at home, he or she will most likely be in a state of convalescence, experiencing limited expectations from family and caretakers. The individual's social functioning has returned to "normal," at least within the limited stresses of his other current environment. The patient will for the most part be symptom-free. What symptoms remain will not, at this phase, seem to affect his or her day-to-day life and will be apparent only upon close examination or questioning.

It is at this time in the recovery process that discharge into community care is planned and/or instituted. Medication is examined with a view to choosing the drug, dosage, and regimen that will best suit the individual in outpatient maintenance care. Usually, a switch is made to a less sedating phenothiazine and a simplified regimen.

Dominant Models

During this superficial recovery phase and succeeding phases, the dominant value of the medical model recedes and adaptational, social, and developmental models become paramount. The medical model still plays a role in the patient's beginning review and appraisal of what has happened.

The adaptational model wil be used in understanding the emerging depression, in assisting the patient with management of abnormal perceptions, and in strengthening cognitive functions. The social model plays an essential role in this and later phases, in the planning, preparation, and implementation of rehabilitation programs. The developmental model, as well, offers a valuable perspective for examining the patient's premorbid level of functioning and current struggles with issues of autonomy/ dependency and passivity/initiative.

Tasks and Interventions

The principal tasks for psychotherapeutic management during this phase include the following.

Review and appraisal. The therapist should initiate, as much as possible, an effort to assist the patient in appraising what has happened. This is merely the initial step of a long psychotherapeutic process of integrating, understanding, and adjusting to the illness. The education of the family and the patient with regard to the illness and aspects of retraining and rehabilitation should be expanded. The family can be engaged in discussions of stress, reactions to stress, and long-term medication. There should be a beginning attempt with the family to distinguish between evidence of psychosis and behavior indicative of the usual array of normal relationship and developmental problems (e.g., adolescent rebellion).

Plan social rehabilitation.   The therapist should encourage more group experiences, resocialization activities, and life-skills training and monitor the development of independence and responsibility. One should guard, however, against over-estimating the patient's level of competence and social functioning. The patient's social skills appear to be better within the safe ward environment than they will prove to be in a less structured environment. Though the patient may not be immediately able to return to work or school, the question of future employment should be raised. Vocational rehabilitation, retraining, and temporary placement in a sheltered workshop can be considered.

Explore developmental dynamics.   The therapist may cautiously explore the patient's autonomy and independence with regard to discharge from the hospital and possible separation from the family. The patient may be establishing new and more functional role relationships with family members, and these should be supported. Family interviews should focus on discharge planning, sharing and agreeing on expectations for the return home, and assessment of the likelihood of success of family placement. If separation from the family appears the better course of action, then the family can be enlisted to aid in this process.

Focus on separation anxiety.   Exacerbation of symptoms should be expected prior to or during the process of discharge. The response need not automatically be an increase of medication and/or delay of discharge.

Allow and reinforce shift in content of communications.   The therapist may help the patient shift abnormal perceptions, experiences, and beliefs in the direction of more universally accepted beliefs. The patient may give up a religious delusion on a gradual and stepwise basis, for example, "I am the Son of God" to "I feel that God has given me a purpose " to "God has put us all on this earth for some kind of purpose." Previous delusional beliefs should not be inquired about or challenged, and with respect to these, an element of saving face should be allowed. The therapist should be alert to the possible emergence of depression.

Strengthen cognitive functioning and assist contextual interpretation.   Therapeutic interventions may help increase the cognitive processes of attending, concentrating, and reality testing. The patient may be given tasks of slowly increasing complexity over several months or asked to practice reading the newspaper for first five then 10 minutes each evening. Therapy sessions may entail lengthy discussions 'of how one should interpret subtle interpersonal cues and complex social transactions.

Special Problems and Issues

Patterns of Recovery

According to McGlashan, Levy, and Carpenter, (1975) schizophrenics may recovery by either "sealing over" or "integration." In the early phases of recovery, patients often demonstrate some combination of these two styles and a few other coping and explanatory mechanisms as well. The most difficult of these responses to deal with is denial or overcompensation. The patient says, "Nothing's wrong with me. I'm fine. I shouldn't have been put in here in the first place" or even, "As soon as I get out of here I'm going back to university and I'm taking up skiing. And politics. I have to get into politics. I have a lot to offer this country."

Denial and overcompensation are usually considered intrapsychic defense mechanisms. They can also be understood from a transactional perspective: The extent to which the young patient must deny or overcompensate for the illness may be partly determined by the extent to which significant others (and the institution) perceive him or her as incapacitated. Denial of illness can be understood as an extreme reaction to parents' distress and pessimism and to the institutions's insistence that the person is incapacitated. Work with the family should be directed toward finding a way of viewing the illness that will foster the right mix of care and support without undue pessimism. The patient's inability to return to work or to school for a few months does not mean that he or she should not be expected to clean his or her room or take out the garbage; in fact, under these circumstances such tasks will be crucial to maintaining an impetus for rehabilitation. The psychotherapeutic task here is to nudge the patient toward a more realistic assessment of his or her position without forcing a showdown or loss of face or, for that matter, without undermining those defense mechanisms that may be highly adaptive.

Extreme denial is not helpful. It usually means that the patient refuses to take medication or attend outpatient appointments. Some degree of denial, however, can be adaptive. A period during which the patient avoids awareness of disabilities, concentrating instead on strengths and plans for the future may be a necessary component of recovery. One author referred to this condition as "life affirmation" in contrast to denial (Beisser, 1979). It is often difficult for the therapist to distinguish one from the other. One must try to support the strengths, hopes, and dreams of the patient while helping him or her adjust to limitations and ongoing medical treatment. The following case exemplifies the vicissitudes of overcompensation and affirmation.

Case Example

A young Italian man, recovering from a severe acute schizophrenic episode, living at home with his parents and unable to hold a dishwashing job, told his therapist that he planned to be a professional musician. He felt he could play the piano quite well, and he looked forward to full employment with a rock band. In reality the patient had sat himself down at the family piano for the first time only two weeks previously. He insisted, though, that his one-hour nightly practice was preparing him for full employment. Following several sessions in which the patient did not deviate from this position, the therapist took him to a piano and asked him to play.

After suffering through two renditions of "Chopsticks," both patient and therapist agreed that it would be some time before he could turn professional. More realistic job hunting resumed.

Several weeks later, however, the patient professed that he had decided to become a professional guitarist instead. The therapist invited him to bring his guitar and demonstrate his skills. When the next appointment arrived, the therapist was surprised to hear some very creditable guitar playing emanating from the waiting room, where a number of staff and patients had gathered around to listen. It turned out that the patient had an untrained, natural ability and could imitate music he heard on the radio.

Hospital Discharge

Superficial recovery is the phase when precipitous discharge and short-range planning can lay the groundwork for inevitable relapse and rehospitalization. This is especially true with the patient who denies illness, disregards the need for follow-up, and thinks unfavorably of the pills he or she is taking. Staff members in their understandable wish to be optimistic, often collude with this attitude and do not make a concerted effort to organize aftercare programs. It is easy to misjudge the patient's level of recovery and social and life skills. As one patient put it, "Sure I was okay on the ward. All we did was play Ping-pong and eat. But when I went back to work, that was a different thing altogether." During hospitalization the patient has learned to function adequately within the simplified context of a psychiatric inpatient unit, protected from the complex social interactions with which he or she had so much difficulty before.

The lesson here is not to overestimate recovery on the basis of ward social interactions and, where possible, to plan a transitional situation. At this point, recreational, social, and vocational activities should approximate those of extrahospital life. Expectations for self-care should be increased. The transition to community care should not be abrupt. As discharge approaches, some anxiety and display of symptoms should be expected. These may be more beneficially alleviated by psychotherapeutic discussion and better-organized aftercare than by increased medication and extended hospitalization.

Secondary Impairment

For the practical purposes of determining treatment and rehabilitation goals, it might be well to adopt Wing's (1975) classification of "primary" impairment, "secondary" impairment, and "extrinsic" factors. "Primary" impairment refers to those dysfunctions produced when the normal biological cycles are disturbed; "secondary" impairments are those behaviors adopted in response to the primary impairment and determined to a great extent by context. Here Wing is referring to the sick role and illness behavior. The full range of compensatory behaviors and psychological reactions discussed earlier can be added to these. "Extrinsic" factors are unrelated to the disease itself but have great influence over susceptibility and recovery. These are the social, individual, and cultural factors that have been mentioned before. Examples of such factors which are known to influence the outcome and relapse rate of schizophrenia are social class, employment, marital status, IQ, education, sex, and family structure. Rehabilitation programs should be devised to reduce secondary impairment and to ameliorate the influences of extrinsic factors.

It is during this phase that the therapist needs to make an accurate appraisal of the patient's life skills and social skills. This can be made through ward observation, participation in occupational therapy activities, direct questioning, life-skill inventories, and an understanding of the patient's premorbid history. The therapist should not be surprised to find the patient, perhaps a 23-year-old man, unable to boil an egg, wash his clothes, or catch the bus. There is no point in sending him job hunting if he cannot find want ads in the newspaper and does not know how to complete an application form. On the other hand, the patient may have some hidden skills or talents, the kind that might have flourished in the context of social isolation and the compensatory mechanisms described previously.

Rehabilitation Goals

Prior to the superficial recovery stage, treatment goals remain relatively clear. The patient is definitely ill and the medical model prevails. The goal of intervention is primarily the eradication of symptoms. Upon reaching this phase, however, other issues must be considered. These include rehabilitation, placement in the community, and adjustment to or overcoming of social disablement. At this phase, planning must move beyond the simple disease concept and the eradication of symptoms to the prevention of disease or relapse and the promotion of health.

The context of social class and culture play an increasing role in determining goals and outcome. It is here that major philosophical questions arise: What is health? What is the appropriate adjustment of an individual afflicted with schizophrenia? How are the goals of rehabilitation determined? What is the role of the physician in this? What cost are we willing to bear for maximal rehabilitation? When we do push people through group therapy, vocational retraining programs, and life-skill exercises, are we simply promoting the values of the status quo? After all, social relations, work, and independent living are cultural values, not absolute prerequisites of "health." It is possible to think of a culture or subculture where these activities are not valued.

One might criticize the extent to which our rehabilitation goals for patients are guided by our own, usually middle- and upper-middle-class, social values. To some extent all therapists promote cultural norms. By working, by receiving money for work, by owning a car and perhaps a house, they are, in the psychotherapeutic context, supporting those particular norms by the simple process of identification. But how actively should training, work, employment, socializing, pairing, and leisure activities be promoted with the reluctant schizophrenic patient? Most mental health institutions implicitly, if not explicitly, promote these values, while some sociologists point out that these activities are not so much treatment as enforcement of the status quo. This criticism is tempered, however, by several factors. Our patients are also usually members of the same society. On the whole, their value systems are not unlike our own. Within a culture that values work and stable relationships, recovered patients have a much better chance of survival if they have jobs and partners.

In rehabilitation planning the goals and expectations of the individual patient must be considered and assessed within the context of a psychotherapeutic relationship. Initially the recovering schizophrenic patient may profess rather grandiose plans or, at the other extreme, may opt entirely for the sick role and recoil from the very thought of planning for the future. Together the therapist and the patient must search for a middle road—one that best accommodates both the patient's aspirations and society's requirements for economic survival.

In summary, then, rehabilitation goals should take into account the following factors: (1) The individual's personal goals and expectations as they evolve in psychotherapeutic discussion, (2) The temporary distortions of these goals by either depression, denial of illness, or adoptions of the sick role; and (3) The cultural norms and social values of the individual's particular sex and social class.

Paranoid Symptoms

Two further methods for managing delusional thinking are described below. These may prove to be of most value in an established and ongoing therapeutic relationship when the patient suffers a relapse or at least a return of symptoms.

Cognitive shapings. With some patients, delusions of persecution and conspiracy, with concomitant misinterpretations of clicks on the phone and shadowy figures in doorways, are exacerbated by periods of anxiety, stress, and transition. Sometimes the patient's persecutory ideas are accurate, if exaggerated; that is, there may be real events in the person's life to validate his or her sense of persecution. In this instance, anxiety can be dampened, either by engagement in a psychotherapeutic relationship and/or appropriate medication. Then rational discussions about the anxiety, life events that produce anxiety, the real evidence of "persecution," and the misinterpreted events can be undertaken in therapy. It is often helpful to normalize the experiences with discussions of the universality of ideas of reference , using the patient's own material for examples. This cognitive framework may help the patient understand and control his or her tendency to respond to anxiety with ideas of reference that become the basis for the development of delusional beliefs.

Case Example

The patient, a young man maintained on a small dose of perphenazine after five hospitalizations, weathered a period of courting and even a wedding with no return of symptoms. On his honeymoon, though, traveling to a strange city by plane for the first time in his life, the patient became suspicious of the behavior of another passenger at the baggage carousel. He concluded that this man in a raincoat was connected with the police, sent to watch him and perhaps arrest him for past sexual crimes.

The patient's heightened anxiety and general disorganization were managed with conjoint therapy sessions and a temporary increase of perphenazine. However, this notion that the man in the raincoat was spying on him lingered after his other symptoms had resolved. The therapist discussed this with the patient, linking the anxiety of marriage, flight, and travel to the patient's arousal and readiness to misinterpret data. It was also pointed out that if a policeman were truly working undercover and spying on him, he (the policeman) would not have been standing elbow to elbow with him at the carousel. The way most people are vulnerable to ideas of reference during times of intense stress was explained as well.

The patient agreed that he could have been mistaken and that his perception might have been paranoid. Still, as he put it, "It may have been a misinterpretation, but it sure felt real at the time."

Entering into the delusions. This process is well described in popular psychoanalytic literature (Lindner, 1976). It would appear to be of some value with intelligent patients who have passed through a period of acute psychosis and/or disorganization and whose residual delusional ideas are of relatively short duration. It would also appear to be most effective when the delusion is maintained with a degree of uncertainty and fuzziness.

In this instance, one of the factors that enables the patient to maintain his or her delusion without coming into conflict with otherwise excellent reality testing is the very fuzziness, vagueness, and selective attention the patient applies to it. If this is the case, then the process of working with the patient to analyze, trace, and understand the details of the "plot" may bring its very inconsistencies to the patient's awareness. The patient may then suggest to the therapist, in some fashion, often obliquely, that he or she would prefer to spend time in psychotherapy sessions discussing more relevant subjects. This approach carries with it the possibility of reinforcing the delusional belief and should not be used without due consideration. It may also unleash depressive affect and/or further disorganization.

Case Example

The young woman believed intensely that a certain young man was sending her messages through others, the radio, newspapers, and television. The young man was purported to be a peson who had jilted her two years previously, and his present interference was ruining her life. This belief survived through hospitalization and several weeks of high-dosage chlorpromzaine. She was discharged improved but still delusional. She spoke vaguely of complaining to the police of the harassment by Joe, but didn't act on this.

It was then that the therapist noted that this otherwise intelligent woman retained her belief in a very vague, inconsistent fashion. She would respond with "Well—you know" to questions about Joe and why she had never looked him up or considered why he might be doing this to her. The therapist then told the patient that he, too, believed the harassment was a terrible thing and that he would be willing to consider with her what action might be taken. He suggested that first they must locate the man, perhaps by going through the telephone book. They must look at ways he was harassisng her and consider why he might be doing this. Finally, the therapist supported the notion of reporting the problem to the police.

Somehow the problem dwindled in importance; the patient seemed to be reluctant to discuss it on those terms. She appeared more perplexed and later depressed. She spent more time discussing her current life situation with the therapist and eventually reported that Joe was no longer bothering her.

Postpsychotic Depression and the Poverty Syndrome

A period of postpsychotic depression frequently emerges following discharge. When it lingers on over weeks and months, with impoverished ideation, blunted affect, and impaired volition, it is often referred to as the "poverty syndrome" (Wing, 1978). It carries with it almost as much discomfort for the therapist as for the patient. When lengthy, it breeds a sense of hopelessness and finally apathy. The therapist gives up, beginning to reflect on the term "dementia praecox" and considering rehospitalization. If the poverty syndrome develops during a prolonged hospitalization, the stage is set for institutionalism.

A common situation in contemporary practice is one in which the patient regularly attends weekly sessions, meekly submits to the bimonthly injection, puts in time at the sheltered workshop, but otherwise remains lifeless. He or she has no overt psychotic symptoms, but has not recovered. The patient is passively obedient, blunted, and flat, intiating nothing. The therapist's questions are answered with single words, sometimes after an exasperating pause. The patient's face is relatively expressionless; he or she may walk without swinging the arms. The optimistic therapist embraces with hope the small smile exchanged toward the end of the interview. The pessimistic therapist is pleased that this patient at least no longer argues about the injection and the need for regular appointments. When this situation drags on for an extended period of time, the patient may become all too painfully aware of his or her impoverished existence and alienation.

Several perspectives on postpsychotic depression have been put forward in the literature, and in practice all are worth considering. Each has explanatory value for some part of the clinical picture confronting the therapist.

Akinetic depression.   The neuroleptic medication may be contributing to, if not causing, this syndrome (Van Putten and May, 1978). Suspicion of this factor may be reinforced by the patient's shuffling gait "chlorpromazine state," or "fluphenazine breathing." Clinicians, however, tend to become desensitized to the minor effects of high-dosage phenothiazines and may overlook them. Sometimes the patient will describe his or her own body experiences using such phrases as, "It's as if I don't own my legs. Like the rhythm's gone and I have to remember which arm to swing." Whether the drugs are a cause or contributing factor, a trial reduction of medication is always in order.

Postpsychotic depression as disease.   A number of authors consider the depressive symptoms, whether postpsychotic, preexisting, or simply contiguous with the illness, to be part of the disease process itself, that is, of primary origin (Rada and Donlon, 1975). For the purposes of treatment, the question of whether or not this syndrome should be considered part of the disease process or secondary to it can be circumvented. The practical issue arising out of this perspective is the possible use of antidepressant medication. The parameters for deciding on tricyclic antidepressant treatment are the same as with other affective illness: Antidepressant medication is most likely to be effective if there are definite and extensive vegetative signs. However, the schizophrenic patient in this situation often sleeps too much rather than too little, eats adequately if not with great appetite, and infrequently responds to antidepressant (Siris, Van Kammen and Docherty, 1978). Antidepressents may be effective in the treatment of a well-defined postpsychotic depression; they are of little value in the treatment of social isolation, chronic apathy, and impoverished ideation.

Depression as reaction.   This perspective, first proposed by Mayer-Gross (1920), views the poverty syndrome and depressive affect as an understandable reaction to major losses. The patient experiences despair and perhaps resignation engendered by the loss of family, friends, hopes, ambitions, dignity, identity, and perhaps of the ego or the mind itself. He or she has experienced a major affront to the sense of self or, to use Sullivan's terminology, a destructive blow to his or her self-system. It is interesting to note that many cultures refer to madness as "loss of mind."

In this perspective, the psychotherapeutic tasks are the same as they would be with other major losses. The patient is helped to review, to reminisce, and to grieve. A postpsychotic depression can be likened to a mourning period, and the therapist and patient should engage in grief work. This third perspective produces some conflict with the second (postpsychotic depression as disease) because here a display of depressive affect would be considered a necessary part of the healing process, not to be quelled with medication.

Posttraumatic neurosis.   A fourth perspective has been put forward by Jeffries (1977). It likens the postpsychotic period of depression and impoverishment to a posttraumatic neurosis. The psychosis, the losing of one's mind, the wild and frightening subjective experiences, and perhaps the whole process of hospitalization and treatment are major traumas that the patient is attempting to block from consciousness. This concept is similar to the recovery style of ''sealing over'' described by McGlashan, except that it suggests that neurotic defense mechanisms are brought into play. Rather than thinking of this as a recovery style or a particular mode of reintegration, Jeffries would consider this clinical state to embody a range of neurotic defense mechanisms brought to bear on the past experience of being psychotic. Within this perspective, the therapist's task would be one of carefully dislodging the protective armor and helping the patient to review, reminisce about, and integrate into total experience the events surrounding his or her breakdown and hospitalization.

Adaptation.   The fifth perspective is related to the last two described and is perhaps the one least often considered, although equally important. This perspective considers the postpsychotic depression, or poverty syndrome, as a range of primitive defense mechanisms brought to bear on the *threat* of losing one's mind, losing control, and becoming psychotic. It postulates that the patient has recently been through an episode in which thinking, feelings, and impulses mushroomed out of his or her control and led to further experiences and events that were at the very least traumatic if not ego-destroying. In this perspective the patient is healing, in a convalescent phase. Active social relationships, social connectedness or intimacy, activity, initiative, and spontaneity will all call forth a range of feelings the patient can no longer control. The patient denies and suppresses affect. He or she sleeps all day, isolates himself or herself, and keeps a safe distance from the therapist.

The above is a psychodynamic explanation, but similar conclusions can be reached by returning to the model proposed in Chapter 1 and by observing the natural development of and recovery from psychosis. Docherty suggested that an early stage of recovery consists of a return to the prepsychotic state of restricted consciousness. If this idea is expanded and the compensatory mechanisms outlined earlier (restriction of communication patterns, withdrawal from social contact) are added, it can be seen that the recovery response of postpsychotic depression may be a variant of the mechanisms that previously existed to maintain continuity, control, and organization. From this perspective the therapist's task is to provide a protective/supportive relationship, encourage the patient to engage in interpersonal/social activities, and discuss with the patient his or her fears, reactions, and experiences.

Nonmedical drugs. Another factor that may contribute to the appearance of blunted affect and absence of volition is the excessive use of marijuana and alcohol. It is wise to be alert to the possible self-administration of stimulant drugs as the patient attempts to overcome his or her sense of deadness, and to talk openly with the patient concerning these possible responses to his other dilemma.

Treatment and Management

Each perspective or diagnosis suggests its own treatment. There are some overriding concerns, however, that will be discussed here.

A common dilemma in the treatment of postpsychotic depression is the problem of deciding if the patient is receiving too much or too little medication. It is often difficult to tell if the patient is constricted, tense, and withdrawn as a way of managing imminent disorganization, and therefore in need of increased neuroleptics, or whether he is dulled, flat, and detached as a direct result of excessive medication. As with most pharmacological agents, the long-term use of neuroleptic drugs is proving more dangerous than previously considered. (e.g., causing tardive dyskinesia). For this reason alone, it is wise to use the lowest possible maintenance dose and to experiment with drug holidays. When antidepressants are used, a danger exists that they will become part of a maintenance polypharmacy. It is not unusual to find a chronic schizophrenic who has been ingesting a mixture of tricyclics, neuroleptics, and antiparkinsonian agents for years. When antidepressants are used, they should be employed to treat a specific, well-defined affective disorder on a time-limited basis.

It is easy to assume, in working with a schizophrenic patient who remains flat, unconcerned, impoverished and dull that he or she has no relationship with the therapist. This conclusion has been legitimized by Freud, who suggested that schizophrenic patients could not develop transference, and by Rado (1962), who claimed they couldn't experience any welfare emotions. Both were mistaken. The schizophrenic patient with poverty syndrome does not express feelings of need and relatedness very well, but he or she is often, without showing it, attached to the therapist to a surprising degree. Although it is difficult for a therapist to maintain an active interest in a patient when the therapist seems to be getting nothing in return, making light of the relationship and ignoring its importance can lead directly to missed appointments and relapse. It is not uncommon for a patient emerging from this state to surprise his or her therapist by clearly referring to an issue the two had discussed at a time when the therapist was convinced the patient was "tuned out" and not listening.

The consideration of postpsychotic depression as a grief reaction is seldom of practical aid. The schizophrenic patient (at this point) is usually unable to engage in grief work. His or her therapist can only ponder the losses and mention them at times and otherwise wait until the patient is ready to discuss them.

During a prolonged postpsychotic depression, the therapist (and treatment team) must resist the temptation of assigning the patient chronic, damaged status, permanently reducing expectations. The therapists's task is to encourage or place the patient into social and rehabilitative situations that may "reawaken" him or her. At some time the patient will begin to talk about his or her recent experiences, and active grieving may occur.

There are a number of complications to this process: The patient is being asked to develop initiative, to become spontaneous, and to think and to make decisions. The decisions he or she finally makes may be contrary to the goals of the therapist. In fact, if the patient is still struggling with dependency/autonomy issues, the patient's goals may have to be contrary to the therapist's. The therapist may spend weeks encouraging an unresponsive patient to attend a vocational assessment course. The patient arrives at one appointment smiling, and announces that he has decided to travel to the West Coast. This particular trip is not what the therapist has had in mind, although the patient's thrust to autonomy may be basically healthy. Should the therapist now quell the patient's initiative, or let him move on to certain drug noncompliance and relapse?

Fortunately, there is often a middle road to follow. The therapist can allow that traveling to the West Coast is an intriguing and exciting idea and that she will certainly see him until the time he has decided to leave and after that if he changes his mind. In this response, the patient's decision making has been supported with other options left open. This patient may than delay his departure and continue in the rehabilitation program. If the patient does leave town, the therapist, by not engaging in a control struggle, has established the basis upon which the patient can someday return.

The poverty syndrome may shade into a chronic sick role. The patient is a dutiful attender, but full of pessimism and caution. He or she begins to worry about anything and everything and dwells on his or her problems. The mother (family, landlady, family doctor) frequently calls to inquire what's to be done. This is often a difficult situation to modify. Reality may make the choice of sick role the best adaptation of several alternatives. Without the sick role the patient may be asked to do things with which he or she feels unable to cope. It becomes very difficult for therapists to determine if the reluctance to try new things is due to real deficits or simply faint heart. We do not really know what a recovering individual can cope with until he or she has had the opportunity to try, within a matrix of support and encouragement. Throughout this trial-and-error period the therapist requires a good working relationship with family, rehabilitation counselors, job placement agencies, and vocational assessment services.

As a patient recovers from the poverty syndrome, whether as a product of time, healing, or medication, his or her feelings may be expressed in an erratic manner. This is especially true if the poverty syndrome has been prolonged. Feelings of relatedness, sexuality, intimacy, and aggression may arise in a somewhat chaotic fashion. Often the schizophrenic patient will have had little opportunity to manage these feelings and their concomitant relationships premorbidly as well.

A male patient may make a rather crude or childlike pass at his therapist, or the mother may call to report that he told her to "fuck off"—something unheard of before his illness. In either case the therapist's task is to resist a crisis reaction—resist the obvious assumption that the patient is decompensating—and help him to express his feelings in a less provocative manner. It is an educative task in which the feelings must be legitimized while the consequences of the manner of expression are explored and alternative expressions offered. Too often the assumption is made that relapse is occurring. Patients are sent back to the hospital, where they learn, with no ambiguity, that their feelings can lead to disastrous consequences.

In discussing the communication of needs and feelings with patients, it is well to remember that they have been hampered for months, if not years, in their ability to discern the cues and signals that control an affective exchange. They often need to be taught very specifically or coached in these kinds of subtle exchanges. Role-playing situations can be very instructive.

In summary, then, when a therapist encounters a chronic poverty syndrome and/or a postpsychotic depression, several perspectives need to be considered: Medical drugs as etiological factors; use of nonmedical drugs; depression as illness; depression as reaction; poverty syndrome as adaptational response; and depression as posture (the sick role).

Psychotherapeutic management guidelines include the following:

1. Maintain the psychotherapeutic relationship despite lack of evidence of progress.
2. Do not underestimate the patient's attachment to the therapist. Maintain active involvement in spite of seeming detachment on the part of the patient. Limiting the time but not the frequency of contacts may be helpful, as may a more informal, chatty style on the part of the therapist.
3. Reawakening from the poverty syndrome may occur anytime from a few days to a few years after psychosis.
4. Within the context of a supportive relationship, place the patient in situations that will evoke feelings and promote relationships.
5. Review psychosis and hospitalization with the patient to aid grief work and assimilation of experiences.
6. Do not overreact to a display of "inappropriate affect."
7. Tutor the patient about the interpretation of interpersonal cues and the expression of affect in a mannner that will promote social integration.

Chapter 10

PHASE FOUR: ADAPTATION AND INTEGRATION

Where to from where?

—anonymous patient

Description

"Rehabilitation" could well be substituted for the words adaptation and integration. The latter have been chosen, however, as words that most clearly reflect the twin processes of this phase of recovery.

Adaptation

Adaptation most closely mirrors the dictionary meaning of rehabilitation, "to restore to a former capacity . . . to a state of health, useful activity, through training, therapy, and guidance." This definition implies change or recovery in the observable behavior of the patient. He or she must learn or regain skills and behaviors that will enable him or her to find a niche in the community.

An internal process of adaptation must occur as well. This is acknowledged in rehabilitation literature in terms of the development of mastery and self-esteem. The schizophrenic patient must also adapt to some image of him- or herself as convalescent, if not handicapped. He or she must also adapt to the new way of being viewed by others. Family, employer, friends, and treatment team will all perceive the patient somewhat differently now than they did before the breakdown. This new identity may be modified over time, but at this point the patient must find a way of adapting to it and perhaps working to change it. The alternative is social isolation.

There are specific activities to which the recovering patient must adapt through this and later phases. These include taking medication, attending outpatient therapy appointments, attending a variety of vocational and rehabilitation programs, perhaps going into a new living situation (group home, apartment, boarding home), and monitoring his or her own symptoms.

The adaptation is rarely unidirectional. While the patient must adapt to some new role within the family or regain his or her old role, family members are faced with the task of adjusting to the return of the patient and perhaps the return of a family member with changed expectations. This situation is complicated by the fact that the family may need to readjust in two seemingly paradoxical directions: On the one hand, they (the family) have had returned to them a convalescent. They may need, at least temporarily, to lower behavioral expectations, to permit idiosyncracies, to tolerate a strange new variety of pills in the medicine cabinet, and perhaps to assist in compliance with medication, appointments, and workshops. On the other hand, they may have developed, through long involvement with the early phases of the illness and through their many fantasies about schizophrenia, a set of behaviors that are far too accepting, too tolerant. They may be willing to excuse too many behaviors as being due to the illness, and they may require help in maintaining or increasing their expectations for socially appropriate behavior.

Integration

The concept of integration refelects a two-way process. First, the convalescing patient's task is to reintegrate him- or herself in the family and community. A dynamic shift in attitudes, cognitive sets, and role relationships is implied. It takes into account the imperatives of family dynamics, community tolerance, and social pressures. As well, it acknowledges the way in which the patient must fit into a complex network of people and their functions.

Second, integration refers to the internal process of accommodating the new information of "being sick," of "having had a breakdown," and a range of subjective experiences not shared by others. Meaning must be found in these experiences, and they must be woven into the fabric of memory. The two extremes—allowing the experience to overwhelm totally, to become the central concept of self, or sealing over, denying the reality altogether—both prohibit satisfactory rehabilitation.

During this phase, then, the central task of therapy is to help the patient adapt to and integrate his or her experiences.

Dominant Models

During this phase of recovery, the medical model should recede to the background in management and rehabilitation planning. Its contribution from this point on is primarily in providing guidelines for assisting the patient to deal with limitations, reactions to the illness, and medication. Conversely, the other three models must gain prominence. The developmental model will continue to provide a frame of reference for understanding and exploring conflicts, impasses, and apparent problems of motivation. The social model will guide attempts to reestablish social patterns, foster new role relationships, and support independence in the patient. The adaptational model will provide a positive perspective for eliminating or   adjusting to specific deficits, and for integrating the experience of psychosis.

Principles of Rehabilitation and Therapy

Lamb (1977), from a review of the literature and his own work, delineated a set of principles of rehabilitation in community mental health. A modified version of his principles will serve us well for the task of rehabilitating schizophrenic patients through the phase of adaptation and integration:

1   Rehabilitation should begin as early as possible.
2.   The distinction between treatment and rehabilitation is artificial. The assignment of status and priority to one activity over another should depend on individual needs (e.g., in some cases psychotherapy may be the most important component; in other cases a vocational program may be).
3.   The best rehabilitation plan is comprehensive, including social and vocational rehabilitation, psychotherapy, medication as required, financial and domiciliary support. This plan implies coordination of a number of community services.
4.   A key component to a successful program is a supportive living situation.
5.   Learning (social skills, life skills, vocational skills) should occur in vivo. It should not be assumed that skills learned in one situation (context) will be transferred to another. On this point, it is well to remember the overwhelming imperatives of context: tightening a bolt in a rehabilitation workshop is altogether different from tightening a bolt at Northwestern Industries.
6.   Rehabilitation efforts should be aimed at the intact portion of the ego. Competence and health are emphasized, deficits compensated for rather than eliminated. Some symptoms tend to diminish when relegated to the sidelines of day-to-day transactions.
7.   High, though realistic, expectations should foster sef-esteem and a sense of competence without ensuring the experience of failure. This is a difficult balance, and more will be said of it later.
8.   ''Psychotherapy should focus on reality issues.'' This statement from Lamb refers to the system of psychotherapy described by Rada, Daniels, and Draper (1969), called, appropriately, ''adaptive psychotherapy.'' The use of the word ''reality'' appears to have been chosen to make a clear distinction from psychoanalytic psychotherapy.
    The focus of psychotherapy with schizophrenic patients should be on current problems and issues of concern within the present tasks of adaptation and integration. Most of these issues will be concrete and

reality-based. Others may be concerned with residual symptoms and long-standing family dynamics. But during this phase the dominant task is to help the patient overcome, control, or adapt to his or her symptoms rather than to explore their content for dynamic meaning. The modalities of therapy that most suit this task are self-help groups, discussion-activity groups, adaptive psychotherapy, cognitive therapy, supportive therapy, and some techniques adapted from behavior therapy.

9. All techniques and programs utilized should have as a goal the development within the patient of a sense of mastery through encouragement, feedback, and specific learning of skills. It is this sense of mastery or competence that will help the patient overcome future stress and challenges.

10. Institutional alliance without overdependence should be fostered. This will aid compliance and provide a means whereby the patient may satisfy some needs without overreliance on other fragile relationships.

11. It should be recognized that approximately 50 percent of disabled schizophrenic patients live with relatives. It is thus the relatives who constitute the primary support group, and therefore it is this group that deserves some help.

During this phase of recovery, if not before, the question of the relative benefit of living at home must be considered. Negative expressed emotion in the family home contributes to a high relapse rate (Brown, Birley and Wing, 1972). In general, the possibility of relapse is reduced when the postdischarge expectations of patient and family are congruent (Serban, Gidynski, and Zimmerman 1976). Whether or not the patient returns to his or her family is often beyond the control of the therapist. Poverty and social disorganization may ensure that the patient will migrate to the boarding homes of the urban center. On the other hand, the long-established reciprocal needs of parents and child may make it impossible for the patient to ever leave home.

Nonetheless, it can be generally agreed that patients with good prognoses and adequate economic circumstances should leave home at a culturally appropriate age. This statement must be weighed against the real deficits of the patient and the quality of community resources.

As demonstrated in the model described in the first chapters, a move away from the family will be symbolic of a major developmental pasage and will be especially difficult for the young schizophrenic. It will take time and may be best accomplished in stages. Such a move may also involve a number of setbacks before completion.

12. Goals must be defined clearly in all aspects of rehabilitation, including psychotherapy. These goals should be known to and negotiated with the patient.

Psychotherapeutic Tasks

The principle psychotherapeutic management tasks of adaptation and integration follow below.

Help the patient deal with limitations.   The patient and the patient's family will continuously need information about the nature and development of the illness and the implications of this illness for their plans and expectations. Attention must be paid to the actual level of functioning of the patient, the tasks he or she could engage in now and in the future. True residual disabilities should be discussed with the patient as they affect functioning at school or work, and these should be distinguished from the sorts of problems and anxieties that afflict everyone in new and difficult situations.

Help the patient with others' reactions to the illness.   The therapist should engage in discussions with the patient about expected reactions of family, teachers, employers, and others to his or her hospitalization and illness.

Help the patient with his or her own reactions to the illness.   Some anxiety and depressive responses may be alleviated by continued working through of the meaning of the acute illness and of its possible long-term effects.

Help the patient with medication.   Specifically, assist him or her with further adjustment to taking and being maintained on long-term medication; discuss expected side-effects.

Prevent overprotectiveness.   Parents should be further engaged in discussions aimed at separating symptoms and issues of illness from expected problems in living. Continued work with the family is necessary at this point to ensure their appropriate response to the patient's apparent vulnerabilities. When a consummate sick role has been accepted by the family and when they have made the necessary rearrangements to adapt to it, certain troublesome but essentially "normal" behaviors and characteristics may be wrongly labeled. Behaviors that in other circumstances would be perceived as willful or lazy are now viewed as traits of illness. For a family and patient settled into this position, the patient's self-assertion and strivings for independence can be confusing and very threatening. This may be the context most likely to produce double-binding. The best attitude is one in which convalescence and handicap are acknowledged without diminution of expectations for behavior in those areas of life not affected by illness.

Case Example

The patient's mother says, her voice tight with frustration, her eyes conveying long suffering, "Will you do something, Doctor? He won't pick up his clothes or clean his room."

"Why don't you order him to do it, if it is a house rule; either that or no television or even no supper."

"I can't do that, Doctor; he's not well, he needs his nutrition."

"It won't hurt him to go without supper one night; maybe he would clean his room the next day."

"He's also growing his hair long, Doctor, and I think he's been using marijuana. I suppose there's nothing to be done."

Often the therapist will be involved with such "no-win" family issues. When this is the case one must promote tolerance and acceptance of those problems and behaviors that are in fact illness-determined, while at the same time helping the family find resolve in dealing with those behaviors that are not. That there is no clear boundary between the two, even in the mind of the therapist, makes this a very difficult task. While being empathic, the therapist must avoid the contagion of the mother's concern and frustration and try to assist her, preferably with the whole family present, to maintain reasonable expectations.

Reestablish social patterns.   The therapist must consider this phase, which may include transition from hospital to community, as one in which there will be a change in role expectations. Part of the psychotherapeutic task is to help the patient reintegrate previously existing role relationships and adapt to some new ones. Where indicated the therapist should work with the school or employer to facilitate a smooth return. The therapist should work to prevent the patient from following the beckoning course of social isolation.

Foster independence.   The therapist should gradually reduce authority and control and encourage the patient to make his or her own decisions.

Foster new role relationships.   If the patient is to return to the family, the actual amount of time spent in contact with the family should be monitored by the therapist with special consideration of the affective climate in the home. If there is a high expression of negative affect within the family, limiting the number of hours per day spent interacting with family members may be less threatening and more obtainable as a goal for the patient now than a complete move to a different living situation. At this time therapy can more openly explore the patient's role in the family (e.g., the parents' tendency to protect and infantilize the patient; the patient's providing gratification for the parents' otherwise impoverished lives.

Explore developmental conflicts.   More intensive work on developmental issues can begin during this phase. This work is based on the patient's previous developmental status and social functioning. Central issues include autonomy, independence, sexuality, and initiative .

Eliminate or adjust to specific deficits.   Attention and concentration deficits may preclude immediate return to school. Modify specific behaviors and expectations as needed. Some patients can be engaged in concentration practice sessions; a homework assignment might include ten minutes of reading each evening, the length of time and complexity of material slowly increasing. Patients can be directly counseled about idiosyncratic behaviors that imperil social acceptance. Some habits may be shaped in therapy sessions by simple informal reinforcement.

Integrate the experience of psychosis.   Help the patient find a way of understanding and integrating the bizarre experiences and strange thoughts of the recent psychosis.

Special Problems and Issues

Therapist's Expectations

It is very difficult to find and maintain an optimal therapeutic attitude during this phase of recovery. It is all too easy to convey an overly optimistic attitude, deny the existence of residual limiting factors and, for example, encourage the recovering patient to return immediately to university and certain failure. On the other hand, pessimistic therapists are often surprised at the accomplishments of their convalescent patients.

Some patients insist on returning to work or school too early. The therapist knows the patient is not ready but does not wish to quell his or her motivation. A compromise may be struck. On the therapist's advice, the patient may elect to return to university in the following semester, after a four-month convalescence. The absence from school is legitimized with the anticipation of a not-too-distant return. The stresses can be further modified with a gradual, stepwise reentry into the student role.

The best balance is a precarious one. The residual deficits should be discussed with the patient frankly in relation to his or her aspirations. These deficits might include difficulty concentrating, low energy, distractability, short attention span, slowed work habits, and perhaps some loss in the ability to comprehend work and study problems. This latter difficulty is often reported by recovering schizophrenics: "I read it and nothing goes in; it's like I've lost a whole year of university." This patient needs to be reassured that his subjective deficit originates from attention and concentration problems rather than from a fundamental decay in intellect and that it will be recovered over time.

Some patients quickly opt for the sick role. They conclude that their deficits are permanent, and they adopt the hospital and its occupational therapy department as home. These people need strong encouragement and sometimes withholding of the institutional envelope. A common pattern is for the patient to want to return to full employment too soon after the first psychotic episode and not at all after the third. These represent the extremes of denial of illness and acquiescence to a permanent sick role.

Case Example

Joe, a 31-year-old third-class stationary engineer, had been hospitalized five times. Despite this, he restituted well after each break and suffered few limitations that were not secondary or reactive. He had originally wanted to become a teacher or a minister, and he suffered his first psychotic episode while studying at a teachers' college. Since that time he had remained at home, but had acquired and retained a well-paying job in the custodial department of a large complex. In therapy he frequently alluded to his thwarted ambitions, never quite sure whether illness, laziness, or immaturity had prevented him from pursuing them. He considered his present job in the same manner. He felt slower than the other workers and always more nervous. The boss watched him closely. Joe considered quitting: "What if there's an emergency at the plant and I go to pieces?" or "I should get my second-class ticket, but I never seem to get around to applying."

This patient needs help to see that, on one hand, the particular pressures of a teaching or ministerial job are of a nature that could precipitate relapse. On the other hand, objectively, despite his fears and concerns, he was managing his present job quite adequately; in an emergency, he would probably perform as well as anybody.

Societal Attitudes

The identity of a "mental patient" may be permanently spoiled (Goffman, 1963). Previous deviant behavior and the stigma of hospitalization may follow the person throughout life. It has been pointed out that, even after active treatment has ended, the person may be socially identified as an "ex-mental patient" (Friedson, 1970). The occurrence of illness in this case seems to imply permanent membership in a particular group; graduation is possible only to alumnus status.

A number of years ago Cumming and Cumming (1957) conducted an experiment in a small community. They wanted to see if attitudes regarding mental illness could be changed for the better by means of education. They were outsiders in this community and, after an initial warm reception, found themselves extruded. The research could not be concluded; the follow-up interviews had to be abandoned. Their conclusion was that the townspeople began to suspect that the preliminary interviews constituted a government method of preparing the community for the construction of a mental hospital. The people did not want a mental hospital near their town. If anything, their attitudes hardened.

This study also supported the labeling perspective that "mental illness" is most commonly defined as an illness that afflicts those people residing in mental hospitals. In a small rural community deviance and eccentricity are not usually considered mental illness until the deviant is hospitalized. "He's not mental; that's just the way John Smith behaves, always been like that." Once taken out of his or her community and hospitalized miles away in a state facility, the subject's community tenure may be fractured, making discharge placement problematic. This is ample reason for mental health workers to be extremely reluctant to hospitalize patients from small and rural communities.

Still, there is contemporary evidence that attitudes are changing. In a number of communities in the Western world, more chronically ill persons are gradually being accepted and integrated. In a sense, though, in this phase of recovery there is concern over a more subtle process: It may be easier for a community to accept the visibly deviant and obviously handicapped than to allow an ex-psychiatric patient to return to full and equal status. The closer one gets to appearing normal or like everyone else, the more closely the person stands as a threat and symbol of everyone's fragility. What progress has occurred may be a result of a growing distinction between the ever-present cultural concept of madness and the simple disease model of schizophrenia.

This is a complex issue, actively investigated by sociologists, psychologists, anthropologists, and even geographers. For the therapist, it remains simply a matter of remembering that others do perceive the "mentally ill patient" differently. They react to him or her differently; they are reluctant to view the passage through psychosis and hospitalization as a temporary aberration.They withhold reassignment of the person's old identity, watching very carefully and, in conversation, avoiding any reference to past events. After a marital separation or a bout with pneumonia, they may say, "Good to see Bill's his old self again," yet only the closest of friends seem to respond this way to the ex-psychiatric patient.

All this can be discussed with the patient; the realities need not be denied. The patient requires support and specific advice on how to tolerate, manage, and sometimess change the response of others. In this process he or she may teach the therapist a thing or two. One patient reported that he had to leave school following his hospitalization because "They all look at me as if I'm a moron. They tiptoe around me; even the teachers—no, especially the teachers." Another reported that, surprisingly, with each month that passed with him doing an adequate (normal) job at work, with no harbingers of relapse whatever, the employer seemed to watch him more closely. It seemed as if the patient would pose a lesser threat if he performed poorly, as expected, and got sick again.

With schizophrenia, finding a way to understand the illness and its meaning for the "self" is a protracted process. The therapist should move with the patient toward what Scheff (1968) has called a "negotiated reality".

Naming and Explaining the Illness

The notion of whether or not the patient has insight about the illness is much too simplistic. He or she may be willing to accept the simple disease concept that the breakdown was principally a biological illness over which the person had no control.But how does this explain the continued need for medication? What does it all have to do with stress? Are shyness, a poor work record, and irritability disease? How can the therapist discuss ways of controlling hallucinations if they are part of disease and therefore not governed by the exercise of will? To what extent and in what manner is the patient willing to accept needed crutches and to acknowledge that without help the patient cannot control the processes of his or her own mind?

These are complex and subtle issues with no simple or permanent answer. The patient's notion of the illness will likely never quite coincide with that of the therapist. The two individuals can only work toward a middle ground—a negotiated reality that will serve the patient well.

Some therapists use diabetes as a model for explanation. Others offer a more general vulnerability-stress concept. Still others talk simply of "when you were sick," leaving descriptive elaboration or interpretation to the patient. The important point here is that the patient needs a way of understanding what has happened that will allow him or her to continue being a patient without having to display excess illness behavior. The illness must be compartmentalized so it does not play a central role in the definition of self and is not used as an explanation for the rest of life's trials, limitations, and excesses.

This issue, which surfaces in each of the phases of illness and recovery, is seldom completely resolved and needs to be discussed again and again. The therapist may feel he or she and the patient have settled into a useful and reliable way of viewing the illness, when, in another context, the patient suddenly says, "You know, I think my basic problem is anxiety. If I hadn't got so anxious, I'd never have wound up in a hospital." It is well to remember that different explanations may suit different needs.

One patient, still trying after four hospitalizations to control his own thought processes without the help of neuroleptics, would refer back to the times "I went off my rocker." He was well aware that he had been insane at those times but persisted in the belief that he could control his illness with the exercise of will power. Another patient, hospitalized nine times and perceived by the staff as being "without insight" and "noncompliant," refused to admit that she had ever been psychotic. When asked for her own explanation, though, she allowed that there were certain circumstances and particular kinds of stress that could make her "flip out." At these times, as distinguished from the experience of anger, she felt she was no longer in control and would usually end up in a hospital. The new therapist accepted the diagnosis of "flipped out." Both agreed that, though it always occurred under trying circumstances, it was a totally unwelcome event. They, the therapist and the patient, agreed also that it would be best to prevent the "flipping out" and that the patient could do with some help in the matter. She was then asked, of all the medications given her in the past, which seemed to help. The patient chose thioridazine in low dosage. This was prescribed for her, and she has remained compliant and functioning well for a two-year follow-up period. It is interesting to note that, a few months later, in discussing problems with her therapist, the patient began to refer to the times in the past when she had "become psychotic."

Family members also need a way of understanding the illness that will serve them as well as the patient. Basically this should be a simple disease concept that excludes such interpersonal, developmental, and social problems as "getting angry at mother," "growing one's hair too long," laziness, sadness, anxiety, tensions, conflicts. One of the most difficult behaviors for the family to deal with is normal adolescent behavior. When the 23 year old, following hospitalization for schizophrenia, begins to stand up to the parents and assert autonomy, is it a sign of illness or delayed development? This situation must be managed by the therapist, helping the parents distinguish between normal reactions to social and developmental stress and the early signs of illness. This circumstance is especially difficult when the young patient has had no previous experience with, say, self-assertion and thus is a little abrupt in his or her accusations. Again, sexual and cultural differences must be considered.

Some therapists teach their patients to be on the watch for early signs of relapse. This can be individualized with the patient telling the therapist about the first things the patient noticed before the previous breakdown. This way the patient gains some control over what was before a frightening premonition. However, it does raise the problem of reinforcing an already too pervasive breakdown vigilance. With overanxious, timid patients it is often better to spend time reassuring them that their flashes of anger, moments of nervousness, and even periods of crying or confusion are *not* illness-related.

Drugs, Psychotherapy, and Compliance

> Without these drugs my head's screwed up. With them my body doesn't work.
>
> —anonymous patient

Rates of non compliance or drug refusal among psychiatric outpatients can be as high as 50 percent. Some causes of noncompliance are peculiar to schizophrenic patients (Van Putten, 1976, 1978) but it is interesting to note that compliance with comparable medical regimens is not much better. When medications have side-effects and their benefits are not immediately apparent (e.g., the treatment of hypertension), compliance is universally poor.

There are three common patterns with neuroleptic compliance. The first of these is represented by the postpsychotic patient who attends passively and obediently, asks no questions, and takes his or her medication as prescribed. This patient is liable, if anything, to question reduction in the medication. This behavior might be considered overcompliance. The passivity will probably extend to all aspects of the patient's life and make rehabilitation problematic. With successful treatment and rehabilitation, the patient may (and perhaps should) become less compliant and obedient. A second and common pattern is that of the young schizophrenic who dislikes taking medication. The patient sees it as some sort of assault on the self, a symbol of a failure to control one's own life. The medication is either refused outwardly or privately used as the patient sees fit. The third pattern is one in which the patient vacillates between overcompliance, passivity, and assertions of independence and noncompliance. He or she may say, "Yes sir," to the doctor but neglect to have a prescription filled.

Amdur (1979) published a thorough and practical article on improving compliance in outpatient psychiatry. His suggestions are comprehensive and difficult to improve upon. They include the following:

1. Prescription of the simplest regimen, integrated with existing daily habits
2. Elimination of all side-effects that can be eliminated, and careful discussion of all others
3. Medication that is easily accessible
4. Drugs that are clearly identified

5.   A clear explanation of the value and benefit of the drugs
6.   The consideration of family and peer attitudes
7.   A physician who is empathic, nonjudgmental, yet clear and enthusiastic about treatment

Psychotherapeutic work, discussed previously, of helping the patient to develop a serviceable concept of his or her illness will enhance compliance. The more the patient understands about the medication and the greater the part played in administration, regulation, and even decisions about dosage, the better. The prescription of medication is a human transaction and, as such, subject to all the nefarious interpersonal rules that govern such exchanges. Pills may be considered an affront or threat to a patient's fragile sense of autonomy. They may also impinge directly on a patient-therapist control issue. These dynamics seem, not surprisingly, especially prevalent with young male patients.

The patient concerned with control issues can be offered the drugs as an option. The medication is fully explained today, but the patient is given the opportunity to think about it until next week. When the patient sees that the pills are not going to be forced upon him or her, they may be accepted. Similarly, the patient with autonomy problems can be given a choice of drug regimen or even dosage. It must be remembered that there is absolutely no point in forcing medication on someone who will not take it. The therapist can also strike a bargain with the reluctant patient, a promise that if the patient still considers the pills of no benefit in four months' time, they will be dicontinued.

Unfortunately, with neuroleptic medication, noncompliance and drug holidays can reinforce further noncompliance. The patient always feels terrific during the first few weeks he or she is drug-free. The only way to minimize this effect is to explain it and to ensure that the patient's regular drug regimen is as free of side-effects as possible. Finally, it is always wise to consider if the patient's drug refusal or noncompliance is really a perfectly rational and insightful rejection of an ineffective, yet toxic, treatment. Therapists are often loathe to admit that, with some patients, neuroleptic medication is of no value, even though the patient had been stating this for years.

In summary, then, the prescription of medication should be considered a transaction, candidly negotiated as a social contract between two adults. The therapist should remember that, in reality, the final choice and control does reside with the patient. Those occasions in which the physician assumes a controlling, authoritative stance should be planned exceptions rather than the rule. When autonomy and control issues play a major role in noncompliance, the patient can be offered some control over the initiation of medication, the regimen and, at times, the choice of drug and dosage.

Rather than being anathema to one another, it is clear that, with schizophrenic patients, drugs make social therapy and psychotherapy possible, and these activities in turn enhance compliance. They are not incompatible. Further, concern that the prescription of medication will interfere with transference is perhaps legitimate, but trivial. What is important is to remember that the prescription of medication is an interpersonal event and, therefore, a component of the relationship between patient and therapist. It can be managed and discussed as such. If need be, it can be separated in time and/or place from the psychotherapy. It may in fact be discussed in the psychotherapy as a concrete action that symbolizes or crystallizes other parameters of the relationhsip.

Case Example

Even after four psychotic episodes and subsequent hospitalizations, Bill, a young man of alternating despair and high aspirations, was having a great deal of trouble accepting the fact of his illness. He was, however, articulate, intelligent, attached to his therapist, and compliant with appointments. The therapist tended to overlook Bill's inability to accept the reality of his illness. There were always more interesting things to talk about. Only with monthly renewal of his prescription did the issue come into focus. Pills represented the handicap Bill was not yet ready to accept.

Family Therapy

It is in this phase of adaptation-integration that more active family therapy could be considered.

The family as patient.   There is no scientific evidence to support the recently popular belief that disturbed families cause schizophrenia. Unfortunately, this belief was the foundation for much of the family therapy provided for schizophrenic patients, inevitably leading to a brand of family therapy that blamed the parents and, if anything, increased family conflict.

The conceptual shift from "he is sick" to "it's his family that is sick" usually carries with it a semantic twist. As long as we use the term "sick" to describe an individual, we can keep the implications of the label to those consistent with a simple disease model. When the word is applied to families and, for that matter, societies, it inevitably takes on connotations of will and morality. In practice, it is often very difficult to be empathic with the parents of your patient.

There is probably no more double-binding or skews and schism in the families of schizophrenics than in the families of others. Yet it is hard to deny the repeated experience of therapists that talking with the families of schizophrenics is very trying. There does seem to occur, too often for coincidence, a mother excessively clinging to her son and a father who seems to have retreated behind a wall of incompetent passivity. The mother smiles too sweetly, her anger denied, her distress quelled. She and her husband are less than candid about the home situation.

Case Vignettes

1.   Telephone call from mother to therapist:

Mother:
"I don't mean to take up your time, Doctor. I know you're a very busy man. I'm so glad that Billy is coming to see you now. I suppose I'm butting in, and it's really too early to ask, and if you're too busy to talk to me now, you just tell me."

Therapist:
"No, no, if Billy knows you've called, we could talk a bit."
Mother:
"Well, then, I know you've only seen him twice, but I wonder what you think of his progress."
Therapist:
"It is early, but I think everything is going fine. I hear from the leader of the group he's attending that their first session went quite well. He seemed to enjoy it."
Mother:
"Well, Doctor, did you know that he's talking about suicide?"

The therapist feels as if he has stepped into quicksand; set up calmly and sweetly and then shot down in flames. He wonders if this mother could drive him crazy as well.

2.   A family session with the patient, a girl of 21, her mother and father:
Father:
(in reference to mother) "She's crazy, Doctor. Always looking for magic. Like the time you got that poison from the old Ukranian for your arthritis. I'd leave if it wasn't for the kids. As soon as they've growed up, I'm gone."
Mother:
(smiling) "Doctor, I wonder if I could ask you what you think of Vitamin B for Joany."
Father:
"You've been pouring so much crap down her throat; she doesn't want it...probably make her more sick. Why don't you just listen to the doctor for a change?"
Mother:
"I have a confession to make, Doctor. I took Joany off your pills four weeks ago. I've been giving her some tea I got from an old medicine man on the reservation. She seems to be better."
Father:
"She's no better. The doctor's pills were helping. You never know what they put in them teabags."
Doctor:
"Why don't we ask Joan what she thinks?" (to Joan) "Joan, which do you think helps you, the pills I've prescribed or the teabags from the reservation?"
Joan:
(faint smile, long pause)
Father:
"Why don't you speak up. Tell the doctor which is better. I can never hear her, Doctor, she talks so soft. I've got partial deafness in my left ear, from the steel mill, you know."
Doctor:
(voice a little patronizing, despite a conscious effort not to be) "Let's give Joan a chance. Joan, which helps most—the pills or that Indian stuff?"
Joan:
(eyes darting to mother, then father, then doctor; soft, weak voice) "I don't know."

The therapist wonders if he wouldn't know either, living between this man and this woman. He wonders why Joan doesn't shout and scream; then he notices her little grin and realizes that, through it all, she seems to be deriving some pleasure in the power she has over these confused adults.

3.   The young man was admitted to the hospital three times, with the symptom, among others, of voices telling him to break some of his mother's possessions. Each time a family history was taken from his mother, and three times she told the interviewer that the present family constellation consisted of herself and her son, left to fend for themselves these past ten years since the boy's father walked out. In an offhand way, she mentioned that she had taken a boarder whom they both referred to as "Old Fred."

Later, in aftercare, the therapist questioned the patient about the role of "Old Fred" in the family. The patient seemed confused; he did remember that "Old Fred" had moved in shortly after his father had left, but he always assumed "Old Fred" was just a boarder. When questioned further, it came to light that the "boarder" and the mother had always shared the same bedroom.

The therapist wonders what it would be like to grow up in a family where the obvious is denied, where pleasant smiles provide a smoke screen for the more important feelings. It wasn't just the "Old Fred" affair that bothered the therapist. The patient's mother was, as is generally the case, consistent; she managed every problem, from the father's disappearance to her son's illness, with the same evasiveness.

4.   The boy was 16, brought to the hospital by his mother and father. He was weeping and trembling, visibly shaking, and he seemed confused and thought-disordered. He had all the signs of "early schizophrenia" that Chapman (1966) had recently described and perhaps, though it wasn't clear through his weeping, some first-rank symptoms as well. He was admitted to the hospital and taken to a pleasant two-bed room on the ward. The doctor was curious to note that the boy's trembling ceased, and though he was not less confused, he now made eye contact. As an experiment, the doctor fetched the two parents and brought them to the boy's room. Immediately the boy began trembling again.

Later the doctor conducted an interview with the two parents in which the father refused to sit. He paced up and down, periodically staring out the window, all the while hurling invective at his wife. She'd been "flat as a board, useless, just like that piece of plastic on the floor" ever since she put herself in the hospital five years ago.

He'd given up; he'd fought with her for 14 years but now he was through "living with a dead person."

Meanwhile, the mother, sitting stiffly, coat still on, smiling tensely, eyes a little vacant, "He stopped talking to me two years ago, Doctor, about the time Peter began to go queer."

Father:

"Sure I did; I gave up. I haven't said a single word to her in two years. Look what she's done to our son."

Cause or effect? Who can know? It seemed the boy, Peter, was an only child, shy and sensitive. The family had moved frequently, and Peter had managed to make only one good friend. This friend had recently been refused entry to the house by the father, partly because of the threat of "bad influence" (the boy was truant) and partly because the father had been ashamed of the condition of the house (the mother's fault). Peter had survived 14 years of his parents' fighting with no apparent ill effects. At least he seemed to manage adequately in school and was never identified as a problem. It was only after his father stopped talking to his mother that Peter developed symptoms. The therapist found it easy to believe that a protracted silent war between these two would be more stressful on the boy than the previous direct verbal abuse.

Discussion. Case 4 would probably not be diagnosed as schizophrenia in Great Britain. Nevertheless, it is included here because, in clinical practice, there is no clear-cut boundary between the schizophrenias and schizophreniform illness. Furthermore, it is recommended here that therapists should avoid searching for parental causes of schizophrenia, although there are exceptions to this rule and this last case would seem to be one of them.

How should the kinds of family aberrations demonstrated in the first three case examples be viewed if there is no proof that family disturbances cause schizophrenia? First, therapist perceptions should be questioned. Are things being read into family interactions that would be considered, in other circumstances, merely troublesome variants in the broad spectrum of normal relationships? This may be the case with the double-bind, which would seem more prevalent in jokes about Jewish mothers than in the families of schizophrenics. Might not the parents of a child suffering from some equivalent medical disease react in a similar manner? The trouble with this comparison is that no physical illness carries with it the same ambiguities and moral dilemmas as schizophrenia.

The issue is not yet resolved. Meanwhile, therapists must work with the troubled families of their schizophrenic patients. In this work, it is not usually helpful to make any connections between family dynamics and cause. Rather, the goal of family work should be enhancement of the family's contribution to the treatment and rehabilitation process. In early phases this may be concrete, specific, and goal-oriented. In later phases it may involve some ventilation, further exploration of the meaning of the illness, and work on those family dynamics that might be limiting rehabilitation and prohibiting reintegration. Thus, for example, the father's role may be supported, and his relationship with the mother explored as a means of providing a structure within which the mother may be able to loosen her grip on her convalescing son.

The most solid evidence of a relationship between family dynamics and recovery from schizophrenia is to be found in the previously referred to work of George Brown and colleagues. They demonstrated that post-hospital schizophrenic patients, taken back into the family, relapse more quickly if the family exhibits "expressed negative emotion." One simple therapeutic repsonse to this finding is to ensure that all schizophrenic patients reentering family homes limit the time spent in direct contact with their families.

One further point from these and other studies (e.g., Gunderson, 1977) should be made. Drugs, sociotherapy, and living situation have an interdependent relationship in rehabilitation and the prevention of relapse. The more ideal (low-stress) the living situation, the more comprehensive the sociotherapy, the less medication required. Again a balance is best: Too little stress and low-grade rehabilitation programs can engender a poverty syndrome, but too much family stress and excessive sociotherapy can precipitate relapse.

Residual symptoms. During this phase, patients can be helped to control those symptoms that cannot be eliminated altogether. Others they can learn to work around. In essence, the social model here takes priority over the medical symptom perspective. Social functioning and subjective well-being are more important than total freedom from symptoms. It is now known that a great many chronic schizophrenic patients can function well in jobs and community despite residual hallucinations or paranoid ideation (Wing, 1978).

One of the more disturbing qualities to hallucinations lies in their intrusiveness. If a patient can learn to bring them under control, at least partially, they lose much of their effect. There are a number of ways to achieve this. All entail a discussion with the patient to discover the particular method best used. Some patients may be able to recognize prodromal experiences and then engage in the kinds of activities (e.g., visiting with a friend or concentrating on housework) that they know reduce the impact of the hallucinations. Others may benefit from simple practice in turning down (and turning up) the volumes of the voices as one would a radio. Imagining knobs and dials may help. Still others may benefit from learning a set of arguments with which to reason themselves out of ideas of reference. Some patients know quite well those particular situations (e.g., drinking, traveling, lack of sleep, arguments about politics, reading pornography) that lead to anxiety and misperceptions. They can be encouraged to avoid their own particular nemesis. There is a secondary benefit here. The more control the patient exercises over his or her own symptoms, the more they seem to recede into memory.

Some patients can also be shown the disastrous social consequences of expressing their delusions and other weird ideas to friends and workmates. They may become willing to keep quiet about unusual experiences and deviant convictions between appointments with their therapists.

These two techniques might be called respectively, "psychofeedback" (to acknowledge a relationship with biofeedback) and "compartmentaliza- tion." A further technique might be called "paradoxical intervention"; this approach is consistent with Jay Haley's "paradoxical intention." It is appropriate only in the context of a well-established psychotherapeutic relationship. In such an instance, when the patient expresses a belief, for example, of being under police surveillance, the therapist unexpectedly pursues this belief to its natural consequences by saying, "Well, then, if the police are watching you, you must be guilty. What are you guilty of? I think you should go down to the police station immediately and turn yourself in". The patient, who has been expecting from the therapist the usual doubt, interpretations, reality testing, empathy, and so forth, is taken by surprise and, for a moment at least, may glimpse the absurdity of the delusion. The therapist can then shift the discussion to the underlying sources of anxiety.

Chapter 11

PHASE FIVE: GROWTH AND CHANGE

I was shy—always had been—but when I grew to have this physical attraction for women I became shy, like really shy.

— anonymous patient

Description

The boundary between the phase of adaptation/integration and the phase of growth and change is not clear. The issues assigned to each phase may arise at different times, be discussed to an apparently satisfying conclusion, and then arise again months later. In practice, the tasks of each phase intermingle, although logically those of growth and change should follow adaptation and integration.

Growth and change is conceptualized as a separate phase in order to highlight a new process and a new set of tasks confronting the "recovered" schizophrenic patient. Through the previous phase, the principal goal of all psychotherapeutic activities and sociotherapy has been to return the patient to normal—to his or her premorbid status. In the phase of growth and change, it is assumed that some of the goals of the previous phase have been achieved. The patient has been stabilized and recovered. He or she is now functioning as well as before the psychosis and hospitalization.

In practice, this often means a return to a level of functioning that is socially limited and developmentally immature. The patient may have lost several years as a result of his or her developing illness, hospitalization, and convalescence. He or she may now be 24 and recovered, but facing the tasks and social problems faced by teenagers. These developmental tasks and social problems remain problematic for the young schizophrenic. He still cannot talk to girls. She still feels like a vulnerable five-year-old in the presence of her father. Otto Will's list of developmental tasks confront the young schizophrenic like a series of very high hurdles. The patient has likely been "burned" once or twice already in confronting these issues, and is more reluctant than ever to pursue independence, develop relationships, and work out his or her own raison d'etre.

It is tempting, at this point, for the therapist or rehabilitation team to consider their work complete. The patient is likely living quietly in the context of the family home or boarding home, compliantly returning to the clinic for medication, may be looking for a job, and at the same time professing lack of interest in other people. Often the patient can neither cook nor wash his or her own clothes.

Although the above description is that of a patient who appears relatively content with what seems to be a rather limited life—a life without any future orientation—it is necessary that the therapist inquire further to obtain an accurate clinical picture. Such a patient may have a hidden interest, an activity or plan that he or she has been reluctant to discuss. This may be a hobby or simply a regular Friday night beer with an old friend. The therapist, if one searches, can often find some ray of hope and fun in the patient's otherwise dull existence. This may be an indicator of the patient's readiness to move toward further growth and change.

The one thing common to all these patients is what Shakow (1963) labeled "neophobia." As described in an earlier chapter, individuals with schizophrenia have special trouble with developmental imperatives and new social situations. This is as true after the acute psychosis as before it.

Dominant Models

The developmental and social models assume dominant positions in identifying and accomplishing the goals and tasks of this phase. The medical model continues to provide a framework for assisting the individual to cope with any long-term limitations or deficits associated with the illness. The adaptational model provides direction for interventions related to resolution of conflict and modification of behaviors inhibiting social integration.

Tasks and Interventions

Principles

Whether or not health and social service presonnel should at this stage of recovery assist the individual to master new tasks or be satisfied with simple readjustment and adaptation depends upon consideration of several related factors: (1) The individual's social and life goals; (2) The resources available; (3) The individual's social and cultural context; and (4) The existing scientific knowledge (limited though it may be) about those circumstances that guard against relapse (Wing, 1978). The therapist must gain an understanding of the interrelationship of these factors over a period of time within the context of a psychotherapeutic relationship.

Postpsychotic patients become ready for developmental progress at different times. The therapist may want to limit psychotherapy and sociotherapy until the patient indicates a readiness to deal with greater change. A stable psychotherapeutic relationship and a satisfying daily activity or vocation are both important in preventing relapse and in readying the individual to take on new challenges. The therapist can assume, with some reservation, that the patient will aspire to many of the same social and vocational goals valued by other members of his or her community. Can (or should) he or she be helped to accomplish these goals?

It must be remembered that while new experiences are the most difficult, they are new only until they have been mastered. Once mastered, a level of stability develops. Although different tasks then become the focus of fear and anxiety, the patient is nonetheless enlarging his or her repertoire and gaining confidence. He or she may have trouble generalizing the new skills (Wallace et al., 1980), but these accomplishments provide an emotional base for further progress.

One of the clinician's major tasks is to make a judgment about the time to promote further advancement in therapy. There is no simple rule governing this decision. During this phase of potential growth and change, some patients need continuing help if only to provide comfort and reduce pain; others can be assisted to successful completion of developmental passages and new social experiences. Some can be helped to resolve a range of neurotic conflicts not directly related to the illness but made especially inhibiting by it; some patients will resist all attempts to improve their existence; and still others are best left alone as their marginal lives contain all the stress they can tolerate.

It often seems paradoxical that some patients, fully recovered and well-endowed with personal and family resources, resist any attempt to help themselves achieve a more mature level of social functioning, while others with severe disabilities, their scars quite visible, struggle daily with social and developmental issues. Two cases examples follow as illustrations.

Case Examples

George is now 25. He has been free of symptoms for four years. He is attractive, polite, and compliant with appointments and medication (now a small single daily dose of trifluoperazine). During the week he maintains full employment in a family firm, and he drives a delivery van on weekends. He lives at home with parents and a younger brother and sister.

He spends no money on himself; he has never washed clothes or cooked food; he has no friends outside the family; and he denies having any interest in sex or women.

Despite his employment record and the long period of being symptom-free, any attempts by the therapist to engage him in discussion and activities that would rectify his developmental lag and his social isolation are met with passive resistance. He doesn't want to learn to cook or to meet people. Life is fine at home.

Arthur is 25. He has been ill since his late teens and hospitalized several times. At his best, he is warm, likeable and intelligent, but able to master only low-level tasks at the rehabilitation workshop. When excited or stressed, he exhibits residual thought disorder. He is constantly on the move and walks from one end of the city to the other every day. This is partly a response to akathisia. His maintenance medication is a relatively high dosage with a balance sought (not all that successfully) between symptom control and side effects.

In spite of this, in group and individual therapy Arthur struggles to grow. His pain touches the therapist and his statements, often somewhat idiosyncratic, carry a special poignancy: "I thought maybe I could do mindwork instead of, you know, handwork. (Laughs) I mean labor, physical labor, maybe a mixture of the two would be best. At the (rehab) center it's like being a cripple. I wanted to, you know, contribute something. All I really want is a car—yes, a car of my own."

Therapist:
"Would you like a girlfriend?"
Arthur:
"A date; like, I'd be happy just to have a date."

It is important that a therapeutic balance be sought between acceptance of the patient's limited life-style and expectations for change and advancement. The recovered schizophrenic patient will respond badly to excess stress. On the other hand, when too little social demand is made, he or she may withdraw into social isolation, poverty syndrome or "institutional neurosis."

At this point, the therapist is faced with the option of leaving this patient alone, recovered and rehabilitated, or working on to nudge the patient through incompleted developmental passages. This is always a difficult choice. The success of such psychotherapeutic work is difficult to predict. Three age-related considerations may help the clinician to make a choice: (1) age of onset of schizophrenia, (2) age in itself as a developmental crisis, and (3) current age of the patient.

Age of onset.   A person who develops schizophrenia relatively late in life (e.g., 25) and who, prior to illness, has socially and developmentally achieved some degree of independent adulthood, is usually perceived as having a good prognosis. Recovery can be equated with regaining premorbid social and vocational status and remaining symptom-free. For this patient, rehabilitation can stop at adaptation and integration.

Unfortunately, schizophrenia usually develops earlier. Most patients usually develop the illness before attaining any independent social and vocational status (age 18 to 24). While such patients will generally be viewed as having poor prognoses, their illness may not be fundamentally more severe than that of the patient reported in the previous paragraph. The difference between the patient who has attained more premorbidly and the one who has accomplished little is that the latter patient will recover only to the stage of development experienced premorbidly, that is, to a preadult level of functioning. The developmental passages already traversed by the former patient await the latter. At this point, the experiences of illness and patienthood make these developmental passages very difficult.

Age as a developmental crisis. It is difficult, however, to deny or avoid developmental issues. The patient is psychologically and to some extent biologically aware of related demands. Family members will not find it an easy task to lower expectations and aspirations. Peers will have moved on to become very visible reminders of his or her own failings. In some ways, the pressure to achieve may be just as stressful as new social experiences themselves.

In this respect, there seem to be certain key ages at which developmental failure becomes most poignant. One might consider the ages, awareness, and tasks suggested by Vaillant and McArthur (1972) and Levinson (1978). In clinical practice, it seems that 30 is rather crucial. Throughout his twenties the young rehabilitated schizophrenic male may be able to justify for himself the realities of his life (still supported by parents, living at home, no sex life or marital prospects, fewer friends each year). He is "still undecided about a career," he "hasn't found anyone to his liking yet," "bachelorhood provides cherished freedom." But around age 30, these rationalizations prove less tenable. The patient finds it more difficult to "be around the neighborhood," to "attend family functions," and to "find someone to roller skate with." Relatives apply more pressure: "We need to fix John up with a girlfriend."

This moment of truth seems equally applicable to the young schizophrenic patient who has compensated for his or her deficits by drifting in and out of cult groups, welfare, walk-ups, alcohol, drugs, and, possibly, repeated hospitalizations. The rationalization may be in the genre of bohemianism or the hippie philosophy of the 1960s. It no longer works at age 30 or 35, when the beard grays, the body shows signs of abuse, the other "kids who dropped out" have gone or have been replaced by a younger group, the poem or novel has not yet been written. The fact of being, in truth, a very handicapped (or else failed and lazy) member of society becomes more clearly apparent.

The purpose of the above discourse is to stress the point that the therapist must make a difficult choice. Leaving a young "recovered" schizophrenic patient alone to live a permanently dependent and socially isolated life with his or her parents may not be a kindness. Time will catch up anyway.

Current age of the patient. The therapist may need to pursue social and developmental progress quite vigorously despite obvious handicaps. In other circumstances it may be more of a kindness to reinforce the patient's denial and rationalization and to help him or her adjust to a limited life-style. This latter choice may depend primarily on the age of the patient. It is usually too late and too stressful to pursue novice-phase issues when the patient is well past 30.

Case Examples

Mike was 25. He had been hospitalized seven times, beginning at age 17, for acute schizophrenic episodes. He lived with his parents and three younger brothers. He had not completed high school and, with the exception of a three-week stint as an after-hours sweeper at a local factory, he had never been employed. Mike was fired from this one job for "carelessness." He spent warm days walking the streets of downtown; cold days were spent sitting at local donut hangouts and pubs. His "buddies" consisted of the familiar faces he watched come and go at these hangouts, people he never exchanged conversation with but who remained an important part of his social world. Although pleasant, likeable, and superficially competent, Mike would become disorganized and thought-disordered under stress. In the five years in which Mike had been in and out of therapy, he had consistently rejected suggestions or invitations to become involved in any kind of rehabilitation program.

The issue had been broached in many different ways by his therapist, but each attempt was rejected with "None of that for me, they're just a bunch of rejects," or "Are you kidding? I'm going to university; my dad always said I would," or "No, thanks, I'm reading up on science and math, I think I'll get a job as an engineer." The alternative plans, as presented by the patient, seemed to get grander as the years passed. As he turned 26 the next year, these plans were presented accompanied by a description of what his friends from the old neighborhood were now accomplishing. One was married and owned a house, one was at university, one was traveling in Europe. Mike's sadness at his own lack of accomplishment became more focused, and his grandiose plans faltered in response to a simple interpretation:

Therapist:
"I guess you would like to have some of those things for yourself."
Mike:
"Yeah, I guess I always thought I'd be further ahead by now. A person hates to feel like a bum."

At this point Mike seemed more able to discuss his feelings of failure, the specific hopes and plans that had never materialized. Eventually he described feelings of inadequacy, "differentness," and concern that "something was wrong with him" that went as far back as early grade school. He acknowledged and asked questions about effects of the illness and finally allowed his therapist to work with him and explore his actual capabilities. Although his therapist had attempted to discuss this in the past, Mike had not become actively engaged until this much later stage. The preliminary introduction of the issues may, however, have helped set the stage for his readiness, while turning 25 or 26 seemed to be the symbolic catalyst for this process.

Currently, Mike functions somewhat marginally in a local sheltered workshop where his job is packaging detergent. He has developed relationships with some of the other workshop employees, and he attends a weekly activity group. Mike's repertoire of self-care skills is increasing. As may often be the case, his extensive denial seemed to be a reaction to extensive disability; the therapy goals for growth and change have been modified accordingly. Mike, in beginning to acknowledge his problem, seems now able to make his personal goals more realistic. Still, it is a painful process. Sadness and pathos are ubiquitous in Mike's struggles.

There are instances in which the therapist's task must be to help the patient accept a limited social life by reinforcing his denial.

Johann was 34. He had been hospitalized several times during his twenties for acute schizophrenic episodes. He lived in a kind of self-contained apartment within his parents' home; he attended a rehabilitation workshop and spent some time visiting his younger, married brother. At his best, he was friendly, talkative, superficially competent. Stressful situations and sometimes even complex questions, however, aggravated a permanent thought disorder.

Two admissions in his thirties seemed to be similarly provoked. Johann had met a girl at a local drop-in center. He fantasized about her for weeks, considered marriage, compared his life with his brother's, and finally found the courage to attend a singles' dance held at the center. It is not clear whether or not he danced with the girl in question that night. Reality and fantasy began to mix, and Johann was admitted to the hospital the next day.

The therapist who began to work with Johann after the second such episode decided to reinforce his rationalizations. He and the patient had lengthy discussions about the benefits of permanent bachelorhood. They agreed that the "carefree" life was best. It was fine to think of women and enjoy their company, but foolish to think about marriage. And yes, masturbation was a perfectly healthy and equally good sexual outlet.

Psychotherapeutic Tasks

With the previously mentioned cautions in mind, the psychotherapeutic management tasks appropriate to the phase of growth and change can be listed as follows.

Help the patient discern and adjust to limitations for vocational, social, and developmental achievements. An issue for psychotherapeutic discussion is the extent to which the illness will inhibit life and developmental changes. Relevant issues include long-term medication and its side effects; how and what to explain in new social relationships about the illness and medications; genetic counseling; general ability to cope with various kinds of stress; the extent to which the difficulty in initiating changes depends on actual illness-produced fragility, as opposed to posttraumatic neurosis and other anxiety/depressive/obsessive reactions to the illness.

Promote development of social and living skills and acquisition of new roles. Typically the young schizophrenic will be blocked at an earlier developmental and social level of functioning and will find each step forward difficult to take. The prominent issues in the psychotherapy program will be adult peer relations, intimacy and primary relationships, dating patterns, sexual relationships and activities, relationship to authority figures, relationship with family, changing roles, autonomy, independence, and responsibility.

The therapist must function as a life-skills coach. The principal style of therapy should be educational. One must explain, tutor, encourage, and review. The clinician must be prepared to assume the role of big brother or big sister and, at times, to use a similar metaphor, "Dutch uncle." Much of the psychotherapeutic work in this period combines an activity and educational stance and involves the learning of new, more adaptive social and life skills. Activity-discussion groups are helpful. Patients can benefit greatly from instructing and encouraging one another. Doing is more powerful than talking about: role playing, direct practice, and experience are effective learning experiences.

Assist the patient with a changing sense of self. One of the psychotherapeutic tasks during this phase may be to assist the patient in becoming comfortable with newly acquired roles and a changing sense of identity. This change should entail a shift from "sick" to "handicapped" to "recovered but vulnerable." With increased social skills and developmental changes, it will also include a new sense of mastery, competence, power, and responsibility. It should be remembered that these positive changes can be just as stressful as negative happenings. In fact, for the young recovering schizophrenic with impaired ability to decipher new context, the progressive, positive changes may be more stressful than overtly traumatic but more simple and discrete changes, such as the loss of a job or the death of a friend. The therapist should provide a supportive matrix and engage in a great deal of explanatory, educative discussion. One's task is to help the patient comprehend the changes and to tolerate new ambiguities.

Resolve conflict and modify noncoping behavior. As the patient struggles with developmental and social issues, some intrapsychic conflicts and concomitant behaviors may surface. These may be specific to schizophrenia or at least the kind of conflicts and behaviors common to people with chronic or disabling illness, or they may be totally unrelated to the disease. The conflicts or dilemmas may be idiosyncratic or universal, but they all tend to have graver consequences for the schizophrenic patient than for someone else.

Examples of the former category of problem would be an excessively dependent relationship on one's mother or extreme difficulty acknowledging anger. Examples of the latter category might include sexual guilt or concerns about homosexuality. The principles of psychodynamic psychotherapy find a place in this phase: A number of issues can be explored, their roots sought, conflicts exposed and overcome. The patient may possess any number of neurotic conflicts that are not primary symptoms of the illness; but the illness and the experience of psychosis can turn a minor psychological struggle into a major impediment. Thus, sexual guilt or an obsessive turn of mind—of mere inconvenience to others—can be crippling to the young schizophrenic. All too often in the past, such liabilities were viewed as etiological. They probably are not; however, the schizophrenic patient will generally still require assistance overcoming them.

The young male patient may feel confused by his ambiguous sexual feelings. He may find himself attracted to males but, having had little experience, not yet be sure of his sexual orientation. He is apt to see this confusion as part of the disorganization of his whole life, and the therapist is likely to view it in kind. The sexual orientation problem may be simply a part of his disorganization and his fear of all relationships. On the other hand, it might have been present at this stage of the young man's life even if he had not developed schizophrenia. Whichever the case, the schizophrenia will make his sexual confusion more ominous, and, in turn, his sexual confusion may heighten his anxiety and thus his vulnerability to psychosis.

The important message here is for the therapist not to assume that the psychosexual or other conflict is directly related to the schizophrenia. In the growth and change phase, such conflict may be approached in the same manner a therapist would approach the conflict with a nonschizophrenic patient. In doing this, one may contract with the patient for a number of sessions devoted to the problem. One should be careful to separate this psychotherapeutic activity from the medical task of monitoring symptoms and prescribing medication. Although one may engage the patient around the conflict distinctly separate from the schizophrenia, one must remember that the processes of uncovering, exploring, behavior modification, and practice are more stressful to the schizophrenic patient than to someone else and may demand more detailed, careful explanation.

Special Problems and Issues

Monitoring the Illness

With the recovering schizophrenic in the phases of growth, change, and continuing care, interpretation of an exacerbation of symptoms is difficult. All too often such a display of old symptoms is viewed by therapists as evidence of decompensation or relapse. A simplistic medical model is brought to the fore to explain the phenomenon: "Joe is decompensating again. It seems to happen each year at this time" or "The meds are no longer holding him. I'm afraid he's deteriorating."

These interpretations may be accurate. While it is not wise to assume automatically under such circumstances that the patient is taking his or her medication as prescribed, some schizophrenics do seem to get worse while maintaining a specific drug regimen. Still others, responding initially to stress, take a downhill course that cannot be blocked until the patient has been hospitalized and given a repeated course of the treatment used during the previous admission. Nonetheless, by the time a patient reaches the growth and change phase, there are at least four other interpretations of "relapse" that should be considered.

The first is to view the new display of symptoms as a specific response to stress. If this perspective seems justified, the stress should be pinpointed and alleviated. Stresses might include too much exposure to family or excessive expectations at the rehabilitation workshop. A temporary increase in medication may be helpful. The therapist should avoid a premature or inaccurate diagnosis of relapse. One should provide increased support and search for possible contributory stressors.

The next perspective—a variant of the first with an important conceptual shift—assumes that abnormal mental phenomena have, by virtue of a protracted psychosis, become easily available to the patient. Hearing voices, developing ideas of reference, being addressed by the television are past experiences well imbedded in memory and now able to be rekindled with minor provocation. They do not contain the intrusive foreignness that helps keep them at bay with other people. In fact, the patient under stress may adopt what Arieti (1976) referred to as the "listening attitude." He or she may welcome the symptoms as an escape from present reality, developing the symptoms and expressing them to the therapist in much the same manner that another patient will discuss anxiety. That is, rather than saying to the therapist, "I'm very anxious. I have spent all my money and I won't get my welfare check for two days," the patient will say instead to the therapist, "My voices have come back."

At this point, it is often useful for the therapist to view the display of symptoms simply as a display of distress, a temporary phenomenon, a communication of anger, worry, or anxiety. One may then ignore the symptom and focus on the reality problem. In attempting to identify the source of stress, it is well to review the basic necessities of life. The symptom has probably arisen as a result of problems in the area of money, housing, job, family, or primary relationship.

A third perspective involves relating the display of symptoms to the progress of psychotherapy or sociotherapy. If the patient is being coaxed into new developmental and social circumstances, he or she must experience stress, and in response may therefore at times display some symptoms. The symptom may be considered in the same light as the anxiety expressed by any other psychotherapy patient.

Lastly, it is well to consider that the display of symptoms is a communication. It is one side of a transaction occurring here and now with the therapist. The symptoms may be engendered by the patient's need to tell the therapist that he or she is having difficulty with the world outside or with the homework prescribed. It may be the patient's way of telling the therapist about being unsure he or she can cope with the new job or rehabilitation program. Or it may constitute a specific communication to the therapist that can best be translated as, "You are expecting too much of me; don't forget I have an illness," or simply, "I still need you." This communication, its content and its style, despite reference to external events, might have meaning only for the therapist-patient relationship; that is, it may be simply the patient's attempt to manage the relationship with his or her therapist.

Images of secondary gain and conscious manipulation come to mind here. Unfortunately, these images often reflect the issues of moral choice and value judgment. These are best ignored: All human transactions entail some conscious awareness of gain and control. Rather, the therapist should consider the symptom as a direct communication to oneself, probably part conscious, part unconscious, and, in turn, speak directly to the core of the issue.

Case Example

Patient:
"I'm getting paranoid again, Doc."
Therapist:
"Are you concerned about the job interview tomorrow, Bill?"
Patient:
"Yeah, but that's not it. I think the police are following me again."

Therapist:
"Well, you're going to be watched very closely when they interview you tomorrow. Maybe you're not ready for it yet."
Patient:
"Yeah, I don't think I'm going. I'll never find the place anyway."
Therapist:
"Maybe we should postpone it for a while. Look for something simpler."
Patient:
"It's a good job, though."

This hypothetical dialogue leads to a very important concept in working with recovering schizophrenic patients and, for that matter, other psychotherapy patients as well: A sense of self is seldom unidimensional. Low self-esteem, for example, often has a "flip side." It may be accompanied by a particular part-identity or valued self-perception that maintains for the person a sense of being "as good as, if not better than others." The notion "I can't cope" is accompanied by the thought "Maybe I can, if only...."

Conflict, or at least ambivalence, is always present. "I can, I can't. I will, I won't." In therapy, patients—especially less psychologically minded patients—often express only one side of the ambivalence. Typically, the therapist will verbalize the other side, and the two proceed to dialogue the dilemma. Problems arise when the therapist recognizes the existence of only the patient's expressed side of the equation. In response to a patient's saying, "Life isn't worth living," the therapist may assume that the patient means just that and engage in a conversation in which he, the therapist, provides pro-life arguments and he or she, the patient, contributes anti-life arguments. In so doing, the therapist has missed the ambivalent nature of the communication and allowed the patient to concentrate on only one representation of his or her concerns. In choosing to argue the other side of that one representation, the therapist begins to "own" it, to harbor the pro-life arguments and inadvertently, through what is essentially debate, to force the patient to dwell on and build his or her anti-life arguments.

Another way of expressing this would be to suggest that the patient's conflict has been externalized and absorbed as currency in an interpersonal relationship. Each participant adopts one point of view and develops his or her complementary role. This process can be very subtle:

Patient:
"I'm hearing voices again, Doc."
Therapist:
"Well, I don't want you back in hospital. Maybe a little more medication and wait a few days."
Patient:
"They're telling me to do things."
Therapist:
"Can you resist them? Can you turn them off?"
Patient:
"I don't know. They're getting stronger."

The patient is asking, not stating, "Can I control my life and my mind? Am I sick or can I really survive out there?"

The question is not asked directly. Rather, it is phrased as the opening gambit for a subtle debate. The outcome of the debate will influence the self-concept of the patient. In this example, the harder the therapist insists that the symptoms can be overcome, the harder the patient might insist that they cannot be. The patient may have to demonstrate to the therapist the strength of the feelings that he or she cannot cope.

A more effective approach entails the therapist's opting for a more neutral stance, ensuring that the patient expresses and owns all sides of his or her ambivalence. In some circumstances the therapist may directly provoke expression of the other side of the problem. For the latter approach the techniques described by Sullivan and Haley offer some guidelines. The therapist can offer confusion, his or her own ambivalence, changeableness, and even paradoxes to provoke the full expression of the equation. Example: "I don't know. It's really a hard choice," "Maybe you're right. I don't know, maybe you're not ready," "Well, you're probably right. I was wrong. The job is too much for you," or "You should probably quit and look for something else. "That job is too much hassle for anybody." Once the patient has expressed all other aspects of the conflict, it can be dealt with more effectively. The patient can be given the lead and can end up deciding for him- or herself, this time anyway, which position should dominate behavior.

Suicide

People with schizophrenia kill themselves at a higher rate than the general population. The same factors that increase the likelihood of suicide in the general population also increase the likelihood with the schizophrenic patient. These include alcoholism, living alone, physical illness, social isolation, and social disorganization—and schizophrenics are more likely to remain single and drift to isolated, unstable environments. Suicide is associated with depression, and depression is ubiquitous to schizophrenia.

Two special factors should also be considered. The first is the rare but dramatic occurrence of the schizophrenic patient's acting upon the bizarre self-destructive instructions of his or her voices or delusions. It is difficult to predict when this might happen. Generally, if the patient is telling the therapist about his or her impulses, the therapist will have time and opportunity to ameliorate them. The urgency of the situation can sometimes be discerned by the degree of intensity of the patient's preoccupations, though the opposite situation can sometimes be misleading. On occasion, a quiet and rather bland schizophrenic patient will unexpectedly act upon his or her delusion. This occurrence is exceptional, however, and should not be used as a rationale for excessive surveillance.

The second situation, of more concern here, is the suicide of a schizophrenic patient that seems to constitute existential choice. Here the young schizophrenic patient is severely disabled and aware of it. Having suffered a psychosis and begun recovering, the patient returned home initially, convalesced, and perhaps dreamed of future successes. As months, even years, pass and he or she remains home with no further improvement, the patient may rationalize his or her failure to make progress by using denial or adopting a sick role. If this role is confirmed—the position supported—he or she may slip into a chronic handicapped status that carries little danger of suicide.

But if the patient is acutely aware of the disablement, conscious of his or her losses and limitations, and if the present situation is untenable, then the option of suicide may be seriously considered. His or her youthful promise has vanished; life is a sterile round of clinics, hospitals, and boarding homes. Friends have deserted him or her, the future looks bleak, and there is a painful awareness of cognitive impairment. Perhaps the family can no longer tolerate the patient, and even his or her therapist has become discouraged. This person is a high suicidal risk, and the only lifeline may be the people he or she meets at the day center or outpatient clinic. Clinical experience shows that this point of anomie can be reached and even provoked during an otherwise successful therapy program. Within the framework presented in this book, it would be most likely to occur during this phase (growth and change) or the preceding one (adaptation/integration).

With sociotherapy, encouragement, support, and psychotherapeutic exploration, the patient may move from the sick role and gain a modicum of independent living. He or she may leave home and settle in an apartment or boarding house. But to move past this point may be very frightening if not beyond his or her resources, and to move back, physically to the parents' home, psychologically to a dependent position, may become intolerable. The patient then is trapped between the rock and the hard place: too frightened to move forward, too discouraged to move back. If the present situation is unbearable, suicide may become an option.

The task of the therapist is to recognize this dilemma and discuss it with the patient. The therapist should remember, again, that success (new job, enrollment in university, engagement) can be as stressful as failure and, in this context, carries with it the extra burden of anticipated failure. The therapist may need to curb expectations and, in the case of programs in which behavior modification is used, temper enthusiasm with the knowledge that one's successful program may be placing the patient in an untenable situation.

The phase of growth and change entails psychotherapeutic work that will be more individualized than the other phases. Each patient will bring different family issues, developmental problems, and social circumstances. The extent of progress and growth will vary tremendously. To illustrate this phase, then, a lengthy case history follows. This case history covers a period of six years, and therefore the information presented will be highly selective. The case spans all phases of psychosis and recovery. Those events and issues pertaining to the phase of growth and change are emphasized.

Case Example

Bill was referred in 1974. At that time, he was 28 years old and living at home with his mother, father, and brother. He had been hospitalized five times since the age of 20 with episodes of paranoid schizophrenia. His brother had also been hospitalized several times with schizophrenia and, as his mother was quick to inform the therapist during the initial interview, there are two cases of schizophrenia on the maternal side of Bill's family.

With family help, Bill had acquired a job and had managed to retain it between episodes of illness. Otherwise his life had become increasingly impoverished developmentally and socially. He had long since lost his friends, and his social life had been reduced to his immediate family and some cousins they would join on family holidays. He had a bedroom next to his mother and father's and a small stereo system with a collection of three records, including one of his school band. He had been a fair trombone player in high school, but had long since packed his instrument away. He owned an automobile and had a large bank account. He had dated once before his illness and once four years later with a nurse he met while hospitalized on a medical ward. (In later psychotherapy sessions with Bill and his brother together, they reminisced about the one date of eight years before as if it had occurred the previous week and with the kind of postdate analysis one would expect from a very shy 17-year-old.)

Bill was a very likeable and intelligent man who was attending first year university when he suffered his first psychotic episode. He was somewhat obsessive, worried a great deal, and was especially concerned about sexual matters. His sexual concerns shifted into ideas of reference, then overt delusions, during his periods of decompensation.

During the first appointment, Bill expressed some strong fears, if not outright convictions, that he was being watched by the police and that the phone of his house was being tapped because of some sexual crimes he might have committed. The crimes were basically masturbation and a fondness for pornographic books depicting spanking. As well, he had a vague idea that he might be responsible for an episode of lingerie stealing reported in a local newspaper years ago.

Bill was left on his current maintenance medication and referred for group therapy on the principle that he needed help in the interpersonal area. This referral required an extended explanation and a fair amount of persuasion. Bill did well in his pregroup interview and attended his first group session. The report from the group therapist indicated that he also functioned rather well in the group.

As would be expected, however, the group discussed confidentiality and decided that what went on in the group was not to be discussed with anybody outside. Bill returned home that evening, and his mother asked him, "What did the doctor say in your therapy?" Bill told her that he couldn't discuss it. His mother insisted, because she was very concerned for his health and his progress and because she was, after all, his mother.

Bill stood firm. He now refused to share something with his mother, with whom he had previously shared everything. She called his former therapist, who had helped Bill through previous psychotic episodes, and told him that Bill had attended one of "those university group sessions" and that he was now getting more and more anxious. The psychiatrist told the mother she had better bring him down to the hospital, and she did this.

By the time Bill reached the hospital he was feeling very anxious and was beginning to wonder if he might in fact be guilty of several sexual offenses.

The interaction between the mother, Bill, and the psychiatrist after the group therapy occurred over a weekend and ended up with hospitalization on a Sunday evening. After a few days Bill was transferred to an inpatient unit at the current therapist's hospital. His symptoms resolved rapidly with antipsychotic medication.

Because it was clear to the hospital treatment team that Bill was too old to be living at home (this judgment influenced by the mother's recent interference), he was sent out to find an apartment. Bill found an apartment; his anxiety level rose; his antipsychotic medication was increased; and he was discharged to outpatient care and a downtown high-rise.

Bill slept in his new apartment, but functioned poorly at work and ate all his meals at home. His anxiety increased, coupled with a strong sense of despair and hopelessness, and soon the therapist began to receive phone calls from the mother pointedly informing him that "Bill's apartment is on the 17th floor and it has a balcony." Bill's psychotic symptoms gradually returned; he became genuinely suicidal and in due course was readmitted.

On this occasion the treatment team moved a little more slowly. After the initial symptoms were resolved, Bill was put on an internal work placement, activity programs, and eventually day care. Family meetings were held, and the family's aid was enlisted in helping Bill find and furnish an apartment.

Bill wanted independence and autonomy, though he quite naturally drifted to his parents' home every night around supper time. His mother seemed an excessively sweet and intrusive woman whose anger and disappointment were controlled beneath a superficially polite demeanor. She told us initially that the father would not attend a family session. He did come, and was quite pleased to be asked, though he turned out to be rather ineffectual and always bowed to his wife's will. (Later Bill expressed a great deal of cautious resentment that his father had never helped him with anything). Mother and sons formed a tight power base and, for the most part, father was excluded. Family sessions were not very successful. Bill's mother was vigilant for any hint of blame or condemnation, and she felt she had to protect her vulnerable sons from any untoward affect. The therapist therefore opted to work with Bill alone and together with his brother, who had by this point been referred to the same outpatient clinic. The fraternal relationship was healthy, if developmentally immature, and the mother seemed to view her two boys almost interchangeably. Past history revealed a seesaw effect in their illnesses. Whenever one was well and making good progress, the other worsened.

Bill was maintained on a low dose of perphenazine. The focus of therapy included basic life skills, social skills, psychosexual education, and issues of autonomy and independence. Two years after these hospitalizations and the beginning of therapy, the following note was written for a case review and presentation:

"Bill has slowly and tentatively increased his independence and autonomy although I suspect he returns home for mother's cooking more often than he tells me. He has learned to shop and cook, in a fashion. He has maintained fairly steady employment. After many lengthy and painful coaching sessions he managed to establish contact with a girl, Elizabeth. He has been dating her steadily for a year now and very recently asked her to marry him. Through these two years he has struggled with ambitions, work relationships, his relationship with his mother and his father, his concerns about his brother. He doesn't sleep well at night alone in his apartment. He thinks he may be in love but he has nothing to compare it with."

He remains chronically anxious and worried. His relationships at work are rather strained. It seems the longer he remains healthy, the more pressure is brought to bear on him at work—that is, stronger implications that he will lose his job if he is not able to cope with it. He wonders whether or not he can handle marriage and he wonders whether or not he can handle children. He wonders if, as someone with schizophrenia, it is fair to marry. He wonders if he should have children, because as he says himself, he wouldn't want anybody to go through what he's been through. He wonders what he should tell the girl's father when he asks Bill what his nervous problem really is.''

Over the succeeding three years since the above paragraphs were written, the frequency of contact with Bill ranged from once every two weeks to once every two months. The problem of developing dependency on the therapist was managed overtly as a joint responsibility.

As his relationship with Elizabeth became serious, a host of issues arose. What would he tell her and her family about his illness? How would he explain the pills he took regularly? Could he handle an intimate relationship? Could he cope with the responsibility of such a relationship? (Bill's attitudes and values about sex, alcohol, religion, minority groups, and duty tended to Middle America, circa 1950.) Could he handle a marriage? What if he married and then lost his job?

He knew that Elizabeth's father watched him very carefully. This made him more nervous in his presence. When Elizabeth's aunt served him tea, his hand shook so badly the teacup rattled. The dating continued, the relationship became more serious; bit by bit he confessed all to Elizabeth. She then came to see the therapist for a discussion about schizophrenia, its implications for Bill and for any children they might have. Afterward, she went off to make her own decision about marriage. They became engaged, with Elizabeth holding Bill to the condition that he have a vasectomy before marriage. There followed a rocky nine-month engagement.

Bill immediately had doubts, and he increased the amount of time he spent with his family. He procrastinated on the vasectomy issue. He doubted his love for Elizabeth and felt himself unworthy. At the same time he was experiencing an adult relationship that involved compromise, discussion, and cooperation, not governed by the rules of childhood. He was struggling with developmental and social issues in his early thirties that are more usual a decade earlier, and in spite of the stress they held for him, he felt more alive than he had for years.

As the wedding date approached, he commented that he could be substituting his dependent relationship with his mother for a possibly equally stultifying situation. At the same time he was experiencing feelings he had never felt before. He even began to express a little anger now and then. This was perhaps the most frightening of all. He would report an argument in which he raised his voice, phrasing this in such a way that he obviously considered it a symptom of his illness and a prelude to decompensation.

Bill and Elizabeth organized an apartment and were married after a year's engagement. He had had his vasectomy too late for intercourse on the honeymoon; it was the first time in a plane for either and the first time booked into a strange hotel in a strange city. Bill became psychotic. He developed ideas of reference and persecutory delusions, and he became thought-disordered. In the midst of this disorganization he also made telling and insightful remarks about his dilemma, his developmental struggle, and the problems his new wife was experiencing. Elizabeth took over and flew them back home to their new apartment. Bill increased his own medication and, with several crisis conjoint sessions, weathered the storm. What is of special interest here is that already, after only a few days of marriage, the spouse was playing the role of healthy caretaker of sick partner and labeling Bill's legitimate complaints about her sexual anxiety as evidence of illness. The conjoint sessions at this point had to tread the fine balance of supporting the appropriate aspects of Elizabeth's caretaking relationship, helping Bill express and legitimize his insights and complaints, and maintaining a sense of partnership and equality in the relationship.

Two years after the wedding, the following was written:

"The couple remain married; each is fully employed. They have probably discussed with one another their sexual needs and their partnership more openly and fully than most 'normal' couples. Bill's separation from his family continues. He no longer considers his parents' house his home. (One of the dilemmas that hit him just before marriage was that he was terrified of the next step forward but could no longer tolerate the thought of going home.) He is becoming more comfortable at work, on occasion speaking up and arguing about union issues, although at one workers' meeting he did argue against 12-hour shifts using his illness as a reason. Needless to say this was not a good encounter."

Discussion

Bill's prognosis was and is good by most parameters, apart from frequent hospitalizations. The limitations he had to adjust to were not that great. Rather, one of the main tasks in working with Bill turned out to be helping prevent his retreat from reasonable expectations. He wanted to become a minister, and in many sessions he returned to this thwarted ambition. He was never quite sure whether illness, laziness, immaturity, or bad luck had prevented him from pursuing this career.

For a long time, as with many other young schizophrenic patients, Bill clung to an idealized image of this profession, but took none of the intervening steps that might place it within reach. (It seems relatively characteristic for young schizophrenic patients to dwell on an idealized future without considering or mastering those developmental and social steps that would be prerequisite. These are, of course, the very steps that the young schizophrenic has most trouble taking.)

Bill's mother was overprotective and vigilant to any signs of impending illness. Bill, though by no means adopting a sick role, had become equally vigilant. The family walked on eggshells. Any conflict or untoward emotion or threat of change carried with it the ominous threat of breakdown and/or suicide. For his part Bill, trapped in a dependent relationship with his mother, his extrafamilial world diminishing, would often share with his mother thoughts or behavior that could be guaranteed to maintain her anxiety. There was little he didn't share with his mother, though he often chastised himself after the fact. Bill had adopted an expression, "I'm not feeling well," as a generic signal of distress. Family and others would think immediately of mental illness.

Thus, one of the principal tasks of psychotherapy with Bill and his family became the process of normalizing. They were helped to distinguish between normal responsive anxiety or anger and symptoms of illness. If anything, the therapist emphasized the other side in order to counteract the effects of eight years of illness interpretation. Thus the statement "I'm not feeling well. I'm too nervous to work today'' would be translated to ''I don't want to go to work today.'' The reasons Bill didn't want to go to work would be discussed. Always rational explanations were sought. Later Bill was able to see how his mother, with the best intentions, undermined his sense of competence and how he ''played into'' this.

Through this phase Bill was given increasing control over his medication. Repeated sessions were spent helping Bill to find a way of defining and coming to grips with his illness. The illness was packaged and separated from the rest of his problems-in-living. The therapist functioned as a life-skills coach or special tutor, helping Bill learn and interpret the transactional rules and rituals of new social relationships.

Change and progress were accompanied by turmoil, some regression, and, on occasion, the presentation of symptoms. Bill would increase contact with his family, worry his mother, and take time off from work. With each step forward came a period of doubt and regret. With major changes the symptoms of paranoia would exacerbate. These were usually perceived by the therapist as this particular patient's way of expressing the universal distress experienced with change, although the temptation to view them as expressions of illness was great.

A point came when Bill, savoring his new experiences and sense of fulfillment, realized that he would never be able to return home. Yet he remained very unsure of the road ahead. Marriage, responsibilities, more independence loomed ahead of him. He wasn't sure he could make it but now found it impossible to settle for less. The two other options of rehospitalization and suicide occurred to Bill, and to his therapist, when the impending marriage brought thoughts of being trapped or failing. The therapist discussed the crisis and dilemma with Bill but chose to ignore the suicidal ideation. Hospitalization would only delay the ''moment of truth'' and probably undermine what sense of competence he had developed.

A specific symptom presented by Bill during times of stress was a delusion of persecution. He felt he was under police surveillance for sexual crimes. Later in therapy Bill would still at times feel he was being watched, but the reasons were unclear to him. He understood by this time that his particular sexual proclivities were not criminal.

Through the long period of working with Bill, this particular symptom was managed by several of the techniques mentioned in this book. Each method was chosen as indicated by the situation in which the symptom arose. On occasion the symptom was simply ignored. Reality issues were discussed instead. At other times the symptom was discussed and linked to particular stresses. The manner in which stress could lead to anxiety, which in turn might lead to ideas of reference and finally misinterpretations, was elaborated. On one occasion the symptom was successfully paradoxed: Bill was told by the therapist that if he felt so strongly that the police were following him, then he must be guilty of something and he should go immediately to the police station and turn himself in. Bill gave the therapist an incredulous look, and, as he reported later, the problem of being followed ''just flew out of my mind.''

Lastly, and without design, an uncovering process has taken place. After four years of therapy, Bill spontaneously reported that he had been thinking about his attraction to spanking and now remembered the first time in his life that he had experienced it. He then related the following story:

He remembered being three or four and, as a daily routine, "helping" his mother change his parents' double bed. His mother stood at the foot of the bed, Bill at the side. The bottom sheet was on the bed, and now his mother threw the top sheet over the bed, holding onto one edge, to let it settle in place. Bill jumped between the sheets. Mother came around the bed, put Bill over her lap, and gently spanked him. Bill remembers the whole episode as a game. Mother was smiling, not really angry. The spanking was fun, part of a secret game between them.

His memories of attaining an erection from thinking about or viewing spanking date from that period. This memory was adopted by therapist and patient alike as a reasonable explanation of how he had come to be sexually aroused by spanking. Pathology was downplayed. Whatever the origin of this particular sexual appetite, it was still only marginally outside average habits. And while the Oedipal story might explain Bill's taste for spanking and his ensuing guilt, it did not explain the ideas of reference, delusions, and further psychotic disorganization. The "neurotic conflict" was separated from the "schizophrenia," partly treated, and partly normalized.

Chapter 12

PHASE SIX: CONTINUING CARE

Not for no purpose or nothing—I go downtown here and there, restaurants and stores and stuff like that, right? That's about the whole kit and kaboodle of what I do from the start of the day.

—anonymous patient

Description

The final phase, continuing care, includes many intervention principles and characteristics overlapping with and repetitive of the previous five phases. It refers to the period of continuing community treatment and management and acknowledges the presence of chronic illness. Chronic disease, as defined by the Commission on Chronic Illness (1957), "comprises all impairments or deviations from normal which have *one* or *more* of the following characteristics: are permanent; leave residual disability; are caused by nonreversible pathological alterations; require special training of the patient for rehabilitation; may be expected to require a long period of supervision, observation or care."

Cogswell and Weir (1966) described how the differences in the course and treatment of acute and chronic conditions have implications for the patient-professional relationship. Their description of the characteristics of chronic, as opposed to acute, care highlights issues of continuing care:

1. The therapeutic goal at this time is containment of social dysfunction and control of symptoms rather than cure.
2. The chronically ill patient will be subject to continuous adjustment of his or her roles and expectations.
3. Rather than being a mere passive recipient of medical care, the chronic patient should be actively responsible for managing components of his or her illness.

156

4. The patient has considerable power in relation to the professional; he or she cannot be forced to participate in treatment; the professional cannot survey the patient's performance at home.
5. Time perspective shifts with chronic care. The patient-health system relationship will be of long-term duration.
6. Environment and contextual concerns change. In managing chronic illness the caregiver becomes less focused on the actual treatment setting and increasingly concerned about the patient's residential and community milieu.
7. While family members may be passively involved at the acute stage, they, along with the patient, can increasingly assume some of the roles of the professional during chronic management.

Because the transition from acute to chronic management of schizophrenia is gradual, some guidelines for intervention have been recommended, in prior chapters, for earlier phases. These become increasingly important considerations as care continues.

Continuing care is generally offered from a community base, from a range of settings including outpatient treatment clinics; social, vocational, and recreational centers; and privately run residences. The nature of interventions required during this phase will depend on progress in previous phases, premorbid functioning, current social setting, patient expectations, and community demands. Patients will have attained varying degrees of recovery at this stage.

A certain percentage of schizophrenic patients require continuing if not lifelong care. More will be learned about specific numbers and their implications over the next decade. Recovery rates have varied greatly and have no doubt been influenced by differing definitions and evaluation procedures and by the introduction of new treatment methodologies. Mayer-Gross (1932) described a 16-year follow-up study in which 33 percent of the patients achieved social recovery. Harris et al. (1956) found that 45 pc cent of patients in their study were socially independent and had few or no symptoms at five-year follow-up. Brown et al. (1966) described their study in which 56 percent of schizophrenic patients were leading independent lives without marked symptoms of schizophrenia at five-year follow-up. Estimates of the outcome of schizophrenia—relapse rates, need for continuing treatment, achievement of community tenure—are influenced by three factors.

Consistency of treatment programs. Only very recently have psychotropic medication and sociotherapy been applied with any degree of consistency and conviction. We cannot yet be certain of the long-term prognosis for patients treated with contemporary, extra-institutional methods.

Social and cultural context. Familial, social, and cultural realities influence the course of schizophrenia, making outcome standardization problematic. It is difficult to compare the prognosis for a schizophrenic in a small, stable African village with that for a patient in New York City. Sartorius, Jablensky, and Shapiro (1977) found that patients from developing countries achieved better outcomes than did those from developed parts of the world. This finding could not be accounted for simply by duration of illness before inclusion in the study; it may be related to the benefits of greater familial and community ties for patients in developing countries and very different social, vocational, and instrumental expectations.

What may be a satisfactory outcome in one culture may be unsatisfactory in another. An assessment of "full recovery without need for continuing care" will be influenced by prevalent cultural values. Is the once schizophrenic woman who slips into the role of "eccentric unmarried daughter living a reclusive life in the family home" fully recovered? One suspects that in some cultures this would be an acceptable outcome, while in others it would be labeled an inferior, if not abnormal, development.

Resources and economics. Assessment of continuing need for treatment and periodic hospitalization will be influenced by the availability of relevant services. An elderly man is discharged from the mental hospital, symptom-free, but friendless, isolated, and preoccupied with old grievances; is he recovered or should clinicians have higher aspirations for his health and welfare? The answer to this question is often determined by local resources and economics.

Until recently, scant attention has been paid to the needs of the chronic mental patient. The President's Commission on Mental Health (1978) noted that, "Despite progress, many persons who should have benefited from these [resource] changes still receive inadequate care. This is especially true of people with chronic mental illness." Even when proposals are developed for improving the care of people with chronic mental illness (e.g., the Joint Commission on Mental Illness and Health, 1961), policy recommendations may be ignored, resources allocated for implementing programs are inadequate, funds diminish over time, and professionals often shift their attention to more rewarding tasks. Work with the severely disabled carries little prestige in psychiatry and is often inherently frustrating and thankless. The particular skills required to do this kind of work effectively are only now being examined.

The extent to which the application of a comprehensive treatment and rehabilitation program as outlined in this book will prevent chronicity has yet to be tested. Many of the individual recommendations have been demonstrated to reduce distress, modify symptoms, prevent relapse, and improve community life. But economics and other realities will continue to inhibit the universal application of what knowledge we do possess. It is one thing to elaborate a treatment and rehabilitation model designed to promote maximal recovery. It is another to find the money and staff to carry it out and patients who will see it through. It is hoped that application of the principles outlined in previous chapters will reduce the number of schizophrenic patients who require intensive, chronic home care or rehospitalization and that comprehensive early treatment will make continuing care, for those who require it, a more efficient and effective process. Styles of care that may be required during the continuing care phase are differentiated according to two major patient groupings: the stable-adaptation group and the marginal-adaptation group.

Stable-Adaptation Group

Having passed through the five previous phases, some patients will have acquired or maintained an adult social and vocational structure and will have achieved a level of stable adaptation. Of these patients, a proportion will require long-term medication to remain symptom-free. Others of this group, while managing much of the time without any treatment, may periodically require medication and/or psychotherapy to assist them in weathering specific life changes or crises. These may include marriage, birth of a child, or death of a parent. Some patients attain a high level of independent functioning and do not require even periodic care.

Marginal-Adaptation Group

At the other end of the spectrum reside those patients who, in spite of hospitalizations, medication, psychotherapy, and social-vocational rehabilitation programs, are barely able to function in the community. Some will have alienated friends and family and be incapable of maintaining employment. Their residential placement is often tenuous; landlady and patient alike may require continuing professional support. Health and social services must often provide a surrogate social and kinship network for such individuals. These patients frequently display idiosyncratic behaviors and overt symptomatology requiring continuous psychosocial and medical interventions. Simple instrumental and social problems, such as a shortage of money or an argument with a housemate, may precipitate a demand for rehospitalization either directly from the patient or from a community caretaker.

A proportion of individuals from the "marginal-adaptation" category will function more adequately than the above description implies. Some will have attained a satisfactory degree of vocational functioning. Others can maintain a facsimile of an independent social network even though this may consist primarily of transients, psychiatric patients, or other fringe groups.

In general, the marginally adapted group of patients will, by definition, present more of a continuing-care problem. These people tend to be more dependent on social and health services, demand more of the service resources, and be more disorganized in utilization of services. Often, their only consistent health service contact is through the hospital emergency room.

Dominant Models

The medical model provides sanction for disability and continues to govern decisions regarding long-term and intermittent use of medication. The adaptational and developmental models assist in responding to life events and coping with stress. The social model is prominent in ensuring maintenance of a social support system (be it natural or constructed) and in guiding vocation-related interventions.

Tasks and Interventions

The following is a partial list of tasks appropriate to this phase:

Differentiate the needs of patients. Patients in continuing care no more constitute a homogeneous group than do schizophrenic individuals in initial phases of illness. The temptation to lump these patients together in maintenance or continuing-care clinics that prescribe limited and uniform treatment should be avoided. Rather, emphasis should be placed on identifying the different groups of patients within the continuing-care category according to shared needs, goals, and levels of functioning. This allows for better allocation of existing resources, more effective interventions, and avoidance of a generalized therapeutic nihilism.

Maintain contact; reach out. Often treatment during the continuing-care phase will entail reaching out to the marginally adapted who might otherwise be too anxious, too disorganized, or too reclusive to maintain follow-up. This will be especially true when follow-up moves from being a contact with one clinic to several contacts spread over various medical and social services. Patients will require extra support and direction through periods of transition or increased expectation.

Chronic patients do not generally choose conventional ways of conveying their need for special understanding and attention. Signals include, among others, missed clinic appointments, appearing at unscheduled times, overt displays of increased symptomatology and distress with therapist or significant others, and failure to appear at the rehabilitation workshop. There are a number of ways of responding to such cues: increasing home visits, arranging additional appointments, reassessing with the patient his or her current program, and making necessary adjustments.

Provide coordinated, community-based care. An organized range of primary services and consultative resources will facilitate community treatment of even marginally functioning individuals with a minimum of dependence on full hospitalization. To achieve this goal, the staff of mental health clinics must perform several functions beyond direct treatment. These functions are described below as five interrelated roles:

Coordinator of care. Continuity may be easily lost during continuing care. The more interventions and management are localized around, for example, hospital care, the easier it is to maintain continuity. But as the locus of treatment moves into the community and encompasses increasingly varied utilization of resources, the more concerted the effort must be to maintain coordination of the different aspects of patient management. Patient conferences, at which all providers are present, can be utilized to maintain clear demarcation of roles and to share goals of patient care. Whenever possible, patients should be included in these conferences. It is necessary to have one person assigned as primary caretaker or coordinator, and the total number of caregivers should be kept relatively small. Community services are seldom well coordinated. The role of coordinator often, by default, falls to the mental health clinic representative. Coordinated care plans, clearly communicated by the group to the patient, will reduce the patient's confusion (and that of the treatment team) and will increase the patient's capacity for understanding and utilizing the various services effectively.

At such conferences the specific roles and responsibilities of each participant should be overtly discussed, agreed upon, and committed to paper (minutes) and a method should be devised to ensure follow-through (e.g., repeat the conference in six months' time).

Supporter of existing community services. Many schizophrenic patients cannot be maintained in the community without the continuing support of a full range of psychiatric, social service, and residential resources. Health services are an additional service requirement of this group, as a disproportionate number of chronic psychiatric patients are known to experience major physical health problems.

Without adequate resources these patients find themselves in a constant state of crisis resulting in repeated hospitalizations, great personal distress, and social and economic cost to the community. Thus, continuing care clinicians must recognize the need to support and foster existing community services. This can be achieved formally by membership on boards of directors, participation in task forces and planning groups, supportive political action and by maintaining responsive working relationships with these agencies.

Consultant and/or liaison to community services. It has long been recommended that psychiatric professionals provide consultation to other mental health resources. This is difficult to achieve: When offered without invitation, it tends to be perceived as a rather arrogant, intrusive stance and often fails to accomplish much of durability. Territorial imperatives and professional rivalry sabotage many beneficient programs of mental health consultation.

A more productive approach is to establish liaisons or formal linkages with those other services of value to the clinic's population. This liaison relationship should be predicated on the basis of mutual benefit. Initially it can focus on information sharing (intake procedures, intake criteria, programs offered) and interface troubleshooting. Later it might develop into a streamlined referral route (both directions) for *appropriate* clients. It may remain at this level and simply provide a vehicle for efficient use of each participating service.

A formal liaison relationship may also provide the matrix of trust and knowledge necessary for the development of relevant consultation. This, too, can function in both directions: the psychiatric clinic may provide medical-psychiatric consultation to a social service; that service in return may provide, for example, budget counseling or life-skills consultation to the clinic. The two services might engage in joint educational ventures or workshops. All these activities enhance the clinic's ability to provide relevant direct care and ensure optimal use of other services.

In certain circumstances the liaison relationship may permit the clinic to go beyond patient-centered consultation to consultee-centered consultation and program consultation. It also provides very valuable information about personnel and policy change in other services, both of which often profoundly affect the behavior of schizophrenic patients. Services of high priority for the establishment of liaison relationships include inpatient units, emergency facilities, supervised boarding homes, family doctors, welfare services, vocational rehabilitation services, workshops, public health nursing, correctional services (probation), and social services (e.g., family service agency).

Advocate for less well-established services. The mental health clinic also serves an advocate function on behalf of less established services, such as group homes, drop-in centers, job-finding agencies, self-help groups, volunteer organizations, and recreation programs. These may operate on short-term funding and require support to ensure their economic and political survival. They are extremely important participants in the network that maintains chronically disabled people in the community. Usually, formal consultative relationships are inadvisable with these groups. Nonprofessionals lose some of their effectiveness when they adopt psychiatric jargon and mimic professional attitudes. Support and encouragement from professionals, though, often helps to keep them functioning effectively. Active liaison with formal services and support for informal services will aid in preventing the patient's community environment from becoming as institutionalized as a mental hospital back ward. Sheltered workshops and boarding or foster homes are particularly susceptible to running this less favorable course (Murphy, Pennee, and Luchins, 1972).

Often the mental health clinic or mental hospital will constitute the patient's major (and/or only) social support. When this is the case and alternatives cannot be arranged, the nature of this relationship should be acknowledged and formalized. Ongoing therapy-activity groups can be especially effective in fulfilling the social support function. Such programs may preclude a revolving-door syndrome of hospitalization. In most cases where a natural support system does not exist, the surrogate social network can be spread out and shared by clinic, rehabilitation workshop, or drop-in center.

Ensure provision and monitoring of medication. Patients who have achieved stable adaptation and require little care in addition to medication may fare best receiving their medication from their general practitioner. This system will reinforce progress made and reduce the negative social consequences of the chronic psychiatric patient role. The decision to discharge a patient from the mental health clinic to the care of the family doctor must be clearly negotiated among patient, therapist, and general practitioner. The mental health clinic may maintain an educational and consultative relationship with the family doctor, providing him or her with information regarding medication dosage, side-effects, drug holidays, and length of treatment.

For both patient and therapist, medications can serve as symbols of a controlling relationship. The patient may refuse medications or demand increases in medication as a means of expressing anxieties and demonstrating dependency conflicts. In turn, the therapist may prescribe or withhold medications as a means of demonstrating power. The following guidelines may assist the therapist in avoiding these particular problems:

Clearly explain and negotiate all medications, giving the patient control over his or her medication wherever possible.

Use the minimum required dosage to adequately control symptoms (reducing potential for side-effects and therapist-created discomfort).

Do not give landladies, workshop supervisors, or other non-health professionals responsibility for holding or dispensing the patient's medications unless absolutely necessary. To do so holds potential for recreating the regressive parent-child relationship of dysfunctional families and ineffective institutions.

When patients are receiving medication in addition to other treatments, such as group or individual therapy, they should be aware that where more than one therapist is involved, clear communication will exist within the team regarding all medication plans and changes.

Provide support and counseling for developmental passages, life events. This intervention may be the sole involvement with a relatively well adapted individual or may make up only one part of a much larger program.

Case Example

Tom, age 34, had been hospitalized on three occasions in his late teens and early twenties for acute psychotic episodes. The first hospitalization came shortly after Tom had left home for the first time and began studying at a university in a nearby town. Following his third admission to the hospital, his efforts to obtain a university degree were abandoned and he returned home to live with his parents and work at a job that had been arranged by his father.

He then managed from age 22 to age 30 without any psychiatric contact, taking regularly during this time a small dose of antipsychotic medication he received from his family doctor. During this almost eight-year period, Tom held a job as a salesman in a hardware store and met and married a young schoolteacher.

Together Tom and his wife established a small but consistent social network and purchased a modest home. Tom's parents maintained a dominant position in the young couple's life, visiting regularly and offering parental advice about their life-style. One theme that frequently came up in the larger family discussions was that of children, and when Tom was 29, Tom and Sue began to talk seriously about pregnancy. Tom felt somewhat insecure at the prospect; nevertheless his wife became pregnant. Around this same time, Tom's father developed serious heart problems and was forced to assume somewhat of an invalid's position, with his wife taking care of him. Through the course of the pregnancy, Tom's anxiety increased. He became unusually distracted, was unable to concentrate on his work, and eventually took to staying in bed all day long. At his wife's recommendation, he visited the family doctor for a little "chat," whereupon the family doctor apparently sympathized with him about the pressures of impending fatherhood, gave him a bit of a pep talk, and chided him to pull it together before the baby came because, "soon he would have two people to take care of."

Tom did not "pull it together." He remained in bed, his speech and thinking became increasingly disordered, and the day his wife was admitted to the hospital to deliver their son, Tom was admitted to the psychiatric ward of the same general hospital exhibiting fully developed symptoms of acute schizophrenia.

In retrospect it seems predictable that Tom might suffer a relapse at a point of developmental stress. Nonetheless, he had managed admirably for eight years, functioning much as would any man of his social background and age group. Everyone involved, Tom and his family doctor included, was surprised by the seemingly sudden recurrence of illness. However, the nine months preceding Tom's rehospitalization bore two changes that would have stressed most people: pregnancy and parental illness. Tom's early history indicates difficulties responding to developmental passages and life changes. It is perhaps most interesting that he did not become ill when he took his first position of employment or formed a relationship with his wife. It must be assumed that these encounters entailed limited role change in comparison to the rather major changes brought about by the combined impact of his wife's changing physiology and his father's illness.

The fact that Tom and his family had never fully acknowledged the seriousness of his earlier illness contributed to their lack of preparedness for what happened. Had the illness been better understood and accepted by the family, steps could have been taken at several points throughout the eight years to equip Tom for taking on new roles and tasks and anticipating stressful events. Life-problem counseling could have been provided by the family doctor, supporting Tom's relatively stable adaptation and "normal" functioning. While such education and counseling cannot ensure prevention of recurrence of all symptoms, it can reduce the likelihood of complete breakdown.

Focus on issues. At the continuing care stage in patient management, an exacerbation of symptoms can be considered in the context of life relationships, changing environments, and other stresses. It may be most helpful to focus on the issues rather than the symptoms, provided that the therapist has an established relationship with the patient and a knowledge of his or her background. By this phase symptoms may have become secondary phenomena, having gained currency as a way of communicating nonspecific distress. It will be more helpful to assist the patient in clarifying the source of the stress than to focus on overt symptoms. Reinforcement of a sense of competence and ability to master situations will emphasize the patient's healthy side.

Maintain an emphasis on normalization. As described earlier, persons who have been assigned the label of "patient," especially "mental patient," need an opportunity to regain a less spoiled sense of themselves as regular community residents. Individuals who, over long periods of time, regularly or periodically require assistance from mental health services need ongoing help to keep a reasonable perspective on their illness and their patient status. Steps should be taken to return individuals to the care of general practitioners and other primary community service delivery systems where possible. Psychiatric consultation can serve as a secondary resource to these services.

While a certain amount of normalization can be carried out by mental health personnel, there is a message in the very context of the service. When the patient relies heavily on the role of mental patient and derives identity and status from his or her madness, a more complete program of de-psychiatrization is in order. As much of this patient's care as possible should be given over to nonpsychiatric services.

Periodically reassess goals (including an evaluation of whether to continue or terminate professional involvement). Throughout all phases of treatment, the therapist is faced with the dilemma of deciding what consitutes realistic patient expectations. While the danger in earlier phases of treatment generally lies in the direction of pushing the patient too far too soon, the opposite is often true in continuing care. By this stage, patient and therapist have often developed a routine format for their interactions. Once the turbulence and uncertainty associated with the psychosis and initial recovery have subsided, everyone—the therapist and patient included—may feel like leaving well enough alone and may unnecessarily limit expectations for future accomplishments. Or, they may prefer to defer discussions of new goals to some undefined later date. This situation is especially likely to arise if the patient is exhibiting the characteristics of the poverty syndrome described earlier.

Regular reassessment of the patient's ambitions, current level of functioning, and potential capabilities must be built into any continuing-care program. The individual's residential and social setting should be as autonomy-engendering as possible, and in the words of Lamb et al. (1976), "The degree of envelopment should be the lowest required."

In spite of varied and concerted efforts at treatment and rehabilitation, some patients show no improvement over a long period of time. Although maintaining an optimistic and hope-engendering stance is taught as the mainstay of the therapeutic alliance, it is difficult for any therapist not to respond to a chronic poverty syndrome by losing faith and essentially giving up. The clinician might even come to view further rehabilitation efforts as useless and the patient's position as intractable. When the therapist feels that treatment is moving in the direction of diminishing returns, it is imperative that it be acknowledged to oneself and one's supervisor. Sometimes reassessment of patient goals will need to include consideration of the usefulness of continuing professional care. Not only is continuing to provide expensive, ineffective treatment impractical, it can also have negative effects on patients and therapists. Both may become discouraged by unrealistic expectations and concomitant continuing failure. Most chronic care clinicians have had a taste of the despair that engulfs these "treatment failures" as they move from one program to another, knowing they are not succeeding at any. The pressure to "make it" builds, while sense of worth diminishes. The process of deciding to reduce, alter, or stop professional intervention must include a full appraisal of the treatment to date and involvement of the patient and all members of the treatment team, including community service workers. If psychiatry clinic contact is required to sustain or back-up the involvement of other community services, it must be continued, though perhaps reduced in time and intensity. Here the role of the mental health worker may become simply that of coordinator and symptom monitor.

Another useful response to therapist burn-out is for another clinic worker to take over the continuing care. Each therapist works more successfully with some patients than with others. A change of therapist may provide the needed impetus for further gains.

If the decision is made to terminate active treatment, this should be transacted with the patient so as to maintain dignity and reinforce the patient's strengths and alternate plans. Failure should be de-emphasized. Generally this negotiation will take several sessions to accomplish. Termination may be gradual, reducing appointments from weekly to monthly to six-month intervals. It should be carried out in a manner that will facilitate later contact, if it becomes necessary.

Special Problems and Issues

Rehospitalization

The focus throughout this book has been on a positive approach to treatment and planning, on a rational approach to the understanding and evaluation of symptoms, and on working to maintain individuals with schizophrenia in the community within as normal and healthy a context as possible. The framework presented here describes four models for guiding interventions throughout the phases of the illness. While this approach implies a continuum of treatment from the hospital, in the initial phases, to the community, in latter phases, it is not meant to suggest that there is not a backward and forward movement at times. Many of the situations that can lead to unnecessary hospitalizations, such as the patient running out of funds or being evicted from a boarding home, can be anticipated and worked through in other ways. While it is assumed that, where possible, individuals should be maintained and treated in the community, there are clearly times when hospitalization is appropriate.

Generally, hospitalization serves to benefit any combination of the patient, the family, the therapist, and the community. The patient may experience an exacerbation of symptoms that will benefit from the structure and controls of a well-timed, well-negotiated and short-term hospital admission. Or a patient may escalate demands and threats of breakdown at a time when the therapist has lowered personal resources (e.g., illness in the family). Hospitalization here may serve first to give the therapist a rest and only indirectly benefit the patient. This needn't be harmful to the patient if kept short and the therapeutic alliance very quickly reestablished. On occasion hospitalization is necessary to demonstrate responsiveness to landladies and families and to give them a brief respite from the patient's behavior. In this case, short-term gains are sacrificed to the more important long-term tenure in the community. The landlady is much more likely to take the patient back if the mental health clinic has been responsive to her distress.

Case Example

For two months a landlady has had in her boarding home a young man who is somewhat eccentric in behavior and disturbing to both the other residents and herself. Yet she has developed a way of interacting with him that makes him fairly manageable, and with the support of the therapist has agreed to let him stay on. One particular Friday, however, the landlady gets sick and goes to stay with her brother, leaving her husband to manage the boarding home. Her husband calls the therapist saying that the young man is acting strangely, bothering other residents, and that he, the husband, doesn't know what to do. Knowing that a weekend without clinic staff lies ahead and anticipating that husband, patient, and other residents will be upset with the landlady away, the therapist visits the boarding home, speaks with her patient, and decides that a short-term hospital stay will preserve the patient's position in the boarding home and relieve the concern of the husband and other residents.

When a patient is to be rehospitalized, several guidelines should be followed:

> The hospitalization should be discussed with the patient beforehand with an emphasis on supporting the patient's strengths and gains and not depicting this event as a major step backward.

> During hospitalization the patient should be allowed to maintain as many of his or her normal roles and functions as possible, with a minimum of regression and institutionalization taking place.

> All steps should be taken to preserve the patient's social, vocational, and residential ties in the community.

> The hospital stay should be as short as possible.

The decision to rehospitalize should be made with thoughtful assessment of the patient's overall circumstances and consideration of both long-term and short-term effects.

REFERENCES

Introduction

Battie, W. *A treatise on madness*. New York: Brunner/Mazel, 1969. (originally published, 1758.)

Berger, P. L., & Luckmann, T. *The social construction of reality: A treatise on the sociology of knowledge*. New York: Anchor Books, 1967.

Caplan, R. B. *Psychiatry and the community in nineteenth century America*. New York: Basic Books, 1969.

Jaspers, K. *General psychopathology*. Chicago: University of Chicago Press, 1963.

Rothman, D. J. *The discovery of the asylum: Social order and disorder in the new reublic*. Boston: Little, Brown, 1971.

van Praag, H. M. *WHO international pilot study of schizophrenia: A multinational study, initial evaluation phase*. Summary (Public Health Paper, No. 63), World Health Organization, 1975.

van Praag, H. M. Impossible concept of schizophrenia. *Comprehensive Psychiatry*, 1976, *17*;481-497.

Wing, J. K. *Reasoning about madness*. Oxford: Oxford University Press, 1978.

Chapter 1

Argyle, M. Non-verbal communication in human social interaction. In R. A. Hinde (Ed.), *Non-verbal communication*. Cambridge, England: Cambridge University Press, 1972.

Bleuler, E. *Dementia praecox or the group of schizophrenias*. New York: International Universities Press, 1950.

Cameron, N. Reasoning, regression and communication in schizophrenics. *Psychological Monographs*, 1938, *50* (1).

Cameron, N. Experimental analysis of schizophrenic thinking. In J. S. Kasanin (Ed.), *Language and thought in schizophrenia*. New York: Norton, 1964.

Chapman, L. J., & Chapman, J. P. *Disordered thought in schizophrenia. In K. MacCorquodale, G. Lindzey, & K. E. Clark (Eds.), Century Psychology Series*. Englewood Cliffs, NJ: Prentice-Hall, 1973.

Cohen, B. D. Referent communication disturbances in schizophrenia. In S. Schwartz (Ed.), *Language and cognition in schizophrenia*. New York: Halsted Press, 1978.

Cohen, B. D., & Camhi, J., Schizophrenic performance in word-communication task. *Journal of Abnormal Psychology*, 1967, *72*, 240-246.

Cohen, B. D., Nachmani, G. & Rosenberg, S. Referent communication disturbances in acute schizophrenia. *Journal of Abnormal Psychology*, 1974, *83*, 1-13.

Cromwell, R. L. Assessment of schizophrenia. *Annual Review of Psychology*, 1975, *26*, 593-619.

Epstein, S. Overinclusive thinking in a schizophrenic and a control group. *Journal of Consulting Psychiatry*, 1953, *17*, 384-388.

Flavell, J. H. *The Development of role-taking and communication skills in children*. Huntington, NY: Krieger, 1975.

Goffman, E. *The presentation of self in everyday life*. New York: Doubleday, 1959.

Goffman, E. *Interaction ritual: Essays on face-to-face behavior*. Garden City, NY: Doubleday, 1967.

Gregory, M., & Carroll S. *Language and situation*. London: Routledge and Kegan, 1978.

Haley, J. *Strategies of psychotherapy*. New York: Grune & Stratton, 1963.

Halliday, M. A. K. *Explorations in the function of language*. London: Edward Arnold, 1973.

Kleist, K. Aphasie und Geisteskrankheit. *Munich med. Wschr.*, 1914, *61* (8).

Kraepelin, E. *Dementia praecox and paraphrenia*. R. M. Barclay (Trans.) Edinburgh: E. & S. Livingstone, 1919.

Lisman, S. A., & Cohen, B. D. Self-editing deficits in schizophrenia: A word-association analogue. *Journal of Abnormal Psychology*, 1972, *79*, 181-188.

Lyons, J. Human language. In Hinde, R.A. (Ed.), *Non-verbal communication*. Cambridge: Cambridge University Press, 1972.

Maher, B. (Ed.) *Contributions to the psychopathology of schizophrenia*. New York: Academic Press, 1977.

Merton, R. K. *Social theory and social structure*. New York: Free Press, 1968.

Parsons, T. *The social system*. Glencoe, ILL: Free Press, 1951.

Payne, R. W. An object classification test as a measure of overinclusive thinking in schizophrenic patients. *British Journal of Clinical Psychology*, 1962, *1*, 313-321.

Piaget, J. *The psychology of intelligence*. New York: Harcourt, Brace, 1950.

Rochester, S. R., Harris, J. & Seeman, M. Sentence processing of schizophrenic listeners. *Journal of Abnormal Psychology*, 1978, *82*, 350-356.

Rochester, S. R., Martin, J. & Thurston, S. Thought process disorder in schizophrenia: The listener's task. *Brain and Language*, 1977, *4*, 95-114.

Schneider, C. *Die Psychologie der Schizophrenen*. Liepsig: Thieme, 1930.

Shakow, D. Psychological deficit in schizophrenia. *Behavioral Sciences*, 1963, *8*, 275-305.

Sullivan, H. S. *Schizophrenia as a human process*. New York: Norton, 1962.

Turner, R. H. Role-taking: Process versus conformity. In A. Rose (Ed.), *Human behavior and social processes*. Boston: Houghton Mifflin, 1962.

Chapter 2

Arieti, S. Psychotherapy of schizophrenia. In L. J. West & D. E. Flinn (Eds.), *Treatment of schizophrenia: Progress and prospects*. New York: Grune & Stratton, 1976.

Bland, R. C. Demographic Aspects of Functional Psychoses in Canada. *Acta Psychiatrica Scandinavia*, 1977, *55*, 369-380.

Bowers, M. B. *Retreat from sanity—The structure of emerging psychosis*. New York: Human Sciences Press, 1974.

Clark, D. H. *Social therapy in psychiatry*. London: Penguin Books, 1974.

Docherty, J. P., Van Kammen, D. P., Siris, S. G., & Marder, S. R., Stages of onset of schizophrenic psychosis. *American Journal of Psychiatry*, 1978, *135*(4), 420-426.

Gruenberg, E. M. The social breakdown syndrome—Some origins. *American Journal of Psychiatry*, 1967, *123*, 1481-1489.

Horowitz, M. J. A cognitive model of hallucinations. *American Journal of Psychiatry*, 1975, *132* (8), 789-795.

Kubie, L. The relation of psychotic disorganization to the neurotic process. *Journal of the American Psychoanalytic Association*, 1967, *15*, 626-640.

Laing, R. D., & Esterson, A. *Sanity, madness, and the family*. Harmondsworth, Middlesex: Penguin, 1970.

Lehmann, H. Schizophrenia: Clinical features. In A. Freedman, H. Kaplan, & B. Sadock, (Eds.), *Comprehensive textbook of psychiatry*. Baltimore: Williams and Wilkins, 1975.

Myers, D. H. Prognosis of schizophrenia. *British Journal of Hospital Medicine*, November 1978, *20*, 516-523.

Orford, J. *The social psychology of mental disorder*. New York: Penguin Books, 1976.

Pasamanick, B., et al. *Schizophrenics in the community: An experimental study in the prevention of hospitalization*. New York: Irvington, 1967.

Paul, G. Chronic mental patient: Current status—future directions. *Psychology Bulletin*, February 1969, *71*.

Phillips, E. L. *The social skills basis of psychopathology*. New York: Grune & Stratton, 1978.

Phillips, L. Case history data and prognosis in schizophrenia. *Journal of Nervous and Mental Disorders*, 1963, *117*, 515-525.

Semrad, E. V. Long-term therapy of schizophrenia. In Usdin (Ed.), *Psychoneurosis and schizophrenia*. Philadelphia: Lippincott, 1966.

Strauss, J., Bolkes, R., & Carpenter W. The course of schizophrenia as a developmental process. In L. C. Wynne, et al. (Eds.), *Nature of schizophrenia: New findings and future strategies*. New York: Wiley, 1978a.

Strauss, J. S., & Carpenter, W. T. Prediction of outcome in schizophrenia. *Archives of General Psychiatry*, 1977, *34*(a), 159-163.

Strauss, J. S., & Carpenter, W. T., Prognosis of schizophrenia: Rationale for multidimensional concept. *Schizophrenia Bulletin*, 1978, *4*, 56-67.

Vonnegut, M. *Eden Express*. New York: Bantam Books, 1976.

Wing, J. *Schizophrenia: Towards a synthesis*. London & New York: Academic Press, 1978.

Wittman, P. Scale for measuring prognosis in schizophrenic patients. *Elgin State Hospital Papers*, 1941, *4*, 20-33.

Chapter 3

Cumming, E. & Cumming, J. *Closed ranks: An experiment in mental health education*. Cambridge, Mass.: Harvard University Press, 1957.

Deutsch, M., & Kraus, R. M. *Theories in social psychiatry*. New York: Basic Books, 1965.

Dohrenwend, B., & Dohrenwend, B., *Stressful life events: Their nature and effects*. New York: Wiley, 1974.

Goffman, E. *The presentation of self in everyday life*. New York: Doubleday, 1959.

Hollingshead, A. B., & Redlich, F. C., *Social class and mental illness*. New York: Wiley, 1958.

Mead, G. H. *Mind, self and society*. C. W. Morris (Ed.), Chicago: University of Chicago Press, 1935.

Mechanic, D. Some factors in identifying and defining mental illness. In T. J. Scheff (Ed.), *Mental illness and social process*. New York: Harper & Row, 1967.

Mechanic, D., & Volkart, E. H., Stress, illness behavior and the sick role. *American Sociological Review*, 1961, *26*, 51-58.

Merton, R. K. *Social theory and social structure*. New York: Free Press, 1968.

Spitzer, S. P., & Denzin, N. K. (Eds.), *The mental patient: studies in the sociology of deviance*. New York: McGraw-Hill, 1968.

Wynne, L. C., Ryckoff, I. M., & Day, J., Pseudomutuality in the family relations of schizophrenics. *Psychiatry*, 1958, *21*, 205-220.

Chapter 4

Bowers, M.B. *Retreat from sanity: The structure of emerging psychosis*. New York: Human Sciences Press, 1974.

Geller, M. P. Sociopathic adaptations in psychotic patients. *Hospital and Community Psychiatry*, 1980, *31*(2), 108-112.

Goffman, E. *The presentation of self in everyday life*. New York: Doubleday, 1959.

Gruenberg, E. M. The social breakdown syndrome—Some origins. *American Journal of Psychiatry*, 1967, *123*, 1481-1489.

Illich, I. *Medical nemesis*. London: Calder & Bayers, 1975.

Kubie, L. The relation of psychotic disorganization to the neurotic process. *Journal of the American Psychoanalytic Association*, 1967, *15*, 626-640.

Levinson, D. J., et al. *The seasons of a man's life*. New York: Ballantine Books, 1979.

Munsinger, H. *The fundamentals of child development*. New York: Holt, 1971.

Parsons, T. *The social system*, Glencoe, ILL: Free Press, 1951.

Rosenham, D. L. Being sane in insane places. *Science*, January 1973, *179*, 250-258.

Scheff, T. Negotiating reality: Notes on power in the assessment of responsibility. *Social Problems*, Summer 1968, *16*(1), 3-17.

Semrad, E. V. Long-term therapy of schizophrenia. In Usdin (Ed.), *Psychoneurosis and schizophrenia*. Philadelphia: Lippincott, 1966.

Spitzer, S., & Denzin, K. *The mental patient: studies in the sociology of deviance*. New York: McGraw-Hill, 1968.

Szasz, T. *The Myth of Mental Illness*. New York: Harper & Row, 1974.

Turner, R. H. Role-taking: Process versus conformity. In A. Rose (Ed.), *Human behavior and social processes*. Boston: Houghton Mifflin, 1962.

Wallace, C. J., et al. A review and critique of social skills training with schizophrenic patients. *Schizophrenia Bulletin*, 1980, *6*, 64-69.

Will, O. Individual psychotherapy of schizophrenia. In R. Cancro (Ed.), *Strategic interventions in schizophrenia: Current developments and treatment*. New York: Human Sciences Press, 1974.

Wing, J. K. Institutionalism in mental hospitals. *British Journal of Social and Clinical Psychology*, 1962, *1*, 38-51.

Chapter 5

Bernstein, N. R. Chronic illness and impairment. *Psychiatric Clinics of North America*, Symposium presented on Liaison Psychiatry, 1979, *2*, (2), 331.

Docherty, J. P., et al. Stages of onset of schizophrenic psychosis. *American Journal of Psychiatry*, 1978, *135* (4), 420-426.

Donlon, P., & Blacker, K., Stages of schizophrenic decompensation and reintegration. *Journal of Nervous and Mental Disorders*, 1973, *157*, 200-209.

Jeffries, J. J. The trauma of being psychotic. *Canadian Psychiatric Association Journal*, 1977, *22*(5), 199-206.

Kimball, C. P. (Ed.) *Psychiatric Clinics of North America*, 1979 *2* (2), 307.

Laing, R. D. *The divided self*. New York: Penguin Books, 1965.

Laing, R. D. *The politics of experience and the bird of paradise*. New York: Penguin Books, 1967.

Levy, S. T., et al. Integration and sealing over as recovery styles from acute psychosis: Metapsychological and dynamic concepts. *Journal of Nervous and Mental Disorders*, 1975, *161*, 307-312.

Mayer-Gross, W. Uber Die Sellungrahme Zur Abgelanfen Akuten Psychose. *Z. Ges Neurol Psychiat.*, 1920, *60*.

McGlashan, T. H., Docherty, J. P., & Siris, S., Integrative and sealing-over recoveries from schizophrenia: Distinguishing case studies. *Psychiatry*, November 1976, *39*, 325-338.

McGlashan, T. H., Levy, S. T., & Carpenter, W. T., Integration and sealing over: Clinically distinct recovery styles from schizophrenia. *Archives of General Psychiatry*, October 1975, *32*, 1269-1272.

Murphy, J. M. Psychiatric labelling in cross-cultural perspective. *Science*, March 12, 1976, *191*, 1019-1028.

Rosenham, D. L. Being sane in insane places. *Science*, January 1973, *179*, 250-258.

Scheff, T. Cultural stereotypes and mental illness. *Sociometry*, 1963, *26*, 438-452.

Scheff, T. *Being mentally ill—A sociological theory*. Chicago: Aldine, 1966.

Scheff, T. *Mental illness and social processes*. New York: Harper & Row, 1967.

Schmale, A. H. Reactions to illness: Convalescence and grieving. *Psychiatric Clinics of North America*, Symposium presented on Liaison Psychiatry. 1979, *2*(2), 321.

Semrad, E., & Zaslow, S. Assisting psychiatric patients to recompensate. *Mental Hospital*, 1964, *15*.

Chapter 6

Frank, J. Therapeutic factors in psychotherapy. *American Journal of Psychotherapy*, 1971, *25*, 350-361.

Greben, S. On being therapeutic. *Canadian Psychiatric Association Journal*, November 1977, *22*(7), 371-380.

Gunderson, J. G. Drugs and psychosocial treatment of schizophrenia revisited. *Journal of Continuing Education in Psychiatry*, December 1977, 15-17.

Havens, L. L. *Approaches to the mind*. Boston: Little, Brown, 1973.

Hogarty, G., Goldberg, S. C., & Schooler, N. R., Drug and sociotherapy in the aftercare of schizophrenic patients. *Archives of General Psychiatry*, 1974, *31*, 54-64.

Marmor, J. Common operational factors in diverse approaches to behaviour change. In A. Burton (Ed.), *What makes behaviour change possible?* New York: Brunner/Mazel, 1976.

May, P. R. A. When, what and why? Psychopharmacotherapy and other treatments in schizophrenia. *Comprehensive Psychiatry*, 1976a, *17*, 683-693.

May, P. R. A. The implications of psychopharmacological research for the treatment of schizophrenia. In L. West & D. Flinn (Eds.), *Treatment of schizophrenia: Progress and prospects*. New York: Grune & Stratton, 1976b.

Mosher, L. R., & Keith, S. J. Psychosocial treatment: Individual, group, family and community support approaches. *Schizophrenia Bulletin*, 1980, *6*(1), 10-41.

Pasamanick, B., et al. *Schizophrenics in the community: An experimental study in the prevention of hospitalization*. New York: Irvington, 1967.

Seeman, M. V., & Cole, H. J. The effect of increasing personal contact in schizophrenia. *Comprehensive Psychiatry*, 1977, *18*(3), 283-293.

Stein, L. I., & Test, M. A., Alternative to mental hospital treatment: I. Conceptual model, treatment program and clinical evaluation. *Archives of General Psychiatry*, 1980, *37*(4), 392-397.

Stein, L. I., Test, M. A. & Marx, A. J. Alternative to hospital: A controlled study. *American Journal of Psychiatry*, 1975, *132*(5), 517-522.

Strupp, H. H., & Hadley, S. W., Specific vs. non-specific factors in psychotherapy. *Archives of General Psychiatry*, 1979, *36*(10), 1125-1136.

Chapter 7

Arieti, S. *Interpretation of schizophrenia*. New York: Brunner, 1955.

Bartolucci, G., Goodman, J. T., & Streiner, D. L. Emergency psychiatric admission to the general hospital. *Canadian Psychiatric Association Journal*, 1975, *20*, 567-565.

Burnham, D. L., Gladstone, A. I. & Gibson, R. W. *Schizophrenia and the need-fear dilemma*. New York: International Universities Press, 1969.

Chodoff, P. The case for involuntary hospitalization of the mentally ill. *American Journal of Psychiatry*, 1976, *133*(5), 497-501.

Ennis, B., & Siegel, L. *The rights of mental patients*. New York: Avon, 1973.

Festinger, L. *A theory of cognitive dissonance*. Evanston, ILL: Row Peterson, 1957.

Fromm-Reichmann, F. Some aspects of psychoanalytic psychotherapy with schizophrenics. In Brodie, E. B., & Redlich, F. C. (Eds.), *Psychotherapy with schizophrenics*. New York: International Universities Press, 1952.

Goffman, E. *Asylums: Essays on the social situation of mental patients and other inmates*. New York: Aldine, 1961.

Goffman, E. *Behavior in public places*. New York: Free Press, 1963.

Hansell, N. *The person in distress: Biosocial dynamics of adaptation*. New York: Human Sciences Press, 1976.

Hill, L. B. *Psychotherapeutic intervention in schizophrenia*. Chicago: University of Chicago Press, 1955.

Horowitz, M. Stress response syndromes: Character style and dynamic psychotherapy. *Archives of General Psychiatry*, December 1974, *31*, 768-781.

Kittrie, N. *The right to be different: Deviance and enforced therapy*. Baltimore: Johns Hopkins University Press, 1972.

Laing, R. D. *Sanity, madness and the family*. Harmondsworth, Middlesex: Pelican Books, 1964.

Mishler, E. G., & Waxler, N. E. *Interaction in families: An experimenal study of family processes and schizophrenia*. New York: Wiley, 1968.

Rosen, J. H. *Direct psychoanalytic psychiatry*. New York: Grune & Stratton, 1962.

Roth, L. H. A commitment law for patients, doctors and lawyers. *American Journal of Psychiatry*, 1979, *136*(9), 1121-1127.

Searles, H. *Collected papers on schizophrenia and related subjects*. New York: International Universities Press, 1965.

Stein, L. I., & Test, M. A., Alternative to mental hospital treatment: I. Conceptual model, treatment program and clinical evaluation. *Archives of General Psychiatry*, 1980, *37*(4), 392-397.

Stein, L. I., Test, M. A., & Marx, A. J. Alternative to hospital: A controlled study. *American Journal of Psychiatry*, 1975, *132*(5), 517-522.

Sullivan, H. S. *Schizophrenia as a human process*. New York: Norton, 1962.

Will, O. Individual psychotherapy of schizophrenia. In R. Cancro (Ed.), *Strategic interventions in schizophrenia: Current developments and treatment*. New York: Human Sciences Press, 1974.

Wing, J. K. *Reasoning about madness*. Oxford: Oxford University Press, 1978.

Chapter 8

Arieti, S. *Interpretation of schizophrenia*. New York: Brunner/Mazel, 1955.

Fenton, F. Tessier, L., & Struening, E. A comparative trial of home and hospital psychiatric care: One year follow-up. *Archives of General Psychiatry*, 1979, *36*(9), 1073-1079.

Lerner, Y., et al. Acute high dose parenteral haloperidol treatment of psychosis. *American Journal of Psychiatry, 197, 136*(8), 1061-1064.
Marder, S., et al. Predicting drug-free improvement in schizophrenic psychosis. *Archives of General Psychiatry*, 1979, *36*(9), 1080-1085.
Pasamanick, B., et al. *Schizophrenics in the community: An experimental study in the prevention of hospitalization.* New York: Irvington, 1967.
Stanton, A. H., & Schwartz, M. S., *The mental hospital.* New York: Basic Books, 1954.
Stein, L. I., & Test, M. A., Alternative to mental hospital treatment. I. Conceptual model, treatment program, and clinical evaluation. *Archives of General Psychiatry*, 1980, *37*(4) 409-412.
Stein, L. I., Test, M. A., & Marx, A. J., Alternative to the hospital: A controlled study. *American Journal of Psychiatry*, 1975, *132*(5), 517-522.

Chapter 9

Beisser, A. Denial and affirmation in illness and health. *American Journal of Psychiatry*, 1979, *136*(8), 1026-1030.
Donlon, P. T., Rada, R. T., & Arora, K. K. Depression and the reintegration phase of acute schizophrenia. *American Journal of Psychiatry*, 1976, *133*(11), 1265-1268.
Jeffries, J. J. The trauma of being psychotic. *Canadian Psychiatric Association Journal*, 1977, *22*(5), 199-206.
Lindner, R. *The fifty-minute hour.* New York: Bantam, 1976.
Mayer-Gross, W. Uber Die Sellungrahme Zur Abgelanfen Akuten Psychose. Z. Ges Neurol Psychiat, 1920, *60*.
McGlashan, T., Levy, H. S. T., & Carpenter, W. T. Integration and sealing over: Clinically distinct recovery styles from schizophrenia. *Archives of General Psychiatry*, 1975, *32*(10), 1269-1272.
Rada, R. T., & Donlon, P. T. Depression and the acute schizophrenic process. *Psychosomatics*, 1975, *XVI*, 116-119.
Rado, S. Schizotypal organization: Preliminary report on a clinical study of schizophrenia. In *Psychoanalysis of Behavior*, Volume 2, Part I. New York: Grune & Stratton, 1962.
Siris, S. G., Van Kammen, D. P., & Docherty, J., Use of antidepressant drugs in schizophrenia. *Archives of General Psychiatry*, 1978, *35*(11), 1368-1375.
Test, M. A. & Stein, L. I., Alternative to Mental hospital treatment: III. Social Cost. *Archives of General Psychiatry*, 1980, *37*(4) 409-412.
Van Putten, T., & May, P. R. A., "Akinetic depression" in schizophrenia. *Archives of General Psychiatry*, 1978, *35*(9), 1101-1107.
Wing, J. K. Impairments in schizophrenia: A rational basis for social treatment. In R. D. Wirt, G. Winokur & M. Roff (Eds.), *Life history research in psychopathology*, Volume 4. Minneapolis: University of Minnesota Press, 1975.
Wing, J. K. The social context of schizophrenia. *American Journal of Psychiatry*, 1978, *135*(10), 1169-1177.

Chapter 10

Amdur, M. A. Medication compliance in outpatient psychiatry. *Comprehensive Psychiatry*, 1979, *20*(4), 339-346.
Brown, G. W., Birley, J. L. T., & Wing, J. K., Influence of family life on the course of schizophrenic disorders: A replication. *British Journal of Psychiatry*, 1972, *121*, 241-258.

Chapman, J. The early symptoms of schizophrenia. *British Journal of Psychiatry*, 1966, *112*, 225-251.

Cumming, E. & Cumming, J. *Closed ranks: An experiment in mental health education.* Cambridge, Mass.: Harvard University Press, 1957.

Freidson, E. The social meanings of illness. In *Profession of Medicine*. New York: Dodd, Mead, 1970.

Goffman, E. *Behavior in public places.* New York: Free Press, 1963.

Gunderson, J. G. Drugs and psychosocial treatment of schizophrenia revisited. *Journal of Continuing Education in Psychiatry*, December 1977, 15-17.

Lamb, H. H. Rehabilitation in community mental health: A recent review of the literature. *Community Mental Health Review*, 1977, *2*(4), 1-8.

Rada, R. T., Daniels, R. S., & Draper, E., An outpatient setting for treating chronically ill psychiatric patients. *American Journal of Psychiatry*, 1969, *126*, 789-795.

Scheff, T. Negotiating reality: Notes on power in the assessment of responsibility. *Social Problems*, 1968, *16*(1), 3-17.

Serban, G. C., Gidynski, G., & Zimmerman, A., Informants' post-discharge expectations of the schizophrenic's community adjustment. *Psychiatry Digest*, September 1976, 15-17.

Van Putten, T., Crumpton, E., & Yale, C. Drug refusal in schizophrenia and the wish to be crazy. *Archives of General Psychiatry*, 1976, *33*(12), 751-753.

Van Putten, T. Drug refusal in schizophrenia: Causes and prescribing hints. *Hospital and Community Psychiatry*, 1978, *29*(2), 110-112.

Wing, J. K. The social context of schizophrenia. *American Journal of Psychiatry*, 1978, *135*, 1169-1177.

Chapter 11

Arieti, S. Psychotherapy of schizophrenia. In L. J. West & D. E. Flinn (Eds.), *Treatment of schizophrenia: Progress and prospects.* New York: Grune & Stratton, 1976.

Levinson, D. J. *The seasons of a man's life.* Maryland: Ballantine Books, 1978.

Shakow, D. Psychological deficit in schizophrenia. *Behavioural Sciences*, 1963, *8*, 275-305.

Vaillant, G. E., & McArthur, C. C. Natural history of male psychological health. *Seminars of Psychiatry*, 1972, *4*, 415.

Wallace, C. J., et al. A review and critique of social skills training with schizophrenic patients. *Schizophrenia Bulletin*, 1980, *6*(1), 64-69.

Wing, J. K. *Schizophrenia: Towards a synthesis.* New York: Grune & Stratton, 1978.

Chapter 12

Brown, G. W., et al. *Schizophrenia and social care.* London: Oxford University Press, 1966.

Cogswell, B. E., & Weir, D. D. A role in process: The development of medical professionals' role in long-term care of chronically diseased patients. *Journal of Health and Human Behavior, 1966, 7.*

Commission on Chronic Illness. *Prevention of chronic illness.* Cambridge, Mass.: Harvard University Press, 1957.

Harris, A., et al. Schizophrenia: A social and prognostic study. *British Journal of Preventive Social Medicine*, 1956, *10*, 107-114.

Joint Commission on Mental Illness and Health. *Action for mental health*. New York: Basic Books, 1961.

Lamb, H. R. et al. *Community survival for long-term patients*. San Francisco: Jossey-Bass, 1976.

Mayer-Gross, W. Die Schizophrenie. In *Handbuch der Geisteskrankheiten*. Berlin: ed. Springer, 1932.

Murphy, H. B., Pennee, B., & Luchins, D., Foster homes: The new back wards? *Canada's Mental Health Supplement,* September/October 1972, *20*(71).

President's Commission on Mental Health, *Report*, Volume I. Washington, D.C.: U. S. Government Printing Office, 1978.

Sartorius, N., Jablensky, A., & Shapiro, R. Two year follow-up of the patients included in the WHO international pilot study of schizophrenia. *Psychological Medicine,* August 1977, *7*, 529-541.

SELECTED BIBLIOGRAPHY

Family Studies and Family Therapy

Bateson, A., Jackson, D. D., Haley, J., & Weakland, J. Toward a theory of schizophrenia. *Behavioral Science,* 1956, *1,* 251-264.

Beels, C. C. Family and social management of schizophrenia. *Schizophrenia Bulletin,* Summer 1975, (13).

Cheek, F. E. The father of the schizophrenic: The function of a peripheral role. *Archives of General Psychiatry,* 1965, *13,* 336-346.

Jones, J. E., Rodnick, E. H., Goldstein, M. J., McPherson, S. R., & West, K. L. Parental transactional style deviance as a possible indicator of risk for schizophrenia. *Archives of General Psychiatry,* 1977, *34*(1), 71-74.

Kohn, M. L. The family and schizophrenia. *American Journal of Psychiatry,* 1976, *133*(2).

Leff, J. P. Schizophrenia and sensitivity to the family environment. *Schizophrenia Bulletin,* 1976, *2,* 566-574.

Lennard, H. L., Beaulieu, M. R., & Embrey, N. G. Interaction in families with a schizophrenic child. *Archives of General Psychiatry,* 1965, *12,* 166-183.

Lewine, R. J. Parents of schizophrenic individuals: What we say is what we see. *Schizophrenia Bulletin,* 1979, *5*(3), 433-434.

Lidz, T., Fleck, S., & Cornelison, A. Schizophrenia and the family. New York: International Universities Press, 1965.

Lidz, T., Fleck, S., & Cornelison, A. Schizophrenia and the family. (2d ed.) New York: International Universities Press, 1975.

Massie, H. N., & Beels, C. C. The outcome of the family treatment of schizophrenia. *Schizophrenia Bulletin,* 1972, *1*(6):24-36.

Mosher, L. R. Family therapy for schizophrenia: Recent trends. In L. J. West & D. E. Flinn (Eds.), *Treatment of schizophrenia: Progress and prospects.* New York: Grune & Stratton, 1976.

Waring, E. M. Family therapy and schizophrenia. *Canadian Psychiatric Association Journal,* 1978, *23*(1), 51-58.

Waxler, N. E. Parent and child effects on cognitive performance: An experimental approach to the etiological and responsive theories of schizophrenia. *Family Process,* 1974, *13,* 1-22.

Wild, C. M., Shapiro, L. N., & Abelin, T. Sampling issues in family studies of schizophrenia. *Archives of General Psychiatry,* 1974, *30,* 211-215.

Wild, C. M., Shapiro, L. N., & Abelin, T. Communication patterns and role structure in families of male schizophrenics. *Archives of General Psychiatry,* 1977, *34*(1), 58-70.

Wynne, L. C. Family and group treatment of schizophrenia: An interim view. In R. Cancro, N. Fox, & L. Shapiro (Eds.), *Strategic Intervention in Schizophrenia.* New York: Behavioral Publications, 1974.

Hospitalization and Partial Hospitalization

Ellsworth, R. B., et al. Hospital and community adjustment as perceived by psychiatric patients, their families and staff. *Journal of Consulting and Clinical Psychology,* 1968, *32*(5), part 2 (Monography Supplement).

Ermutlu, I. M. Effect of hospitalization on guilt and shame feelings. *Psychiatric Forum,* 1977, *6,* 18-22.

Glick, I. D., Hargreaves, W. A., Drues, J., & Showstack, J. A. Short vs. long hospitalization: Schizophrenic patients. *American Journal of Psychiatry,* 1976, *133,* 509-514.

Gunderson, J. G. A reevaluation of milieu therapy for nonchronic schizophrenic patients. *Schizophrenia Bulletin,* 1980, *6*(1), 64-69.

Linn, M. W., Caffey, E. M., Klett, C. J., Hogarty, G. E. & Lamb, H. R. Day treatment and psychotropic drugs in the aftercare of schizophrenic patients. *Archives of General Psychiatry,* 1979, *36*(10).

Ratcliffe, W., Nixon, G. W., Dyck, R. J., & Hassan, F. A. Utilization of an evening/night hospital: First two years of operation. *Canadian Psychiatric Association Journal,* 1977, *22.*

Voineskos, G. Part-time hospitalization programs: Neglected field of community psychiatry. *Canadian Medical Association Journal,* 1976, *114,* 320-324.

Wilder, J. F., Levin. G., & Zwerling, I. [A] two-year follow-up evaluation of acute psychotic patients treated in a day hospital. *American Journal of Psychiatry,* 1966, *122,* 1095-1101.

Language and Disordered Thinking

Andreasen, N. C., & Powers, P. S. Psychosis, thought disorder, and regression. *American Journal of Psychiatry,* 1976, *133*(5), 522-529.

deSilva, W. P., & Hemsley, D. R. [The] influence of context on language perception in schizophrenia. *British Journal of Social and Clinical Psychology,* 1977, *16,* 337-345.

Gerver, D. Linguistic rules and the perception and recall of speech by schizophrenic patients. *British Journal of Social Linguistic Psychology,* 1967, *6,* 204-211.

Gregory, M., & Carroll, S. *Language and situation.* London, Henley and Boston: Routledge and Kegan, 1978.

Harrow, M. & Quinlan, D. Is disordered thinking unique to schizophrenia? *Archives of General Psychiatry,* 1977, *34*(1), 15-21.

Hemsley, D. R. What have cognitive deficits to do with schizophrenic symptoms? *British Journal of Psychiatry,* 1977, *130,* 167-173.

Lawson, J. S., McGhie, A., & Chapman, J. Perception of speech in schizophrenia. *British Journal of Psychiatry,* 1964, *110,* 357-383.

Martin, J., & Rochester, S. R. Cohesion and reference in schizophrenic speech. In A. Makkai & V. B. Makkai (Eds.), *The first LACUS forum 1974.* Columbia, SC: Hornbeam Press, 1975, 302-311.

McGhie, A., & Chapman, J. Disorders of attention and perception in early schizophrenia. *British Journal of Medical Psychology,* 1961, *34,* 103-116. *British Journal of Medical Psychology,* 1961, *34,* 103-116.

Payne, R. W., Caird, W. K., & Laverty, S. G. Overinclusive thinking and delusions in schizophrenic patients. *Journal of Abnormal and Social Psychology,* 1964, *68,* 562-566.

Piaget, J. *The language and thought of the child.* New York: Harcourt, Brace, 1926.

Rochester, S. R. The role of information processing in the sentence decoding of schizophrenic listeners. *Journal of Nervous and Mental Disorders,* 1973, *157,* 217-223.

Rochester, S. R. Are language disorders in acute schizophrenia actually information processing problems? In Wynne, L. C., Cromwell, R. L. & Matthysse S. (Eds.), *Nature of schizophrenia: New approaches to research and treatment,* New York: Wiley, 1978.

Rochester, S. R. & Martin J. The art of referring: The speaker's use of noun phrases to instruct the listener. In R. Frudle (Ed.), *Discourse comprehension and production,* (Vol. 1). Norwood, NJ: Ablex Publishing Corp., 1977, 245-269.

Salzinger, K., Portnoy, S., & Feldman, R. S. Intrusions in schizophrenic speech: The immediacy hypothesis vs. the lapse of attention hypothesis. *Comprehensive Psychiatry,* 1977, *18*(3), 255-261.

Shakow, D. Segmental set. *Archives of General Psychiatry,* 1962, *6,* 1-17.

Shakow, D. Psychological deficit in schizophrenia. *Behavioral Science,* 1963, *8,* 275-305.

Shands, H. C. Coping with novelty. *Archives of General Psychiatry,* 1969, *20*(1), 64-70.

Truscott, I. P. Contextual constraint and schizophrenia language. *Journal of Consulting and Clinical Psychology,* 1970, *35,* 189-194.

Wynne, L. C., & Singer, M. T. Thought disorder and the family relations of schizophrenics. II. Classifications of forms of thinking. *Archives of General Psychiatry,* 1963, *9,* 199-206.

Neuroleptic and Psychosocial Treatment

Chien, C. Drugs and rehabilitation in schizophrenia. In M. Greenblatt (Ed.), *Drugs in combination with other therapies,* New York: Grune & Stratton, 1975.

Goldberg, S., Schooler, N., Hogarty, G., & Roper, M. Prediction of relapse in schizophrenia out-patients treated by drugs and sociotherapy. *Archives of General Psychiatry,* 1977, *34*(2), 171-184.

Goldstein, M., Rodnick, E., Evans, J., May, P., & Steinberg, M. Drug and family therapy in the aftercare of acute schizophrenics. *Archives of General Psychiatry,* 1978, *35*(10), 1169-1177.

Hogarty, G., & Goldberg, S. C. Drug and sociotherapy and the post hospital maintenance of schizophrenia. *Archives of General Psychiatry,* 1973, *24*(1), 54-64.

Payn, S. B. Group pharmacotherapy for withdrawn schizophrenic patients. *Canadian Psychiatric Association Journal,* 1978, *23,* 97-99.

Schooler, N. R. Antipsychotic drugs and psychological treatment in schizophrenia. In M. A. Lipton, A. DiMascio, & K. D. Killam (Eds.), *Psychopharmacology: A generation of progress.* New York: Raven Press, 1978.

Schooler, N. R. Neuroleptics and psychosocial treatment. *Schizophrenia Bulletin,* 1980, *6*(1), 131-134.

Outcome and Prognosis

Bellak, L., & Strauss, J. S. The heuristic need for subgroups of the schizophrenic syndrome. *Schizophrenia Bulletin,* 1979, *5*(3), 441-442.

Birley, J. L., & Brown, G. W. Crisis and life changes preceding the onset or relapse of acute schizophrenia: Clinical aspects. *British Journal of Psychiatry,* 1970, *116,* 326-334.

Bland, R. C., & Orn, H. Schizophrenia: diagnostic criteria and outcome. *British Journal of Psychiatry,* 1979, *134,* 34-38.

Bleuler, M. The long-term course of the schizophrenic psychosis. *Psychological Medicine*, 1974, *4*, 244-254.

Durell, J., & Katz, M. M. The changing clinical picture of schizophrenia. *Schizophrenia Bulletin*, 1977, *3*, 528-530.

Evans, J. R., Goldstein, M. J. & Rodnick, E. H. Premorbid adjustment, paranoid diagnosis and remission in acute schizophrenics treated in a community mental health center. *Archives of General Psychiatry*, 1973, *28*, 666-672.

Garmezy, N. Process and reactive schizophrenia: Some conceptions and issues. *Schizophrenia Bulletin*, 1970, *2*, 30-74.

Goldstein, M. J. Premorbid adjustment, paranoid status, and patterns of response to phenothiazine in acute schizophrenia. *Schizophrenia Bulletin*, 1970, *3*, 24-37.

Goldstein, M. J. Further data concerning the relation between premorbid adjustment and paranoid symptomatology. *Schizophrenia Bulletin*, 1978, *4*, 236-243.

Hanson, D. R., Gottesman, I. I., & Heston, L. L. Childhood indicators of adult schizophrenia inferred from children of schizophrenics. *British Journal of Psychiatry*, 1976, *129*, 142-154.

Harrow, M. & Silverstein, M. L. Psychotic symptoms in schizophrenia after the acute phase. *Schizophrenia Bulletin*, 1977, *3*, 608-616.

Hogarty, G. E. Temporal effects of drug and placebo in delaying relapse in schizophrenic outpatients. *Archives of General Psychiatry*, 1977, *34*(3), 297-301.

Johnson, D. A. W. Expectation of outcome from maintenance therapy in chronic schizophrenic patients. *British Journal of Psychiatry*, 1976, *128*, 246-250.

Kayton, L., Beck, J., & Koh, S. D. Postpsychotic state, convalescent environment, and therapeutic relationship in schizophrenic outcome. *American Journal of Psychiatry*, 1976, *133*(11), 1269-1274.

Kendell, R. E., Brockington, I. F., & Leff, J. P. Prognostic implications of six alternative definitions of schizophrenia. *Archives of General Psychiatry*, 1979, *36*(1), 25-31.

Klorman, R., Strauss, J. S., & Kokes, R. F. Premorbid adjustment in schizophrenia. *Schizophrenia Bulletin*, 1977, *3*, 214-225.

Marder, S. R., van Kammen, D. P., Docherty, J. P., Rayner, J., & Bunney, W. E. Predicting drug-free improvement in schizophrenic psychosis. *Archives of General Psychiatry*, 1979, *36*(10), 1080-1085.

McCabe, M. S. Reactive psychoses and schizophrenia with good prognosis. *Archives of General Psychiatry*, 1976, *33*, 571-576.

Meltzer, H. Y. Biology of schizophrenia subtypes: A review and proposal for method of study. *Schizophrenia Bulletin*, 1979, *5*(3), 460-479.

Miller, H. R., Streiner, D. L., & Woodward, C. A. An attempt to develop a process-reactive scale for males and females. *Canadian Journal of Behavioral Science/Rev. Canadian Sci. Comp.*, 1978, *10*(1), 60-67.

Roff, J. D. Long-term outcome for a set of schizophrenic subtypes. In R. D. Wirt, G. Winokur, & M. Roff (Eds.), *Life History Research in Psychopathology*, (Vol. 4). Minneapolis: University of Minnesota Press, 1975.

Sartorius, N., Jablensky, A., & Shapiro, R. Two year follow-up of the patients included in the WHO international pilot study of schizophrenia. *Psychological Medicine*, 1977, *7*, 529-541.

Silverstein, M., & Harrow, M. First-rank symptoms in the postacute schizophrenic: A follow-up study. *American Journal of Psychiatry*, 1978, *135*(12), 1481-1486.

Strauss, J., et al. Premorbid adjustment in schizophrenia: Concepts, measures and implications. *Schizophrenia Bulletin*, 1977, *3*, 182-185.

Strauss, J., Korman, R., & Kokes, R. F. Premorbid adjustment in schizophrenia: Implications of findings for understanding, research, and application. *Schizophrenia Bulletin,* 1977, *3,* 240-244.

Strauss, J. S., & Carpenter, W. Prediction of outcome in schizophrenia. *Archives of General Psychiatry,* 1977, *34,* 159-163.

Strauss, J. S., & Docherty, J. P. Subtypes of schizophrenia: Descriptive models. *Schizophrenia Bullletin,* 1979, *5*(3), 447-452.

Tsuang, M. T., & Dempsey, G. M. Long-term outcome of major psychoses. II. Schizoaffective disorder compared with schizophrenia, affective disorders and a sugical control group. *Archives of General Psychiatry,* 1979, *36*(11), 1302-1304.

Zigler, E., et al. Premorbid social competence and paranoid-nonparanoid status in female schizophrenic patients. *Journal of nervous and mental disorders,* 1977, *164,* 333-339.

Outpatient Care

Fenton, F. R., Tessier, L., & Struening, E. L. A comparative trial of home and hospital psychiatric care. *Archives of General Psychiatry,* 1979, *36*(10), 1073-1079.

Levenson, A. J. Acute schizophrenia: Efficacious out-patient treatment approach as alternative to full-time hospitalization. *Diseases of the Nervous System,* 1977, *38,* 242-245.

Linn, M. W., Caffey, E. M., Klett, J. C., & Hogarty, G. Hospital vs. community (foster) care for psychiatric patients. *Archives of General Psychiatry,* 1977, *34,* 78-83.

Modlin, H. C. The discharged mental patient in the community. *Psychiatry Digest,* 1976, *37*(6), 13-22.

Strauss, J. S. The treatment of outpatient schizophrenics. J.C.E. *Psychiatry,* October, 1977.

Paranoid Symptomatology

Di Bella, G., & Williston, A. Educating staff to manage threatening paranoid patients. *American Journal of Psychiatry,* 1979, *136*(3), 333-335.

Freeman, A. M., & Melges, F. T. Temporal disorganization, depersonalization, and persecutory ideation in acute mental illnes. *American Journal of Psychiatry,* 1978, *135*(1), 123-124.

Lansky, M. R. Schizophrenic delusional phenomena. *Comprehensive Psychiatry,* 1977, *18,* 157-168.

Larkin, A. R. The form and content of schizophrenic hallucinations. *American Journal of Psychiatry,* 1979, *136*(7), 940-943.

Psychotherapy

Benedetti, G. What is psychotherapy of psychosis? Proceeds of the 9th International Congress of Psychotherapy, OSLO 1973. *Psychotherapy Psychosomatic,* 1974, *24,* 327-336.

Birnie, W. A., & Littman, S. K. Obsessionality and schizophrenia. *Canadian Psychiatric Association Journal,* 1978, *23*(2), 77-81.

Dyrud, J. E., & Holsom, P. S. The psychotherapy of schizophrenia: Does it work? *American Journal of Psychiatry,* 1973, *130,* 670-673.

Fromm-Reichmann, F. Some aspects of psychoanalytic psychotherapy with schizophrenics. In E. B. Brodie & F. C. Redlich (Eds.), *Psychotherapy with schizophrenics.* New York: International Universities Press, 1952.

Garfield, S. L. Basic ingredients or common factors in psychotherapy. *Journal of Consulting and Clinical Psychology,* 1973, *41,* 9-12.

Hayward, M. L., & Taylor, J. E. A schizophrenic patient describes the action of intensive psychotherapy. *Psychiatric Quarterly,* 1956, *30,* 211-248.

Hill, L. B. *Psychotherapeutic intervention in schizophrenia.* Chicago: University of Chicago Press, 1955.

Lidz, R. W., & Lidz, T. Therapeutic considerations arising from the intense symbiotic needs of schizophrenic patients. In E. B. Brodie & F. C. Redlich (Eds.), *Psychotherapy with schizophrenics.* New York: International Universities Press, 1952.

Lidz, T. *Origin and treatment of schizophrenic disorders.* New York: Basic Books, 1973.

May, P. R. Psychotherapy research in schizophrenia—Another view of present reality. *Schizophrenia Bulletin,* 1974, *9,* 126-132.

Mintz, J., O'Brien, C., & Luborsky, L. Predicting the outcome of psychotherapy for schizophrenics. *Archives of General Psychiatry,* 1976, *24*(33), 1230-1233.

Schulz, C. G. An individualized psychotherapeutic approach with the schizophrenic patient. *Schizophrenia Bulletin,* 1975, *13*(1), 46-69.

Schulz, C. G. Sullivan's clinical contribution during Sheppard-Pratt era—1923 to 1930. *Psychiatry,* 1978, *41,* 117-128.

Rehabilitation

Beisser, A. R. Models of helping and training for incapacity. *American Journal of Orthopsychiatry,* 1973, *43*(4), 586-594.

Cotton, P., Bene-Kociemba, A., & Starker, L. A mental health center's aftercare specialty service for discharged state hospital patients. *Hospital and Community Psychiatry,* 1980, *31*(6).

Fairweather, G. W., Sanders, D. H., Maynard, H., & Cressler, D. L. *Community life for the mentally ill: An alternative to institutional care.* Chicago: Aldine, 1969.

Lamb, H. R. In Heath & Downing (Eds.), *Handbook of community mental health practice: The San Mateo experience.* San Francisco: Jossey-Bass, 1969.

Lamb, H. R. New asylums in community. *Archives of General Psychiatry,* 1979, *36,* 129-134.

Menuck, M. Rehabilitation of psychiatric patients. *Canadian Psychiatric Association Journal,* 1978, *23*(2), 111-119.

Pattison, E. M. Clinical social systems interventions. *Psychiatry Digest,* April 1977, 25-33.

INDEX